ESP, SEERS & PSYCHICS

MILBOURNE CHRISTOPHER

ESP,
SEERS & PSYCHICS

THOMAS Y. CROWELL COMPANY

New York   Established 1834

Designed by Abigail Moseley

Manufactured in the United States of America
L.C. Card 78-127607
ISBN 0-690-26815-7
5 6 7 8 9 10

For Roland Winder

Whose excellent antiquarian library is never disturbed by "ghostes and spirites walking by nyght."

CONTENTS

ILLUSTRATIONS

THE OCCULT

The Right Reverend James A. Pike, former Episcopal Bishop of California, did more to arouse public curiosity about the occult than any man of his time. During a séance with the Reverend Arthur Ford, a minister of the Disciples of Christ Church and the best-known American trance medium, which was televised in Toronto, September 17, 1967, Pike affirmed that the message relayed by the entranced psychic from his dead son was authentic.

The noted churchman, whose unorthodox religious views almost led to a trial for heresy, admitted later he had consulted other mediums and through them received consoling words from the young man, who had shot and killed himself in New York a year earlier.

Pike said he had seen poltergeist phenomena, too. Books seemed to vanish and reappear, safety pins were found open and placed to indicate the hour of 8:19, the approximate time his son died. Half of the clothes in a closet were discovered disarranged and heaped up while the remainder were in perfect order.

The story of the Canadian telecast was front-page news in the *New York Times*; the tape of the séance was televised in New York less than a month later. Arthur Ford had been in the headlines with another spirit communication almost forty years earlier. In January 1929 he had delivered a message from Houdini, the magician who was the archenemy of mediumistic fraud, to his widow and convinced her—temporarily. At the time of the séance Beatrice Houdini was under a doctor's care; the papers reported she had been having hallucinations. When she recovered, she disavowed her earlier endorsement. Houdini never spoke through Ford again.

Bishop Pike resigned his high post to study mysteries that were beyond the range of usual theological thought. With his second wife, the former Diane Kennedy, who collaborated with him in the writing of a book about his mystical experiences, *The Other Side*, he went to Israel in 1969. Their car became stuck after they took a wrong turn in the Judean desert. They walked under the blazing sun until he became exhausted; she went on for ten hours until she found help.

Days of search for the fifty-six-year-old clergyman were futile. Ford sent word to Mrs. Pike that, in a vision, he had seen Pike alive in a desert cave. Mrs. Ena Twigg, a London medium who had given Pike messages from his dead son, phoned from England to say that the churchman "was on the border trying to make the transmission." She offered no clue as to where he could be found. Mrs. Margot Klausner, a Tel Aviv medium, suspended a pendulum over two maps and marked the spot in the desert where searchers could find him. She also held a pen and, without conscious effort, wrote a communication from Edgar Cayce, the late American mystic. It said Pike was in a coma.

The day before the former bishop's body was found on a ledge in a canyon, not in a cave or at the location indicated by the pendulum, Mrs. Pike herself had a vision. She saw the spirit of her husband emerge vaporlike from his body, then ascend into the sky where a great crowd greeted him. His son was there and several of his old friends; in the background she recognized Bobby Kennedy

Since then her husband has spoken to Diane Pike in dreams, but as yet there have been no other manifestations.

Interest in ESP and in seers and psychics is at a new high. *Time, Life, Look,* and *Newsweek* have reported the burgeoning popularity of occultism. A special issue of *McCall's* in March 1970 covered ESP, spirit séances, astrology, and kindred topics; *Esquire* that month ran twenty-five pages on occult evils in California. A five-day ESP seminar on NBC-TV's "For Women Only" program in January 1970 had Aline Saarinen's studio audience more excited than any topic since The Pill. Clairvoyants, crystal gazers, and astrologers are frequent guests with TV hosts Johnny Carson, Mike Douglas, Merv Griffin, and David Susskind. Linda Goodman, whose *Sun Signs* was the first astrology volume to make the *New York Times* best-seller list, studied Carson's chart when she visited his program and predicted he would have another child in the fall of 1969. Perhaps her interpretation of the planetary influences was at fault; the year ended without the announced addition to his family.

New national magazines *Psychic, Occult, Beyond,* and *Astroview* share newsstand space with *Fate* and the many astrology periodicals. Marcia Seligson's "Publishing Enters the Age of Aquarius" in the September 28, 1969, *New York Times Book Review* and Nora Ephron's "Publishing Prophets for Profits," which appeared in the same publication in August 1968, heralded the avalanche of books on almost every phase of occultism. Hans Holzer alone has produced twenty-three volumes on subjects ranging from haunted houses to prophecy, from spirit photographs to thought transference. His attitude is never critical; many publishers believe that only books with affirmative viewpoints enjoy extensive sales.

The story of Jeane Dixon, a Washingtonian who predicts presidential elections, future wars, and the fates of people in the news, is a sure-fire seller. It has been told by Jess Stearn in *The Doorway to the Future,* Ruth Montgomery in *A Gift of Prophecy,* and by the seeress herself in *My Life and Prophecies. A Gift of Prophecy* sold more than 260,000 copies in its clothbound editions and 2,800,000 as a paperback.

A front-page feature in the October 24, 1969, issue of the *Wall Street Journal,* "Strange Doings: Americans Show Burst of Interest in Witches, Other Occult Matters," said that mysticism was not only a national craze but also a "booming business." Sybil Leek, a self-proclaimed British witch who now lives in Florida, is so busy writing books and a monthly astrology column, making personal appearances on TV panel shows and the lecture circuit, that she has little time to stir her cauldron.

Ouija boards, the *Journal* reports, are bought by 2,000,000 customers each year, and Time Pattern Institute, a firm in Valley Stream, Long Island, New York, merchandized more than 250,000 personalized astrological forecasts for 1969. Another company, Zodiactronics, advertised, in a full-page display in the February 6, 1970, *New York Post*, a twenty-four-hour, dial-in service. "Our computer is fed by a staff of world-famous astrologers (including Linda Goodman and Charles Cooke) who translate every possible juxtaposition of the planets into clear, up-to-date information you can use." For three dollars the potential subscriber was to receive a "printed personality profile" and four phone-call readings in the first month. After that another dollar each month paid for four more phone-ins.

Maurice Woodruff, the British clairvoyant-astrologer, had his own hour-long syndicated TV series produced by David Susskind in 1969. Carroll Righter, the Hollywood horoscope caster, appeared on the cover of the March 21, 1969, *Time*. In addition to his widely syndicated daily newspaper forecasts and books, Righter now tapes his daily predictions for radio use.

A volatile younger generation, champions of world peace, academic reform, human rights, sexual freedom, and long hair, is as intrigued with mysticism as a disillusioned older segment of our society. The failure of organized religion to satisfy the basic needs of inquiring minds has brought on a resurgence of interest in what was once called psychical research but is now also known as parapsychology. Dr. Joseph Banks Rhine, with his extrasensory perception experiments at Duke University, was the first prophet of the new order. His disciples are eager to experience the occult on their own.

High school sudents test their ESP powers with symbol cards;

they stage séances and table-tilting sessions. University undergraduates test the effectiveness of ancient black magic formulas, try to
project themselves astrally, then discuss their frustrations at
psychic study clubs. Recently a girl who is pursuing less controver-
sial subjects at a New York college phoned me to ask where a
qualified spirit medium could be found. She was nineteen and had
had her first encounter with "psychic forces" during a séance in an
old tomb on her father's estate. A boy at the table had fallen forward, with blood gushing from a wound on his neck. There were,
she insisted, no loose stones in the ceiling of the vault yet "something" had struck him. She had joined the Rosicrucians, a California study-by-mail cult which claims to teach the "inner power" of
the mind; now, she said, she was ready to appreciate the work of a
gifted psychic.

Periodically the press tells of poltergeist disturbances—objects
hurled in rooms reportedly empty—and strange sounds and sights
in houses that are said to be haunted. Stories are printed of people
who claim to see the future, and of those who had premonitions of
events that came to pass.

Spiritual Frontiers Fellowship, a religious group, was formed
in 1956 "to sponsor, explore and interpret the growing interest in
psychic phenomena and mystical experiences within the church,
wherever these experiences relate to effective prayers, spiritual
healing and personal survival." What more impressive confirmation
of the spiritual nature of man could be offered than scientific proof
of his spiritual powers?

"We live in an age of Buck Rogers!" the Reverend William V.
Rauscher, then the group's president, wrote in the April 1966 *Gate
Way*. "An age when we can orbit the earth. An age when research
in consciousness will gain momentum . . . . An age which is ready
for enlightenment as never before."

The Association for Research and Enlightenment perpetuates
the teaching of the late Edgar Cayce. He is said to have projected
his consciousness hundreds of miles to diagnose and prescribe for
his ailing followers. The A.R.E. files are filled with testimonials to

the recuperative powers of his remedies. Faith is a great healer. An expert in astral projection would be a valuable secret weapon for any government; he could be sent to report on high-level military conferences in hostile countries. Cayce's astral powers were never put to a formal test, but the Reverend Gilbert N. Holloway, who claims the same out-of-body expertise, made two invisible trips for me—one less than four miles away, the other halfway around the world to India. I tell what happened in another chapter.

Other startling wonders are regularly reported in the national magazines devoted to the mystic arts, and more scholarly accounts appear in the journals of the British and American Societies for Psychical Research and the periodical published by the Parapsychology Association.

During my travels across the United States and in sixty-eight countries abroad, I have had an excellent opportunity to see and study marvels that most people know about only through reading. Lady, the "talking" horse in Virginia which Dr. Rhine believed was "the greatest thing since radio," spelled out answers to my questions. Achille D'Angelo, the Italian mystic, produced chill breezes and "psychic thrusts" in my presence. I looked on while Rahman Bey and Chundra Bey were buried alive. I observed fire walking in Asia as well as Haiti.

I have been in séance rooms when raps were heard and objects were moved apparently by invisible forces. I have stood beside a man who elongated his body until he added an extra eight inches to his height—a specialty of the nineteenth-century psychic Daniel Dunglas Home, "the medium who was never exposed."

I have visited houses where poltergeists had terrorized the residents, though none manifested themselves while I was there. I have spent the night in rooms where ghosts were seen.

I have had my future told by clairvoyants, mediums, gypsies, and soothsayers of many sorts. And, unlike most people who consult them, I made careful notes of their prophecies. Dowsing rods have twitched and turned in my hands; pendulums have swung over thought-of-objects when I tried to hold them motionless;

tables have tilted at my touch; and indicators on Ouija boards have spelled out curious messages when I was not conscious of directing their movements.

I have a special interest in ESP and in seers and psychics. For more than thirty-five years I have been a professional magician— and it requires arduous work to create illusions, though to the audience the performer seems to work without effort. Mental and physical labor plus practice are necessary before a routine is perfected. A magician's fingers must be as supple as those of a concert pianist, and the magician, like the pianist, must practice constantly or he will lose his dexterity. I often thought how wonderful it would be if I could produce my illusions through the powers of my mind alone. So much time, trouble, and drudgery would be saved! For this reason I began my study of the occult. I saw many things which were overlooked by those who were not familiar with the psychology of deception. The results of my studies over a period of many years may surprise, even shock, some people, but it is my hope that my experiences and findings will help the readers of this book to evaluate better the wonders of the occult world.

EXTRASENSORY PERCEPTION

I had a strange feeling that morning as though something terrible was about to happen. I sat at the kitchen table and looked at the front page of the newspaper. There was a story about President Kennedy's trip to Texas. I *knew* then what would happen. I switched on the radio and waited. Soon the music was interrupted. An excited voice said: "We bring you a special bulletin from Dallas—"

I woke up suddenly. I thought I heard my husband scream. I turned on the bedside lamp. It was 3.30 A.M. Harry was still working on the night shift at the plant. I tried to read, but couldn't. I kept waiting for the telephone to ring. When it did, Harry's boss was on the line. Ten minutes before my husband had fallen from the top of a 30-foot ladder.

Reports such as these are not unusual. Many people on sudden impulse have canceled reservations on ships that sank, planes that crashed. Others say they have known instinctively when their sons were killed in Vietnam or Germany. Premonitions are difficult to authenticate. Few who have them make notes immediately of their thoughts and of the time and date of their occurrence. Skeptics who have tried to check out reports of premonitions usually find little, if any, firm evidence to document them.

Dr. Gardner Murphy is not a skeptic. The president of the American Society for Psychical Research has been actively investigating phenomena since the early 1920's. For fifteen years he was the research director of the Menninger Foundation in Topeka,

Kansas. He is now Professor of Psychology at Georgetown University in Washington, D.C. He is convinced that people can be aware of events before they happen. He believes that telepathy and clairvoyance are not only possible but a natural part of human life.

Precognition, the ability to foresee the future; telepathy, mental communication between two or more minds; and clairvoyance, knowledge of events that happen elsewhere, are all facets of what is known today as extrasensory perception.

For almost ninety years, data has been accumulating on extrasensory perception experiments. In 1876 William Fletcher Barrett, Professor of Psychics at the Royal College of Science in Ireland, asked the British Association to appoint a commission to study the subject. His request was ignored, and his paper "On Some Phenomena Associated with Abnormal Conditions of the Mind" was not published in the association's *Proceedings.*

Irked by the hostile reaction of his fellow scientists, Barrett and several academic friends formed the Society for Psychical Research. Henry Sidgwick, Lecturer on Moral Philosophy at Cambridge, was the first president. In his speech at the initial general meeting July 17, 1882, in London, he expressed regret that so many learned men disputed "the reality of these marvelous phenomena —of which it is quite impossible to exaggerate the scientific importance, if only a tenth of what has been alleged by generally credible witnesses could be shown to be true."

He warned that the society must "guard against the danger of illusion and deception" but, once convinced that something was true, they should force skeptics either to disprove their findings or "to accuse the investigators, either of lying or cheating or of a blindness or forgetfulness incompatible with any intellectual conditions except lunacy."

At this session Barrett, as chairman of the thought-reading committee, presented a report which Sidgwick said he hoped would precede many others "which may have reached the same point of conclusiveness."

Barrett was eloquent. He and two former Fellows of Trinity College, Cambridge, Edmund Gurney and Frederic W. H. Myers, had seen some incredible demonstrations at the home of the Reverend Andrew Macreight Creery in Buxton, Derbyshire. Four of the clergyman's teen-age daughters—Mary, Alice, Maud, and Kathleen —along with Jane Dean, the family's young servant girl, could apparently communicate without using "the ordinary channels of sensation." When one was out of the room and the committee members chose an object, number, name, or playing card, the girl frequently could name it on her return.

A white penknife and a box of almonds had been guessed immediately, though a threepenny piece and a box of chocolates had not been identified. When playing cards were used, the girls were more perceptive. Five cards in a row were called correctly. "The odds against this," Barrett stressed, "were over a million to one." Another time eight successive cards and eight consecutive names were correctly identified. The odds against the former were "142 million to one and . . . the latter something incalculably greater."

Psychic research was off to a fine start. Or was it? In June, Barrett, Gurney, and Myers had written a glowing account of their adventures with the Creerys in *The Nineteenth Century*. The July number carried a scorching criticism by Dr. Henry Donkin, a physician who delighted in deflating miracle hunters. Why, the girls hadn't even been blindfolded, Donkin jibed. Obviously, he said, they could have used signals. It wasn't uncommon for children and family maids to play tricks on their elders. They wouldn't have needed a sophisticated code since the naive investigators announced each category—cards, objects, or names—in advance. There were, Donkin emphasized, professional entertainers who exhibited far more baffling mental tricks.

This was—and is—true. As early as 1781, Philip Breslaw, the German conjurer, sent, to quote his handbills, "the thoughts of any person to another without the use of speech or writing" during an engagement in London. Three years later in the Theatre Royal, Haymarket, the wife of Giuseppe Pinetti, the celebrated magician, would sit "in one of the front boxes with a handkerchief over her eyes and guess at anything imagined and proposed to her, by any person in the company." She rarely made a mistake.

That children were as clever in this line as adults was demonstrated by Louis Gordon M'Kean, an eight-year-old boy from Inverness. In 1831 the kilted "Double-sighted Phaenomenon" stood blindfolded, his face away from the audience, and described coins, watches, snuffboxes, and trinkets. Though people would whisper so quietly that even those close by could not hear, young Gordon—at a distance of a hundred yards—could repeat their words.

Twelve-year-old Emile, the son of Robert-Houdin, the famous French illusionist, would sit blindfolded on a stool and describe minutely any object which was tendered to his father. Inscriptions on medallions and words written in foreign languages never fazed him. Between 1848 and 1853, Queen Victoria saw him perform three times. In his memoirs Robert-Houdin said he got the inspiration for the feat, "to which I owed my reputation," by watching his young sons play a game in which one with a handkerchief tied over his eyes described an object which the other held. A good memory, Robert-Houdin went on, was essential. "Women," he added, "daily perform far more astonishing feats. . . . I can safely assert that a lady seeing another pass at full speed in a carriage, will have had time to analyze her toilette from her bonnet to her shoes, and be able to describe not only the fashion, and qualities of the stuffs, but also say if the lace is real, or machine-made."

Gamblers were communicating without words even before magicians. In the sixteenth century a popular signaling device was the "organum." Pressure on a loose floor panel caused it to rise under a confederate's shoes. The organist played a simple tune—so many taps—to send suits and pips. Patrick Hurley, who cued his accomplice by the position of his finger on his nose or on a table and by blinking his eyes, earned a hundred thousand pounds with his sly tricks, which are noted in *Authentic Memoirs Relating to the Lives and Adventures of the Most Eminent Gamesters and Sharpers from the Restoration of King Charles*, London, 1744.

The members of the first Society for Psychical Research investigative committee were well versed in many classical studies but totally unfamiliar with the theory and practice of deception. Perhaps they thought such specialized knowledge was unnecessary as they were not dealing with professional charlatans but the daughters of "a clergyman of unblemished character," girls "as free as possible from morbid or hysterical symptoms" who were "in manner perfectly simple and childlike."

For four years the Creery sisters repeated their private demonstrations with such remarkable success that when Gurney, Myers, and Frank Podmore, another member of the committee, wrote *Phantasms of the Living* in 1886, they said it was to the Creery tests "that we owe our own conviction of the possibility of genuine thought-reading between persons in a normal state."

Shortly before his death in 1888, Gurney contributed his last article to the *Proceedings of the Society for Psychical Research*. Its title, "Notes Relating to some of the Published Experiments in Thought-Transference," gave no hint of its explosive content. In the course of a demonstration at Cambridge for Sidgwick, his wife, and Gurney, two of the Creery girls "were detected in the use of a code of signals, and a third has confessed to a certain amount of signalling in the earlier series."

When one of the sisters could see another, they used visual cues. Glances up, down, to the right or left to indicate the suits of playing cards. If one was behind a screen, they switched to another system. Sighs, yawns, coughs, and the noise their shoes made on the carpet conveyed data. "The sisters were very restless," Gurney explained, "which made their movements less obvious than they would otherwise have been."

It had taken a group of intelligent men six years to discover the secret. Once they were aware of the deception, before they told the girls of their discovery, they could interpret the codes themselves. "Their success," Gurney concluded, "afforded a complete proof of the use of signals."

Apologists have maintained that this exposure did not invalidate *all* of the early tests. The will to believe in the wonderful exceeds logic.

The second report of the committee, in the 1882 *Proceedings*, revealed that two men had been found who could send and receive thoughts. Gurney and Myers had gone to Brighton to test the powers of George Albert Smith and Douglas Blackburn. G. A. Smith, aged eighteen, was an entertainer who had puzzled the townspeople of the popular seaside resort with his exhibitions of hypnosis and thought reading. Blackburn, aged twenty-five, the editor of *The Brightonian,* was Smith's most enthusiastic publicist and the sender of the thoughts which Smith received.

As Gurney and Myers looked on, Smith was blindfolded. He sat in a chair with his face toward a wall. When one of the investigators chose a number, Blackburn would take Smith's hand and Smith would reveal the number. Tests were also made with selected colors. Communication between sender and receiver ceased when the sender went to another room. It resumed when the hand-to-hand link was made. Sometimes, when words were thought of, Smith received them in incomplete form. "Queen Anne" became first "Queechy," then "Queen," and Wissencraft developed from "Wissie" to "Wissenaft." Even simple drawings could be transmitted. The investigators said these tests gave them "the most important and valuable insight into the manner of the mental transfer of a picture which we have yet obtained."

The third committee report in Part I of the 1882–83 *Proceedings* covered two series of Smith-Blackburn tests made at the society's rooms in London. The Brighton mentalists communicated now without physical contact. While the blindfolded Smith sat in one room, Blackburn was shown a sketch in another. Blackburn studied it intently, closed his eyes to visualize it more completely, then was led back to the testing chamber. He stood two feet or so behind his partner and obviously strained to convey the picture in his mind. Eventually Smith reached for a pencil and attempted to duplicate the design. Sometimes he scrawled with his eyes still bandaged; other times he pulled the handkerchief down so that he could draw with more care. The target sketches and Smith's versions of them were published for comparison.

Why Smith and Blackburn severed their partnership after the London tests is not clear. Smith became Gurney's secretary and an associate member of the society. Later he participated in other telepathy tests as a hypnotist who entranced subjects. Blackburn returned to his work on the Brighton newspaper. He wrote an interesting paperbound book in 1884, *Thought Reading; or, Modern Mysteries Explained.* In it he described among other things a thought-projection feat during which the receiver, eyes bandaged, duplicated a sketch then in the sender's mind. Perhaps members of the S.P.R. committee never saw the volume. There was no mention of it in the *Proceedings,* and the Smith-Blackburn tests faded temporarily from public view.

Blackburn went on to South Africa and wrote six novels on African life. More than twenty years passed before the Smith-Blackburn tests became a subject of speculation again. Dr. Donkin, the physician who had criticized the S.P.R. investigators so scathingly during the Creery sisters' experiments, revealed in the November 26, 1907, issue of *The Westminster Gazette* an important sequence of the Smith-Blackburn research in London which had been omitted in the committee report. When proper precautions were taken to insure that neither sound nor sight cues were used, the marvelous phenomena abruptly ceased. Mrs. E. M. Sidgwick's reply, printed three days later, asked for more details about the alleged incident which she didn't remember and in the *Gazette* of January 29, 1908, Sir James Crichton-Browne supplied them. He had been present as an observer. When a rough drawing of an owl had been the target, Smith drew an owl, but it was quite a different owl from the original. Crichton-Browne suspected the word "owl" had been cued. He and George Romanes collaborated on an odd design that could not be identified by a single word, or by a dozen for that matter. When the sender, Blackburn, saw it, "his face fell." He stood behind Smith with his hands in his pocket, and after several minutes Smith drew something "but there was not the slightest approach to the figure drawn."

Though he was not familiar with the Morse code, Crichton-Browne supposed something of the sort was used. He had noticed that when Blackburn stood with his hands in his pocket he clinked the coins together. Although she was not mentioned in the report, a woman had sat facing Smith. It would have been possible, he said, for Blackburn to wink his eyes to flash the code, she in turn could have passed it on to Smith. These were mere suppositions but Crichton-Browne's next step, the ruling out of sight or sound cues, provided evidence that signals of some sort were used.

As anyone who has played Pin the Tail on the Donkey knows, it is easy to peek down when a handkerchief is tied over the eyes. Crichton-Browne sent out for some cotton wool to remedy this defect. The cotton wool was packed tightly in and around Smith's eye sockets; his ears were plugged; and a large handkerchief bound the added material in place.

When experiments of the sort that had been successful earlier were tried again: "There was no more flashing of images into his mind. His pencil was idle. Thought-transference was somehow interrupted."

At the end of the session Frederic Myers made a statement: "It must be allowed that this demonstration has been a total failure, and I attribute that to the offensive incredulity of Dr. Crichton-Browne." This produced an equally blunt retort: "I hope I will always show offensive incredulity when I find myself in the presence of patent imposture."

Once the long silence about the Smith-Blackburn tests had been breached, Blackburn wrote six revealing articles in *John Bull*; the first was printed December 5, 1908. Then, almost two years later, in the September 1, 1911, issue of the *Daily News*, he again gave his side of the story. As "the sole survivor of that group of investigators" he believed his exposures would be an object lesson for those who accepted without question avowals of marvelous phenomena from men who were not qualified to recognize fraud. The former telepathist said: "The principal cause of belief in psychic phenomena is the inability of the average man to observe accurately and estimate the value of evidence, plus a bias in favor of the phenomena being real."

Myers and Gurney were sincere, but as they did not know how the tricks were done, it was almost impossible for them to describe the feats accurately. They made many mistakes in their reports. They had written that Blackburn never touched Smith in one experiment, but Blackburn said he had touched his former partner eight times, "that being the only way in which our code then worked."

They had only a week's intensive practice before Myers and Gurney arrived in Brighton. The committee members were so eager to get data confirming telepathy that they had permitted the mentalists to make their own conditions for the tests. By the time of the London tests they had worked out various other codes.

A change in strategy was necessary when, as under Crichton-Browne's direction, Smith was put in situations where he could neither see nor hear. Yet with ingenuity even these obstacles could be overcome.

On one occasion, Blackburn wrote, wool covered Smith's eyes, and folded kid gloves were put over the wool before a heavy cloth was tied in place. Wool and bits of putty were inserted in Smith's ears; then two thick blankets covered him almost completely as he sat in his chair. The target drawing Myers asked Blackburn to send was "a tangle of heavy black lines, interlaced, some curved, some straight, the sort of thing an infant playing with a pen or pencil might produce."

Blackburn walked back and forth behind Smith, stopping occasionally to aid his concentration by drawing a copy of the complicated figure. He would stare intently at the figure, then toward the blanket-swathed man in the chair. Finally Smith's hand came from under the blanket to reach for his pencil, and he made an almost perfect copy.

Before the test they had practiced their moves thoroughly. With vision and hearing obscured a new ruse was needed to pass on the information. When Blackburn, apparently by accident, stumbled against the edge of rug near Smith's chair, Smith felt the vibration. This was his signal to shout, "I have it," extend his hand from the blanket, and reach for the pencil. Blackburn, who by then "was fairly expert in palming," pushed a pencil across the table to Smith. This was the pencil he had earlier used to draw the image as a focal point for his concentration. While he had openly drawn a large design, he secretly had made a smaller one on cigarette paper. During his pacing, Blackburn had crumpled the cigarette paper and inserted it in the brass end of his pencil.

Under the blanket, where no one could see him, Smith forced up the material over his eyes, removed the paper from the pencil, and read it by placing it flat against a luminous piece of slate that he carried in his pocket. The wadded cigarette paper and the slate were stashed away in his pocket; the bandage was pulled back in place; and he was ready to demonstrate that his powers as a thought reader had not been hampered by the rigorous precautions against cheating. He had had to remember the design for only a matter of seconds before beginning to draw the large facsimile.

Blackburn's series in *John Bull* caused no furor among the members of the Society for Psychical Research. Perhaps none of them ever read this publication. The *Daily News* article, however, did. The strongest objector was a former S.P.R. member who now owned an amusement area in Brighton—Blackburn's one-time partner, George Albert Smith. Quite naturally he told a reporter from the *News* that the piece was "a tissue of errors." Blackburn replied that he was "pleased to learn that the bright, amusing and ingenious confrère of thirty years ago is in the prime of life." Blackburn said he had heard while abroad that Smith had died. However, if Smith wished to prove he had authentic telepathic ability, he should demonstrate it in London. Smith did not accept the suggestion.

Those who wish to learn more about Smith's involvement with

the Society for Psychical Research should read Trevor Hall's *The Strange Case of Edmund Gurney*, published by Gerald Duckworth & Co. Ltd. in London in 1964. Hall saw a letter that Sir Oliver Lodge, the distinguished physicist and staunch believer in psychic phenomena, wrote concerning the Smith-Blackburn experiments on December 5, 1908. As Lodge recalled it, Gurney became aware that a code was being used, though this is not mentioned in any of his printed reports, when either Blackburn didn't cue Smith that they were doing a test with pictures rather than numbers or Smith failed to get the cue. Blackburn concentrated on the sketch of a cat. Smith, after due effort, seized a pencil and wrote 3120. The third letter of the alphabet is *C*; the first is *A*; and the twentieth is *T*.

The first investigation of extrasensory perception in an American university began at Stanford in Palo Alto, California, in 1915. Thomas Welton Stanford, the founder's brother who lived in Melbourne, Australia, had given the university fifty thousand dollars for psychical research four years earlier. An annual five hundred dollars supplementary gift was added for the purchase of relevant books and periodicals.

John E. Coover, Stanford's first Fellow in Psychical Research, was made an Associate Professor in the Psychology Department. By March 1917, Coover had completed 12,900 ESP experiments to test the theory, advanced by Charles Richet, the French physiologist, that everyone has a measurable capacity for extrasensory perception. A thousand more experiments were made at Stanford to evaluate another Richet theory—that professed psychics have a greater ESP potential than normal folk. One of Richet's subjects, Leonie B., a medium who had been hypnotized, identified five of twenty-five playing cards individually sealed in envelopes by him in Paris in 1888. When similar tests with Leonie were repeated in London, her score dropped to a pure chance average.

As it had been suggested that subliminal impressions might possibly have been a factor in previous experiments, 15,485 tests were made by Coover in this area. Several experiments in long-distance telepathy were also recorded. Later in 1917 a 600-page report was published. Coover had found no scientific evidence for ESP.

After the death of Dr. Richard Hodgson, secretary of the American branch of the Society for Psychical Research in 1905, friends donated a memorial fund to finance experiments in mental and psychical phenomena at Harvard. A later gift from Mrs. John Wallace Riddle was made on the proviso that the long-delayed investigation begin immediately. Late in 1916 Professor Leonard Troland began making plans for a laboratory study of telepathy and clairvoyance in the psychology department. His announced aims were:

> to insure the accurate determination and reproducibility of experimental conditions, to eliminate the personal equation of the investigator and to obtain quantitative data which shall be clearly amenable to mathematical, statistical treatment.

Gardner Murphy, a graduate student, assisted him in selecting and arranging the equipment. Troland's 605 tests for telepathy were too few to be conclusive. In 1920, with the arrival of William McDougall, the British psychologist, Harvard became a center for ESP activity. Professor McDougall, then president of the Society for Psychical Research in England, was elected president of the American group the following year.

Gardner Murphy, who in the meantime had received his doctorate, began research under the Hodgson fellowship in 1922 and for three years devoted a large share of his time to experiments in telepathy. Dr. G. H. Estabrooks, the next Hodgson Fellow, also probed the sending and receiving of thoughts. Though the students he used for his subjects frequently scored high at the start, the longer they were tested the lower their scores dropped. Apparently ESP was not a talent that increased with experience.

In June 1926, Dr. Joseph Banks Rhine and his wife, Louisa, arrived in Cambridge. Psychical research interested them greatly. They planned to spend a year at Harvard, studying psychology and philosophy, and hoped Professor McDougall would aid them in understanding the puzzling areas of extrasensory perception which perplexed them.

Rhine, who was to become America's most famous parapsychologist, was born in Juniata County, Pennsylvania, in 1895. When his family moved to Ohio, he met and went to school with the girl he later married. They completed their undergraduate studies at the University of Chicago and received doctorates in biology there. Rhine had once hoped to become a Protestant minister. Louisa shared his belief that men had powers which seemed to be beyond the five senses.

They had heard Sir Arthur Conan Doyle lecture in the 1920's during his American crusade for spiritualism. The tall, moustached British writer had a serenity rare among men. He was convinced that there was an afterlife. He said he had talked with dead friends through mediums, and he had seen psychics perform marvels that could be explained by no accepted scientific laws. Rhine was stimulated by Conan Doyle's words; if there was only a spark of truth in what this man said it would be of tremendous significance. "This mere possibility," Rhine wrote later, "was the most exhilarating thought I had had in years."

He and Louisa attended séances and sat in dark rooms while mediums seemed to summon up the dead, but rapping sounds, floating tables, and luminous forms didn't impress them. In Boston they visited the home of Dr. Le Roi Goddard Crandon, a respected surgeon, whose wife Mina was known to the public as Margery. She had been the principal contender for the award offered by the *Scientific American* to any medium who could convince the magazine committee of experts that his or her manifestations were of supernatural origin. Professor McDougall, Houdini the magician, Dr. Walter Franklin Prince, and Dr. Daniel Fisk Comstock had cast four negative votes to Hereward Carrington's single affirmative to grant her the award. After an evening in the dark, upstairs séance chamber on Lime Street, the Rhines agreed that Margery had practiced "brazen trickery."

During the Rhines' year at Harvard, Dr. Prince, of the Boston

Society for Psychical Research, was their mentor, McDougall having accepted an offer from Duke University to establish a department of psychology there. In 1927 they, too, went to Durham, North Carolina. McDougall thought telepathy and clairvoyance were worthy of academic study. Rhine was eager to devise and carry out laboratory experiments; he wrote later that McDougall gave him encouragement, which he doubted he would have received in any other American institution of higher learning.

The Rhines' first published report in the ESP area concerned a horse, not a human. They traveled with McDougall in late 1927 to a barn near Richmond, Virginia, to investigate Lady, a "talking" mare; Lady answered questions by pushing alphabet and number blocks with her nose. Convinced that the three-year-old equine had telepathic powers, they wrote "An Investigation of a 'Mind-Reading' Horse" which was printed in the *Journal of Abnormal and Social Psychology* in 1929, Volume 23, page 449. Later that year, in Volume 24, page 287, in a follow-up study, they said that later visits to Richmond convinced them that the mare had lost her psychic ability during the interim.

The first of the card-guessing tests that were to bring Rhine to prominence was made with the youngsters at a summer camp in 1930. The children were told to write the first digit that came to their minds as the thirty-five-year-old psychologist from Duke stared at a numbered card in his hand. In a thousand trials not a single child scored high enough to warrant further investigation.

At the university sixteen hundred trials were conducted by Rhine and Dr. K. E. Zener with undergraduates attempting to guess either letters of the alphabet or numbers that had been sealed in opaque envelopes. The total of accurate guesses was so close to chance that a less dedicated man might have abandoned the project.

Instead a change in procedure was made. Someone had the brilliant idea of using five target symbols—thus the guesser had a 1 in 5 break. The symbols chosen were a circle, star, rectangle, wavy lines, and a plus sign. Decks of twenty-five cards, each symbol repeated five times, were prepared. Tests were made after the pack had been shuffled but without the cards being enclosed in envelopes. Today these decks, which are called Zener cards—after Rhine's associate—or ESP cards, are a standard testing unit throughout the world. Five correct guesses in twenty-five are expected by chance.

Even with the symbol cards the scores seldom were far enough above the results that one would expect from chance guessing. The big breakthrough came one afternoon in late May 1931. Adam J. Linzmayer, a psychology student, was relaxing on a couch in the laboratory. Rhine shuffled a pack and walked to a nearby window. He looked at the top card and challenged the young man to name it. Linzmayer did. Rhine urged him on, and he made nine correct calls in a row. This many consecutive hits had never before been made at Duke. Student and instructor were so elated that the next day they ran through a series of three hundred cards. Again Linzmayer called nine successive cards accurately, but his hits dwindled the longer they persisted. By the end of the day Linzmayer's right guesses had dropped to the level of chance.

Unfortunately the student was leaving Durham to work at a summer job. The intensive three-hundred-card session had shown that his ESP was not at its best under pressure. His last day on the campus Rhine took him for a drive. The instructor pulled his car to the side of a road and with the motor still running began another test. Again Linzmayer, who sat beside him on the front seat, relaxed, his head back and his eyes closed. Rhine cut a pack of symbol cards, took the top one and tilted it enough to see it, then put it face down on the notebook in Linzmayer's lap.

"Circle," called Linzmayer. "Right," Rhine verified. "Plus Sign." Another right and the student went on to name 15 correct symbols in a row. In that epic run he scored 6 more successes—21 of a possible 25. They spent the rest of the afternoon driving, testing, starting, stopping. The mathematical odds Rhine quoted on the 15 in a row triumph were thirty billion to one. As to naming 21 of 25, the odds would boggle the imagination.

Seven other students, among the hundreds tested, made incredibly high scores. For example, when George Zirkle, whose telepathy scores with other senders had not been notable, was tested with his fiancée, Sara Ownbey, it became obvious they were in tune mentally as well as emotionally. When she was ready to concentrate she pressed a telegraph key, signaling to Zirkle two rooms away. He responded at the signal. Linzmayer's record toppled. Zirkle correctly identified 23 of a possible 25, 85 of a possible 100, and averaged 16 hits for each 25 in 250 tries. He was, Rhine enthused, by far the best receiver of telepathic impressions yet.

When they changed places and George sent while Sara received, it soon became clear that theirs was not a two-way system.

"Was Prof. J. B. Rhine Hoodwinked?" asked the headline on the front page of *The Jinx*. In the August 1938 edition of his magic journal, editor Ted Annemann explained how it would have been easy for the students in the room-to-room test to get their high scores. First, two people practice counting silently until their counts are in unison. Then they give the five symbols numerical values. For example, plus sign—two, wavy lines—three, and square—four. At the start of the test the receiver writes any symbol that comes to his mind for the first entry, but the moment the sending key is pressed both sender and receiver begin counting silently. If the next card is a plus sign, the sender presses the telegraph key after counting two; if a square, after counting four. As sender and receiver are silently counting at the same pace, the receiver gets the second and the next twenty-three cards on cue, and should he make a lucky guess on the first card he can score a perfect result. Without the lucky guess, a 24 out of 25 is possible, though wise deceptionists would play it cozy and not strain credulity by calling so many correctly.

Sara Ownbey told Dr. Rhine that while she was alone she had shuffled a pack of ESP cards, put them face down on a table, then, clairvoyantly, predicted their order from top to bottom. She said that once she had named all twenty-five correctly in advance. Rhine wrote that she was the best scorer in a test of this sort Duke had ever produced "if we take her unwitnessed records, as I am fully prepared to do."

Another prime exhibit on Rhine's roster of ESP experiments at the North Carolina university was the Pearce-Pratt series. Hubert E. Pearce, Jr., a young Methodist, was a divinity student at Duke's School of Religion. Psychic abilities, he said, were prevalent on his mother's side of the family. Once, according to Pearce, she had had a table tilting so vigorously that it took the combined strength of two men to hold their side down, though she touched it only with her fingers.

Rhine arranged for Pearce to be tested by his assistant, J. Gaither Pratt. Though Pratt had experimented with other students, he had never recorded unusually high scores until he began working with Pearce in 1932. During their early sessions together, nine or ten correct calls per twenty-five were common. Pearce continued to maintain this average score for a year, except when he was ill or when special experimental situations were arranged. When he was given a drug, for example, his average score fell. The tests, according to Rhine's own description of them, were far from being foolproof. Pearce and Pratt sat facing each other across a small table in the Duke laboratory. On the table were a dozen or more packs of ESP cards and a record book. Pearce, the person being tested, was actually allowed to handle the cards most of the time. First he shuffled the deck and placed the pack face down on the table. After Pratt cut and restored the deck, Pearce picked it up and, one by one, removed the top cards, called them while their faces were down and put them aside. Pratt entered the calls in the record book. When the run had been completed Pratt turned the cards face up and compared their order with the notes he had made. Rhine wrote that an "alert" tester could not have been deceived again and again by sleight of hand during this process. Of course, Rhine emphasized Pearce was not even an amateur conjurer.

Actually there are at least a dozen ways a subject who wished to cheat under the conditions Rhine described could deceive the investigator. Not the least effective is a gambler's ruse which has been employed for at least two hundred years. Attached to the ball of the right ring finger of the dealer's hand by a bit of wax is a small *shiner,* a reflecting disk. As the gambler holds a card face down in his right hand the lower right number and suit are reflected in the shiner and there the dealer sees it. I have tried the technique with ESP cards and because of their large bold symbols it works equally well. It should be noted that in the early eighteenth century some sharpsters spilled a drop of the liquid they were quaffing on the table, and later used it as their reflector. No sleight of hand was necessary. If Rhine will offer a subject who can consistently match Pearce's high scores under exactly the same circumstances while members of the Occult Investigation Committee of the Society of American Magicians look on, I guarantee to produce a sleight-of-hand performer who will equal or better the scores without his method being detected by Rhine.

The only magician Rhine mentioned in his report as observer for a Pearce ESP test was Wallace Lee, "Wallace the Magician," who lived in Durham. While he looked on Pearce made 55 hits in 275 calls, an average of 5.0—pure chance. Before the magician arrived and after he left, the scores were higher, 7.5 and 7.4 respectively.

Pearce's impressive scores at long-distance clairvoyance were made while he was in another building across campus. Pratt sat in his office in the Physics Building, shuffled an ESP pack, cut the cards, then put one face down in a target position on a book resting on the table. Each card was left in place for a minute, then removed, still face down, from the book and put to one side. Pratt's and Pearce's watches were synchronized. Pratt, looking from the window of his office, could see Pearce as he crossed the campus and entered the library building. The tests were timed so that Pearce could reach his reading cubicle in the library before Pratt began the sending procedure in his office.

Pearce would make a guess, jot down a symbol, wait until a minute passed, then write another. Two packs of 25 cards were used. After Pratt had finished his part of the "sending work" he would turn the cards face up, enter their order on one piece of paper, then make a copy on a second. Pearce's task was less complicated. As he already had one list he had only to make a copy. Pratt and Pearce then folded their record sheets sealed them in envelopes and dated the envelopes. The first three hundred trials were made with Pratt about a 100 yards away from Pearce; eleven hundred were made at a greater distance—250 yards with Pratt in another office in the Medical Building. The final three hundred tests were completed with Pratt back in his own office. Pearce's hits in the first 100-yard test averaged 9.9; at 250 yards they dropped to 6.7; and rose again for the last 100-yard runs to 7.3. In the last 150 cards in the final test Pearce reached a new high —9.3.

Mathematically the result of the combined long-distance experiments was overwhelming. To quote Pratt's figures: "the chance odds are 1 in 10,000,000,000,000,000,000,000,000."

Rhine's first book, *Extra-Sensory Perception* (there was a hyphen in the first word in those days), was published in 1934. His analysis of ninety thousand trials over a period of some three years led him to conclude that ESP was now "an actual and demonstrable occurrence." Enthusiastic articles in newspapers and magazines convinced the man in the street that Dr. Rhine of Duke University had scientifically confirmed a suspicion many people had harbored for years. The academic world was more cautious in its appraisal. Could the "actual and demonstrable" experiments be repeated? Not, it was soon evident, at Princeton, Johns Hopkins, Colgate, Southern Methodist, or Brown.

Scholarly critics offered a long list of objections to Rhine's conclusion. First, there was no plausible theory to account for ESP. The detail expected in a scientific report was lacking. How, precisely, were the cards shuffled in the various tests? What steps had been taken to eliminate possible fraud in the long-distance experiments? Rhine claimed that all of Pearce's work had "been carefully witnessed." No observer had been with Pearce in the remote library cubicle. Had anyone thought to measure any difference in elapsed time between each tap of the telegraph key in the Zirkle-Ownbey tests?

In the four-page appendix to the British edition of his book, Rhine wrote that in the year and a half that had passed since he had finished his report "a special condition" had been successfully arranged "that completely eliminates all chance for deception" aside from the collusion of all who worked on the project. He did not describe this "special condition" which could protect against *all* possible fraud.

Henry L. Mencken was suspicious of both ESP and the Durham investigator. The high scores, the Baltimore iconoclast suggested, were either a matter of luck or the knack of the subjects to recognize minute differences on the backs of the ESP cards. "Next to English physicists, American psychologists seem to be the easiest marks on earth for transcendental wizardry—and Professor Rhine, observe sadly, is of the psychological faculty."

Official Duke University ESP testing cards, approved by Dr. Rhine, were manufactured and offered for sale in 1937. Both scientists and magicians were quick to discover that some of the symbols could be read from the back. The stamp of symbol dies had made a perceptible difference on the reverse sides. Other cards were "edge readers"; designs near the edges on the backs had been machine trimmed so that a close observer could tell those bearing one symbol from another. Rhine's *Journal of Parapsychology* in 1937 mentioned that imperfections had been noted, though they were not specified. Those who had the faulty packs were advised to "screen" the cards, that is, not let the people being tested see the backs. Charges that the ESP cards were marked haunted Rhine and his associates for years.

Most magicians have logical minds. John Mulholland pondered the staggering odds Rhine had quoted against the success of his experiments and wondered just how accurate they were. He approached his friend Professor Walter G. Pitkin at Columbia University and asked him if anyone could call long runs of successive symbols just by chance? How did one determine the odds against matching pairs? Pitkin didn't know but the problem intrigued him. Mulholland and Pitkin arranged for a large-scale random test.

As Rhine had used five symbols, they had the cards for their experiment marked from one to five, forty thousand of each, two hundred thousand in all. Half of the cards were red; the other hundred thousand were white. Each set was mechanically shuffled, then fed through a machine which read and printed their numbers on sheets of paper. The task then was to check the sequences of the red cards with those of the white.

The results were interesting. Sometimes there was not a single match in thirty-two successive numbers; by accepted odds there should have been six. Runs of five matching pairs were 25 percent under the expected occurrence, but six matches in a row rose the same proportion above chance. Sequences of seven pairs were 59 percent more frequent than expected, and there were some runs of twenty-five to fifty numbers with approximately half paired. The mechanical card shuffling and processing were carried out by the International Business Machines Corporation.

Summing up the experiment Mulholland said: "The total number of pairs in the entire one hundred thousand was less than 2 per cent away from what was to be expected. The total, by the way, was under mathematical expectancy."

Rhine too had noted that though a rare subject scored high, eventually the average dropped to chance. When, because of the criticisms, more precautions were taken to block possible sensory cues at Duke, high-scoring subjects who could equal the early records of Linzmayer, Pearce, Zirkle, and Ownbey could not be found.

S. G. Soal, a British mathematician, was Rhine's most persistent critic. In his opinion the early high scores were due not to gifted subjects but to lax testing conditions. Soal knew from experience how easily a man could be deceived. He had been amazed in 1929 when Pascal Fortuny, a French psychic who was then in England, called the first three letters of his last name, though they hadn't been formally introduced. Later he learned that Fortuny at lunch that day had asked and been told the name of the man who would see him in the afternoon. Fortuny also asked if Soal remembered someone named Geddes from the days when he was a schoolboy. Soal did indeed. Geddes had been his drawing instructor when he was fifteen. This seemed spectacular evidence of ESP until Soal discovered the French mystic had tried the same name on two other sitters. In neither case was there an association. Soal reasoned it was a name the medium thought would be applicable to his British clients.

Soal was not amused "by Rhine's discovery of a telepathic horse . . . by the card-guessing feats of Pearce while sitting in a motor car and similar marvels." If things of this sort occurred in Britain they would be "quickly exposed as frauds or conjuring tricks," he said, but in Rhine's country "they are proclaimed genuine with a blare of trumpets."

He did not deny the existence of ESP but endeavored to confirm it with foolproof tests. By 1939 Soal had made 120,000 trials with more than 140 people of varied backgrounds and I.Q.'s; he tested Chinese, Greeks, Indians, and Egyptians as well as Britons but found no confirmatory data. When it was suggested that he reevaluate his records and check the number of hits that proceeded or followed each call he found two of his early subjects scored high in these areas.

Further experiments were made in 1941 with Basil Shackleton as a subject on this premise. Mrs. K. M. Goldney, of the Society for Psychical Research, assisted Soal. Shackleton, a professional photographer, made 1,101 right guesses in a run of 3,789 cards. The right guesses were, however, not on target but one ahead; for example, each correct answer matched not with the card being called for, but with the next card in the run. When the tests were speeded up, Shackleton's right guesses jumped to two cards ahead. In 794 trials, by this method of scoring, 236 hits were made.

Four years later, Mrs. Gloria Stewart, the second of the high scorers in the earlier tests by the new evaluation, made 9,410 correct calls in 37,100 trials. These were right on the button, not calls before or after. In *Modern Experiments in Telepathy* (New Haven & London, Yale University Press, 1954) which Soal wrote with Frederick Bateman, it is noted that no "ultra-rigorous precautions on fraud" were carried out "on the part of the experimenters" because if they "are not to be trusted, there is no point whatever in their doing experiments." Another Soal comment, published in *Ciba Foundation Symposium on Extrasensory Perception* (Boston, Little, Brown and Company, 1956), is illuminating: "But it never entered my mind that Mrs. Stewart or Mr. Shackleton would try consciously to cheat, they are not the sort of people who cheat."

A new series of away-from-the-laboratory experiments began in August 1955. Soal's subjects were Glyn and Ieuan Jones, two thirteen-year-old boys who lived with their parents near Capel Curig, a small village in North Wales. Tests in the family cottage were most informal. Packs of animal cards—one of Soal's early innovations—made up of five penguins and a like number of elephants, zebras, lions, and giraffes were used. Soal mixed the cards, then showed them one by one to one of the schoolboys. The other youngster sat across the table which had a suitcase lengthwise on its top to prevent him from seeing the other boy's face. The first runs were disappointing. When Soal offered an incentive for success, however, ESP began to be apparent. He promised each boy a shilling if 9 correct calls were made in 25, two shillings for 10, four for 11, and so on. Before the summer was over each of the Jones boys had earned fifteen pounds thirteen shillings, or $43.82 apiece.

They were so successful that Soal set up a new payment plan. Sixpence for 9, a shilling for 10, another sixpence for each point higher until 18. Odds were so high against 18 that he offered a pound (then $2.80) thirty shillings ($4.20) for 19, and on up to four pounds ($11.20) for a perfect score of 25.

In October, Soal brought the boys to London for a series of tests at the Society for Psychical Research headquarters. The first day the Welsh wonders were not in good form, but in the next three series they were back on target. Two 18-correct runs were recorded.

When the boys were tested again in Wales that November, control conditions were tightened. A carpet was draped over one end of the table so that Glyn could not see Ieuan's legs. Scores plummeted. Ieuan, who had shown no sign of so much as a sniffle earlier, began coughing. Mrs. Goldney became aware that the boy's chair creaked three times as he concentrated on lion cards and each time Glyn guessed right. Shades of the Creery sisters and their downfall at Cambridge so many years before! The boys, like the girls, confessed. After they promised their parents that they would not cheat, the tests resumed. Even without the obvious coughs and creaks they again made high scores.

On their third visit to London a man they did not know conducted the first three sittings. The tall, balding man made few changes in the usual procedure, but when he offered a suggestion, they followed it. One of the boys was put in one room, the other in an adjacent chamber. A blanket was suspended across the open doorway so that one youngster could not see the other's movements. Their chairs faced, but they were more than twenty feet apart. Their scores for the first two sittings were far above chance and for the third they soared to 21, 20, 18, and 19 for 25-card runs.

For the first time they learned that the man who had been supervising these tests was Jack Salvin, chairman of the Occult Investigation Committee of the London Magic Circle. He signed statements after each sitting admitting he found no evidence of chicanery. To quote from one: "Code or trickery in the experimental conditions I witnessed is impossible." No one in England knew more about the methods gamblers use to convey card information than the late Jack Salvin, and he and his wife sometimes presented a mental act during which she revealed his unspoken thoughts.

After the Welsh boys learned his identity, a strange thing happened. He conducted the next three sittings, and each day their scores sagged below chance expectation. If the boys were using trickery, why hadn't Salvin detected it? If the solution offered by C. E. M. Hansel is correct, Salvin overlooked one possible explanation. Hansel, Professor of Psychology at the University College of Swansea, University of Wales, suspected that a silent dog whistle was the signaling device. Its blasts cannot be heard by men of Salvin's age, though dogs, children, and some young adults with an acute sense of sound are immediately aware of the high-pitched sounds. Hansel cut off most of the body of a silent whistle and to the business end fixed a length of rubber tubing. To the far end of the tube he fastened a rubber ball. With the whistle dangling down his trouser leg and the bulb in his trouser pocket, he was ready to test his theory. He supposed that the father of one of the Jones boys, who was in the room in London during the tests, could have used the device, or the sender could have operated it. Hansel chose two Welsh girls for an open-air experiment. One was eight, the other nine. The girl who was to be the sender peeped at the first card as Hansel pressed the bulb in his pocket. She and the receiver both heard the "silent" blast and began counting mentally. He continued pressing the bulb until the number which indicated the proper card was reached. At this point the girl who had looked at the card made a slight movement with her foot. Hansel released the bulb, and the other girl, hearing no more sounds, knew the number. After a quarter-hour practice the girls scored 16 hits in 25 cards.

Hansel went further. He found he could control the "test" even when he was not on the scene. While watching the girls from the second floor window of a house, he signaled to them with the whistle, which could be heard perhaps fifty feet away. Indoors, he worked with a nine-year-old Welsh boy. Sometimes he gave the cues when he stood by as an observer, other times when he played the part of the sender. None of the people who saw the tests had any idea that a trick was being done, let alone how it was done.

The researchers who tested the Jones boys, Hansel pointed out, were closer to seventy than forty, so it was highly unlikely that a silent whistle would have been detected.

Jack Salvin was in charge of another London series of experiments in March 1959. This time Christopher Scott and his wife, in a similar setting to that used in the Jones tests, were sender and receiver. Scott cued his wife with a concealed silent dog whistle. Salvin admitted frankly he saw no evidence of deception.

The Jones boys, like the best subjects at Duke and those Soal had tested previously, lost their telepathic powers. In April 1957, Soal decided there was no point in arranging further tests.

Hansel today is the most active critic of ESP. He will accept no experiment as valid, no matter how distinguished the researcher, unless every precaution was taken against possible fraud. It is difficult now for him to prove that deception was used in the early experiments but he delights in explaining how trickery could have been used. In *ESP—A Scientific Evaluation,* published in New York by Charles Scribner's Sons in 1966, he tells how while he was a Senior Lecturer in Psychology at the University of Manchester he came to Durham, North Carolina, to study Dr. Rhine's work. The Pearce-Pratt cross-campus tests intrigued him, but the published reports had been much too skimpy in detail. Dr. Rhine arranged for a grant to cover Hansel's expenses and he, Dr. Pratt, and other members of the Duke staff were eager to fill in the missing facts though sometimes the answers were not available. Soal asked Pratt which cubicle in the library Pearce had used as his post. Pratt couldn't remember. He did take Hansel to the room in the old Physics Building that had been his office for the 100-yards-away tests. He put a table and a chair in the positions they had occupied then and mentioned that the room had been remodeled, that a wall now cut off a smaller area. At the time of the experiments it had been a part of the room in which they stood.

In the smaller room Hansel noticed a window about two feet wide and equally high. Its lower ledge was approximately five feet ten inches above the floor. Across the corridor other offices had similar windows. He entered one office and discovered he could look through its window into the small room and, had not the new wall intervened, possibly down on the table where, after the tests,

Pratt turned the cards face up so he could write the sequences in his reports. What, Hansel wondered, would have prevented Pearce from leaving the library and making his way to this room across the hall in time to see the cards as Pratt turned them face up? If Pearce had done this, he could have quickly written enough hit symbols on his sheets to bring his score far above chance. Pratt would have been busily occupied first in listing the order of the face-up cards, then in making a copy of this list. Pratt and Rhine had seen Pearce enter the library building, but they would not have been staring out the window constantly during the test: their attention must have been on the target cards. This explanation, Hansel admitted, was just a conjecture.

He could, however, test to see if such a procedure would have worked. He asked one of the men on Rhine's staff to sit at a table and go through the sending and recording routine precisely as Pratt had done. Hansel said he would concentrate in another room down the hall. The man did as he had been asked. After he finished making a copy of the recorded symbols, he unlocked his door, and Hansel returned. The staff member now compared Hansel's symbols with those he had recorded. He found 22 in 25 correct and confessed he had no idea how the British psychologist had made such a score. The skeptic explained his deception. He had not gone to a room at the end of the hall; instead he had entered the one next door. Standing on a chair, he had peeked into the office through a crack at the top of the door between the two rooms. Once he had seen the face-up cards he had quickly filled in his report.

Hansel also visited the room in the Medical Building which Pratt had used during the 250-yard-distance test. It too had been remodeled, but there was a trap door in the ceiling directly over the position Pratt's table had once occupied. Couldn't Pearce have gone to the room above while he was supposed to be in the library, Hansel conjectured, and peeked down at the cards?

Dr. Bernard F. Riess, a psychologist at Hunter College, had

been fascinated by, and dubious of, the high scores reported in the Pearce-Pratt distance tests at Duke. One of his students knew a girl who was said to be psychic. She lived a quarter of a mile or so from his home in White Plains, New York. The girl was willing to participate in a house-to-house series of experiments. She agreed to be ready at 9 P.M. on nights that were convenient to them both. Riess in his study went through two packs of ESP cards, and the girl at her home wrote her impressions. Her scores, like so many others, were unpromising on the first run. From the second day on they began improving. When Riess checked her calls against his records for 1,800 cards, he found she had an average of 18.23 hits for each 25! This was the greatest score ever achieved in an extensive test of ESP, far better than that made by the star subjects of either Rhine or Soal. In 1937, Riess published a report in the *Journal of Parapsychology*, Volume 1, Number 4. In a second series of 250 calls her score returned to a more normal ratio: 5.30 per 25 cards. When scholars sought verification from the girl a year later, no one could find her. Dr. Riess said her health had deteriorated and she had "disappeared" somewhere in the Middle West. By then Riess had experimented with sixty-seven Hunter students; none had a score higher than chance.

Despite the melancholy saga of ESP research, many people still can't help thinking there is something in it. They ponder over their own experiences, forgetting the hundreds of times their hunches fizzled and remembering only the rare occasions when they came true. "I knew my sister would be on the phone that night with the news that her daughter had died after the cancer operation," a woman told me in Pittsburgh. With her niece in a critical condition, it seems reasonable that a late-night phone call would have come from her sister and that if her sister called the news would not be good. "I frequently know what my wife will say before she opens her mouth," a young man told me after my lecture at the University of Wisconsin. So do I. When two people live together they share so many experiences that it is not unusual for one, triggered by a news item, a passage in a book, or a household incident, to say something which the other at precisely that second is either thinking or about to say.

Despite the lack of confirmable evidence for ESP, many people think that eventually it will be proved. Meanwhile, you can amuse your friends with a feat that makes it appear you can anticipate their thoughts. Write several words secretly on a piece of paper. Fold it and put it under an ashtray or a glass. Announce you are about to make a psychological experiment. When you snap your fingers, your friend is to answer immediately—without a second thought—the question you pose. Snap your fingers and say, "Name a color." Immediately after the reply, snap them again, and say, "A piece of furniture." Finally, snap them a third time, "Name a flower." If you have written red, chair, and rose, the odds are that you will have two, if not all three, correct.

When Professor Rhine retired at the age of seventy, his famous Parapsychology Laboratory at Duke University closed. The equipment and records were moved off campus to the new Institute for Parapsychology in 1966. This is a project of the Foundation for Research on the Nature of Man, established by his supporters, some of whom had given funds for his work at the university. Here, under his direction, the experiments continue. Many of his former aides at Duke are associated with other organizations. Dr. William G. Roll is project director for the Psychical Research Foundation, which was founded in 1961. Its headquarters are also in Durham. He is more interested in poltergeists and mediumistic phenomena than tests for telepathy and clairvoyance. Dr. Karlis Osis is research director for the American Society for Psychical Research. He is evaluating the results of local and long-distance ESP tests, investigating the work of psychics, and visiting houses that are said to be haunted. Dr. J. Gaither Pratt is on the staff of the new Division of Parapsychology in the Department of Psychiatry at the University of Virginia School of Medicine.

A generous donor made the grant which led to the establishment of a Research Professorship in Psychiatry at the University of

Virginia, a post that psychical researcher Dr. Ian Stevenson now holds, and the creation of the Division of Parapsychology. The same donor practically doubled the endowment of the American Society for Psychical Research and provided most of the money for its research programs. Their laboratory on West 73 Street in New York City, equipped with closed-circuit TV for room-to-room ESP tests and a computer, now bears his name. Chester F. Carlson, the inventor of the Xerox process died December 4, 1968. He was intensely interested in scientific investigations of the occult. This interest many share, but few have the means to sponsor it on such a grand scale.

Dr. Rhine in a recent radio interview said he still looks forward to the day when parapsychology will be accepted as a "respectable" science. Dr. Pratt predicts that a revolution in thinking will lead to this acceptance. Professor Hansel still waits patiently for a single conclusive, repeatable ESP experiment. He thinks future scientists should devote their time "to more worthwhile research."

A large share of the public has been so misled that they offer telepathy as a valid explanation when one person seems to know what another is thinking. Yet many brilliant men have investigated the subject for almost ninety years, and they have yet to find a single person who can, without trickery, receive even the simplest three-letter word under test conditions.

At the start of this chapter it was said that Dr. Gardner Murphy, the president of the American Society for Psychical Research, is convinced that ESP exists. Belief and proof are not, however, synonymous. He was quoted in the January 1970 A.S.P.R. *Journal*: "in a strict sense there are no hard facts," and he admitted in the February 1970 issue of *Psychic* that most of the phenomena one hears about casually are "just rubbish." People do not realize, he continued, "that the most bizarre coincidences do happen." An Associated Press story in the February 27, 1970, issue of the *New York Post* offers an excellent example. Mrs. Jack Greenway, while playing bridge at the Cocoa-Rockledge Country Club in Cocoa, Florida, dealt herself thirteen spades. Mrs. James Purgason received thirteen diamonds; Mrs. R. B. Deaton, thirteen hearts; and Mrs. Myron Stevens, thirteen clubs. The *Post* article continues: "*The Guinness Book of World Records* says: 'If all the people in the world were grouped in bridge fours and each four were dealt 120 hands per day, it would require 1,000,000,000,000 years before one "perfect" deal could be expected to recur.'"

ESP IN ANIMALS

Extrasensory-perception tests were not limited to human beings during the days that Dr. J. B. Rhine had his Parapsychology Laboratory at Duke University. In the 1950's, Dr. Karlis Osis and Mrs. Esther Foster experimented with cats. While one researcher watched a cat make a choice of food from two similar plates, the other, hidden by a screen, tried to direct the tabby mentally. In another series for clairvoyance, the cat on its own was to find which of two pans contained food. The results were not impressive.

A dog named Chris made phenomenal scores at symbol-card guessing. He indicated his choice by pawing once for a circle, twice for a plus sign, and so on. The results were never documented under conditions acceptable to skeptical scientists. Rigid control was impossible as Chris performed in the home of his owner, G. H. Wood, in Warwick, Rhode Island. Two of Rhine's associates, Dr. Remi J. Cadoret and Dr. J. Gaither Pratt, on several occasions between 1957 and 1960 traveled there to observe. In his book *Parapsychology: An Insider's View* (E. P. Dutton and Co., Inc., 1966), Pratt offered three possible explanations for the dog's remarkable performance. The first, and most satisfactory to him, was ESP. The second was "the successful agents were unconsciously giving sensory information . . . to the person working with Chris." The third was "some honest mistake in interpreting

39

the rules they were supposed to follow." The latter two, Pratt concluded, "are hardly within the bounds of reason." A fourth possibility may occur to the reader before he finishes this chapter.

The most discussed animal marvel of recent times was Lady, a benign mare who performed in a red barn near Richmond, Virginia. Though widely heralded as a talking horse with occult powers, Lady offered no more than an occasional whinny or snort. She communicated by spelling out words with large letters of the alphabet which she raised with a shove of her nose.

"She can read minds, predict the future and converse in Chinese," said an article in the New York *World* in 1927. A quarter of a century later, Les Leiber reported in *This Week* that he had arrived at the barn without an appointment and had written his name on a piece of paper which he kept clutched in his hand. The equine marvel spelled out L-E-S. It was enough, he confessed, "to have given me the willies."

Mrs. Claudia Fonda, the horse's owner, bought the filly two weeks after she had been foaled. She told me that she raised Lady as she would a child. The animal was not a thoroughbred or even striking in appearance; her only idiosyncrasy was a fondness for bananas. The horse, however, was a quick learner. Mrs. Fonda said she taught her how to count, master the alphabet, then perform simple feats of mathematics. No calculus—just practical everyday arithmetic. Proud of her prodigy, Mrs. Fonda decided to show her off to the world, at least that part of the world which drove by the farm on Petersburg Pike, three miles south of Richmond, Virginia.

A roadside sign announced that the Wonder Horse could spell, add, subtract, multiply, divide, tell time, and answer questions. Most people knew the time, and children were delighted when she solved math problems; but her answers to questions intrigued everyone and eventually made Lady a Richmond celebrity. Admission to the barn, which was open to the public afternoons and evenings, was reasonable: fifty cents for children, a dollar for adults.

Motorists on the pike, a section of Route One that extended

from New York to Florida, spread the story of the mare's amazing ability not only along the East Coast but throughout the United States. Most people asked personal questions: When would they marry? Should they take their doctor's advice? Was their husband true to them? How should they invest their money? Lady's prediction that Dempsey would trounce Sharkey attracted widespread comment. Sportsmen came to Virginia with serious queries. Who would win the Preakness? Which team would take the World Series banner? The mare was as well informed about Midwestern baseball as she was about the big leagues. She correctly prophesied that the Terre Haute, Indiana, club would capture the Three-I pennant in 1932. She had more success picking the annual winner of the Army-Navy football game than most professional sportswriters. An advertising man told me that he had three winners in a single afternoon at the Havre de Grace racetrack. It wasn't just chance, he went on, he had the tips straight from a horse's mouth. The horse, of course, was Lady.

Few horses devote much time to politics. They are more interested in oats, pastures, and other horses. Lady was never hesitant to give her opinion on the outcome of an election—local, statewide, or national. She singled out Franklin D. Roosevelt as the winner of the 1932 presidential campaign even before he received the Democratic nomination, and galloped from the Virginia limelight to the pages of the national press.

She was not impressed by Thomas Dewey when he ran against Harry Truman, the man from Missouri, nor, it developed, were a majority of the voters. It was said that senators and congressmen drove down from Washington to get her advice on pending bills and that fortunes had been made when her tips on the stock market were followed, but no evidence was ever offered to prove that this was true.

Dr. Joseph Banks Rhine, who later was to head the Parapsychology Laboratory at Duke University, firmly believed that Lady had psychic ability, or ESP as he termed it. He pitched a tent near the barn so that he could study her talents scientifically.

Life lamented in 1940 that the fifteen-year-old mare's days as a gifted psychic were over. Her misses were outtotaling her hits; she was better at grazing than prophesying. Yesterday's animal marvel was today's old horse.

Then, late in 1952, America's most famous four-legged prophet was in the headlines again, reaping the biggest press coverage of her long career. A man came south to confront her with a problem that had stymied the police of Norfolk County, Massachusetts. A four-year-old boy had vanished without a trace. Intensive searches by state troopers and volunteer citizen groups had failed to find even a shred of his clothing. There were many ways to pose the question. Had he been kidnapped? Had he met with a serious accident? Had he run away from home? The man chose the direct approach. Where was the boy now? As Mrs. Fonda stood by Lady's side in the barn, the twenty-seven-year-old former oracle bent her head over the lettered oblongs and spelled out "Pittsfield Water Wheel." The man knew there was no water wheel in Pittsfield, Massachusetts; he returned home disappointed. Too bad the old horse wasn't as psychic as she used to be.

A police captain who learned of Lady's prediction stared at the words after he wrote them on a piece of paper. The ancient oracles of Greece had been known to give messages that required considerable interpretation. Pittsfield Water Wheel. As he stared, his mind rearranged the syllables: Field Wheel Water Pitt. No, that wasn't quite right. It should be Field and Wilde Water Pit. Eureka! There was an old quarry which people knew by this name filled with water. They had looked everywhere else. Why not there? Dragging operations began, and eventually the body of the missing youngster was pulled from beneath the murky surface.

Lady made a comeback of spectacular proportions. It was the first time that *Life* ever publicly apologized to a four-footed animal. Two pages of pictures announced her return to the magazine's good graces. More people than ever began taking a detour to Virginia to seek the psychic horse's counsel. Reporters from the West Coast as well as the East coaxed Lady to find other missing persons or solve local crimes. One woman visitor was more interested in the horse's welfare than her talent. She asked the old mare a personal question. How did she like her work? Lady, bored by now with nuzzling out answers to queries, flipped up the letters to spell "Don't."

By 1956, Mrs. Fonda had shortened the time the famous horse was available to the public. The mare could be seen then only in the afternoon. Her evenings were free. One day I had a phone call from my friend John Kobler. The *Saturday Evening Post* was sending him to Richmond to do an article on Lady. Was I available to go with him, as one who was familiar with the techniques of deception, to act as a consultant? I was.

On the plane down I suggested that he introduce me to Mrs. Fonda as John Banks. She might have read my comments on Lady in the Baltimore *Sun,* and besides my assumed name had a special significance that I would explain later. We drove in a rented car out to the Petersburg Pike and turned left at the roadside sign. I had a camera with me, and it seemed logical to assume that Mrs. Fonda would accept me as a photographer associate of the writer.

We talked with Mrs. Fonda in her frame farmhouse. She told us how impressed Dr. Rhine had been with Lady and let us read a letter he had written her stating that the animal was "the greatest thing since radio." I asked if Lady answered questions that came by mail. No, she answered, she didn't want any trouble with the government post office. Once the Richmond authorities had tried to make her pay the thousand-dollar yearly fee imposed on fortune-tellers, but she had convinced them that she was exhibiting an educated animal and the annual license in that category was fifty dollars.

While we were talking, some schoolchildren knocked on the front door. They wanted to ask Lady a few questions. She told them to come back later. She adjusted her glasses when I asked her if she planned to train another horse to replace Lady when the horse died. No, she answered, it had been fun working with Lady as a girl, but she would never go through it again.

We walked across the lawn to the red building with "Lady

Wonder Horse" lettered in white on its side. She unlocked the door. At one end of the structure was a pipework frame stall, with open sides and a rope tied across its front. In it stood the celebrated swaybacked mare. There was a "typewriter" between us and the horse.

To a thick plank were fastened two horizontal metal rods. Half the letters of the alphabet were flat on the horse's side of the rods, the other half extended flat toward us. Each of the metal oblongs that bore the letters rested on a lever. By pressing one of the levers, a letter could be raised to stand on end or drop vertically in place on our side. There was no trick to the simple mechanism. A bar on the right was pulled after words had been spelled and the letters were forced flat again for the next round.

Mrs. Fonda stood to our right by the horse with a rod, similar to a riding crop, in her right hand.

"What is my name?" I asked the mare. Lady moved her head, lowered it so that her nose pressed on a lever and B popped up to be followed by A-N-K-S.

"When will my brother come back from Europe?" Lady spelled out S-U-M-M-E-R.

I was disenchanted. I had been introduced to Mrs. Fonda as John Banks. I had used this name because a showman named Banks had exhibited the first famous talking horse in the seventeenth century, and I don't have a brother!

After Kobler had asked several questions, we were given pads and pencils. We could write any numbers and the clairvoyant horse would flip them up, Mrs. Fonda said. We stood far away from the stall to write. Neither the horse nor its owner could see the faces of the pads. John's numbers were immediately nosed up. I wrote several numbers. Some were correctly indicated, others not, and there was a good reason why they were not. For example, I wrote a 2, which Lady flipped up, then a 1 which Lady gave as 9. I wrote the 2 as anyone would, but when I wrote the 1, I went through the motions of writing a 9 but only touched my pencil to the paper for the downstroke.

It was obvious that a trick employed by mediums was being used. This is the technique known as pencil reading. The medium doesn't see the surface of the pad, but she can see the long end of the pencil. By following its movements, numbers and letters can be detected many feet away.

Mrs. Fonda had simplified the method; she had given us long, narrow pads. A wider pad or shorter pencil would make it difficult for her to follow the pencil movements. I still have the slips on which I wrote. They are 2½ inches wide and 8¾ inches long. The paper is yellow with thin, blue, ruled lines. Three pads of this width can be made by cutting a school tablet in three vertical parts.

I have read many accounts of others who visited Lady. In a few it was mentioned that questions were written, but not one, Rhine's included, noted the special long pads or the long pencils. Obviously the investigators were not aware of the pencil-reading system.

If Dr. Rhine was interested in testing for ESP, he should have ignored the horse and studied Mrs. Fonda.

There is an amusing sidelight to my visit to the talking horse. Tacked to one side of the barn was a notice. Mrs. Fonda's pet dog had run away. She offered a reward for its return. Here was Lady answering questions, telling where lost people could be found and not cooperating in the search for the missing family pet.

The trainers of talking animals deserve credit for infinite patience. The most successful insist on remaining in the background, focusing attention and applause on their pupils, just as ventriloquist Edgar Bergen insisted that Charlie McCarthy, his dummy, was the clever member of the team.

The trainer's basic problem is to get his animal accustomed to the cues that trigger the actions. Every successful circus has a riding master who can make his steed kneel, stand, trot, and stop with no visible signals. Silent commands can be given with the slight movement of a foot, head, hand, whip, or, in Mrs. Fonda's case, with the stick she held in her right hand. A horse does not see ahead. Lady's vision to the left included Mrs. Fonda who stood by her side. A good performer apparently remains idle with his eyes on the animal while the four-footed marvel seems to do all the work. Lady was trained to move her head back and forth above the board bearing the letters. When she was over the right lever, a slight movement of Mrs. Fonda's stick cued her to lower her head and touch the proper lever.

As animals, unlike humans, are not interested in money or fame, their rewards are in the form of food. No trainer feeds his protégé before a performance. Tidbits are given after feats have been accomplished, for once the animal has been fed, the work incentive disappears.

Early in the twentieth century a horse convinced his master that no signals were necessary for him to stamp out answers to questions. Clever Hans was the horse; Wilhelm Von Osten, an elderly Berliner, was his owner. Learned professors were convinced that Hans could work out his own solutions to mathematical problems and had a better knowledge of world affairs than most fourteen-year-old children. Oskar Pfungst was determined to find a more rational explanation. Had Hans's master been a charlatan he would have blocked the intensive investigation by the Berlin psychologist, but Von Osten shared the general opinion that his horse was a phenomenon.

Pfungst's study revealed that the horse could give a correct answer only if the questioner knew it. When Pfungst shielded the eyes of the animal, the hoof remained still. It was reasonable to suppose at this point that Von Osten was cuing Hans subconsciously. Further study ruled out signals by touch or sound. Pfungst now centered his observations on the questioner. He discovered that Hans started stamping when the questioner leaned forward ever so slightly to see the hoof in action. Hans stopped when the man relaxed even a fraction. The other investigators had never noticed this; their attention had been focused on the horse.

Then Pfungst played horse himself. He rapped with his right hand as friends posed queries. Twenty-three out of twenty-five questioners gave the starting and stopping cue without realizing it. Pfungst's answers were as baffling to them as the horse's had been.

The psychologist published his findings in 1904. Von Osten refused to accept them. Before he died four years later, he willed Hans to his friend Karl Krall, an Elberfeld merchant and horse fancier, who believed as he did that the animal had remarkable reasoning powers.

Krall had the time and the money to develop the talent of other equines. The Elberfeld horses became world famous. The Arabian stallion Muhamed mastered mathematics in less than two weeks; it had taken Von Osten three years to "educate" Hans. Krall simplified the answer system. One rap of Muhamed's left hoof indicated tens, while the right hoof tapped ones. Four left stomps and one right, for example, represented the figure 41. Muhamed worked out square roots and complicated equations which were as far beyond Hans's capacities as Krall's were beyond Von Osten's.

Other Krall horses, especially Zarif and Mustapha, approached Muhamed in brilliance. Professor E. Claparéde, who came from the University of Geneva to study the Elberfeld horses, was as awestruck as Dr. Rhine was to be in Richmond. He proclaimed: "These horses are the most sensational event which has ever appeared in the field of animal psychology—perhaps, indeed, in the whole realm of psychology."

Dr. Stefan von Maday took the opposite view. One by one he struck down Krall's points of evidence, then went on to analyze the human behind the horses. Krall, he said, was driven by a desire for importance. He was an animal lover and thought through them to achieve a greatness not possible in the business world where he had accumulated his wealth.

Krall's horses were more cautious than Lady. None seems to have predicted the date of its death. Lady, years before her end, said she would live thirty years. She died in 1957 at the age of thirty-two.

I had chosen to be introduced to Mrs. Fonda as John Banks because I thought that if Lady were really clairvoyant she would spell out my own name rather than that of the man who had exhibited "the white oat-eater" Morocco in the seventeenth century. Morocco, like the Elberfeld marvels, answered questions by stamping his hoof. With popular belief in witchcraft, sorcerers, and seers widespread, his performances were greeted with awe and some apprehension. The steed would rap out the totals of two rolled dice, though the dice were hidden from his view. He would give a quick count of the pence in a piece of silver which any spectator could put in his master's hand, and he was as well posted on the value of French money as he was of English.

Sentenced to be burned at the stake in Orléans, the marvelous animal saved his own hide and the skin of Banks by kneeling in submission before a high authority of the church. The charge of witchcraft was dismissed on the grounds that no emissary of the devil could come that close to a wearer of the holy cross.

History does not record where Banks and his talking horse met their fates, but there are tales in old books that, despite their narrow escape in France, they were eventually burned to a crisp for dealing with demons.

Another famed equine was the "Learned Little Horse" which a Mr. Zucker exhibited in Glasgow in 1764. This horse, in addition to his talent for "speaking," had more than his share of bad habits. He played cards with spectators, enjoyed a game of dice, and ended each performance by drinking a toast to the audience's health.

A less riotous-living stallion was Mr. Henley's "Military Horse of Knowledge." I have a 1780 handbill that describes his performance in glowing terms. This popular quadruped performed feats of multiplication, fired a pistol, and charmed his viewers with a repertoire of card tricks. "If any person takes a pack of cards in his own hand and shuffles and cuts them ever so often, the creature will with his mouth draw a single card and tell the number of spots on it to the amazement of the spectators."

This steed was perhaps the most patriotic of his breed. If Mr. Henley jokingly remarked that he should serve the king of France or Spain the animal—British to the core—would seize his master's arm with his teeth. When, however, Mr. Henley asked if he would fight for the English sovereign, the Military Horse of Knowledge demonstrated his great enthusiasm by rearing back on his hind legs "and returning thanks."

He, like Lady, could tell the hours and the minutes by a timepiece and "agreeably entertain the company with several other diversions, too tedious to mention." Let's hope they were not too tedious to enjoy.

Almost a century and a half ago when ventriloquism was still a mystery to the average person, Signor Antonio Blitz, one of the most celebrated voice throwers of his day, used to amuse himself by strolling through a town and holding conversations with the horses he found tied at sidewalk hitching posts. As if this weren't startling enough, Blitz once discussed the state of the weather with a dead mackerel in a fish market and almost created a panic.

The best-known talking horse of yesteryear in America caused astonishment by his appearance as well as his talent. Spottie, "an African horse," was spotted like a leopard—and in four colors. He had a tail "like an elephant," and this appendage was prominently mentioned in the advertisements for his performances. At Mr. Cook's tavern in Baltimore in 1807, you could quaff a few beers, then for twenty-five cents watch Spottie stamp out the time and give the totals of figures suggested by those who looked on. He personalized his demonstrations by striking the floor once for every button on a gentleman's coat.

Sunday circus performances were illegal in New York in 1892. When E. L. Probasco was arrested in May for exhibiting his educated horse Mahomet on the Sabbath at Huber's dime museum, the brown stallion was the principal witness for the defense. He was not sworn in; the judge transferred his session to the doorsteps of the courthouse so that Mahomet could testify. Probasco's lawyer had contended that the exhibition was "of an intellectual character." "How old are you?" the judge asked. The horse struck his right forefoot five times on the ground. He then tapped out that for three years he had appeared before the public. When the judge pulled out his pocket watch and asked Mahomet the time, the horse immediately stamped out the hour. The New York *Herald* reported that the judge "seemed to be of the opinion that Huber's exhibition was not an infraction of the law, yet he felt constrained to hold him for trial." The outcome of the case is not known, but it was the first time a horse was accepted as a qualified witness by an American court.

Two years later in London, Probasco, who was then exhibiting Mahomet in British music halls, admitted to a writer from *The Sketch* that for centuries trainers had cued their animals to stamp once for "yes" and twice for "no" by a simple movement of their whip. An affirmative reply was signaled by tilting the far end toward the shoulder; a negative answer was indicated by tipping the whip forward. He had worked with Mahomet so long, and the Australian horse was so intelligent that he now dispensed with the whip and sent his signals so unobtrusively that no one could detect them.

One of the features of the stage performance was an addition test. Each of four spectators wrote a four-digit number on a blackboard. Mahomet glanced at the numbers and stamped out the total. The horse was equally skillful, many credulous spectators thought, at subtraction and division.

A talking horse named Captain was one of the attractions at the San Francisco Exposition of 1915. Captain finished his act by playing popular tunes on a set of chimes. He nuzzled the keys of an ingenious control board, not unlike the one in Lady's Virginia barn.

Despite the accomplishments of these famous equines, scientists say that horses are not unusually intelligent animals. George John Romanes in his *Animal Intelligence* claims that horses as a species are rather dull creatures, far less perceptive than elephants. Dogs, on the other hand, are quick learners, and a long line of talking dogs has matched and even surpassed their equine rivals.

Don Carlos, "The Double-Sighted Dog," was a great draw in

England during the 1830's. The handsome spaniel gave a command performance before King William and the royal family at the Brighton Pavilion. The knowledgeable animal added fun to the proceedings by pointing out the loveliest lady present and "the gentleman most partial to the ladies." It must have been with considerable regret that his owner, Mr. Harrington, eventually offered him for sale at fifty guineas ($262.50).

Munito, another clever early-nineteenth-century canine, answered questions pertaining to geography, botany, and natural history in France and England. While Signor Castelli urged him on, he would pick up lettered cards between his teeth to spell out the answers. Fond parents brought lackadaisical youngsters to see the show, hoping that Munito's talents would serve as an object lesson.

Munito had another claim to fame. He proudly wore a gold medal attached to his collar. It had been awarded to him with proper ceremony by the British Humane Society "for having saved the life of a lady in the most extraordinary manner." He had gripped her dress between his teeth and pulled her ashore before she drowned.

There are records in the French Academy of a dog who actually talked. According to Leibniz, the celebrated scholar, this animal, which was owned by a peasant in Saxony, had a vocabulary of thirty words, which was put to effective use when he wanted something specific to eat or drink. Academicians admitted that if someone of lesser importance than Leibniz had vouched for the dog they would have considered the matter unworthy of their consideration.

Charles L. Burlingame, a Chicago magic dealer at the turn of the century, had a talking cat of sorts. The conjurer's tabby would purr in different tones for milk, meat, or water. Beyond this the feline never spoke.

"Learned pigs" were strong attractions at Bartholomew Fair in London and other British festivals. Generations of Englishmen paid their shillings to see the sapient porkers. The public had been intrigued by the wonderful horses and dogs, but it was absolutely

entranced by the savants of the sty. Grunting and waddling, the gross animals went through the routines made popular by their predecessors. One pig, learned or not, looks pretty much like another. When the reigning star became too old to exhibit, he wound up on a dining table, and another took his place in the exhibition booth.

The Mr. Nicholson who toured through Scotland with a learned pig in 1787 also taught a turtle to fetch, a hare to beat a drum, and six turkeycocks to do a country dance. The S.P.C.A. will be unhappy to learn that many a callous showman who exhibited dancing chickens skipped the usual training period and relied on a heated metal stage. Once the tender-footed performers touched the hot plate, they "danced" to keep from being burned.

Bostonians saw their first pig pundit in January 1798. William Fredrick Pinchbeck announced that his attraction had been imported from England by way of Philadelphia. He said he had paid a whopping big price for it—a thousand dollars.

Realizing that canny Yankees might be dubious about his prodigious pig, he offered a money-back guarantee if anyone could prove that his wonder wasn't a bonafide, in-the-flesh animal. No one ever got a refund; his claims were true. Pinchbeck wrote and published *The Expositer; or Many Mysteries Unravelled* in 1805 "to oppose the idea of the supernatural agency in any production of man." Its principal feature was a series of lessons which instructed the reader how to teach a "Pig of Knowledge."

"Take a pig, seven or eight weeks old, let him have free access to the inferior part of your house, until he shall become in some measure domesticated," Pinchbeck began. Each day put a card in the animal's mouth and try to make the pig understand that he must hold it firmly until you take it away. Three lessons daily will soon produce results. Each time the animal follows your instructions, he went on, you should reward him with a piece of bread or a slice of apple, whichever he prefers.

Next the pig should be taught to pick up a card from the floor. Bend a corner of it, hold the animal's head down, and put the corner in his mouth. More practice and more tidbits, and the pig will learn to pick up the card by himself. Now with three cards on the floor the porker is taught not to pick up the card nearest him—his natural tendency—but to move his head and bend it down only when you sniff through your nose.

Finally spread a dozen or more cards in a circle with a four-inch space between them, and after several weeks of rehearsal the pig will be ready to perform in public. When the pig has been properly trained, it will move around the circle with his snout just above the cards. Hearing the sniff signal, he will pick up the proper card immediately. Pinchbeck suggested that it may be necessary at first to tie a string around the animal's neck when training him to walk in a circle, but this can be dispensed with when the pig fully understands what you expect him to do. "That animal, who in his rude state appears the most stupid, with the least share of tractability amongst all other quadrupeds," Pinchbeck wrote, "will be found sapient, docile, and gentle."

While evidence of talking pigs abounds, I have come across only one "goat of knowledge," though surely there must have been more. This billy was not as balky as his brothers and went through the same paces as the animals that had preceded him in taverns up and down the populated centers of the eastern seacoast early in the nineteenth century.

Many birds have been taught to tell time and to find cards selected by their audiences. A Sieur Rea had a pair of "minous . . . from Botany Bay" in England in the fall of 1810. "They are much superior in Knowledge to the Learned Pig," Rea boasted in his handbills. I have seen birds in Hong Kong and Japan which street fortune-tellers had taught to pick out slips of paper bearing advice for the future from heaps carried in baskets and boxes.

Houdini was so taken with a handbill advertising "Learned Goose" that he made a tracing from the original in the British Museum. Eight years ago I found another original. This feathered marvel offered feats "most prodigiously and certainly unbelieving to those who know the intellects of a goose" at the shop of Mr.

Beckett, a London trunkmaker who plied his trade at No. 31 Haymarket. The goose was advertised to tell "the number of ladies and gentlemen in the company or any person's thoughts." This is the first bird I have found who performed the feat of picking up a chosen card while wearing a blindfold.

A second learned goose was exhibited later at No. 5 Pantechnicon Arcade, Belgrade Square, in London. "The curious may be highly gratified with a very extraordinary performance by one of the most silly and stupid Animals in Creation . . . no one would believe, unless they see him, that such an Animal as a Goose could be taught to display feats of intelligence." Talking Goose No. 2 added a new mystifier to the ones earlier animals had shown: "any person may put Figures in a Box, and make what Number they please, and this Curious Bird will tell the number made before the Box is opened." The conjuring trick was even more mysterious when the performer was a goose.

I have known two exhibitors of trained fleas who amazed audiences when their insects pulled tiny carriages and carried tinier flags, but neither claimed their fleas could read thoughts and as yet no parapsychologist has attempted to measure a flea's ESP quotient.

THOUGHT READING

A proficient thought reader carries out the unspoken directions of his subjects. Parapsychologists say that in the future everyone will be using untapped areas of the human brain. The potential is there, they claim, but it must be developed. Unlike the patient experimenters in scientific laboratories, professional thought readers rarely fail to achieve a perfect score in their demonstrations. They are willing to bet heavily on their ability to perform seemingly impossible feats.

George Kreskin ended his week on the Mike Douglas television show in November 1969 with the statement that he would either find the hidden check for his salary or go without compensation. A committee from the studio audience had secreted the valuable piece of paper while he was in another room. In the final minutes of the program he seized the hand of a woman, who thought of the hiding place, and quickly led her to a man who was sitting with the other spectators. Kreskin asked the man to stand, then ran his free hand up and down a few inches away from the man's body. Just before the final commercial the thought reader triumphantly pulled the envelope containing his pay from the man's left shoe.

For many years this effective finale was the climax of Franz J. Polgar's routine. Despite the trepidations of his agent, who constantly feared he might lose his commission, the Hungarian-born showman never missed. During Polgar's cross-country tours he found his elusive checks in some unlikely places. Once he took a rolled-up check from the gun of a Texas police chief; another time he found one which had been sealed in a tennis ball. He didn't hesitate to break open the hollowed-out heel of a woman's slipper, which had been glued back in place containing the tightly folded paper, but he was reluctant to reach for another check which had been hidden in a girl's brassiere.

Look magazine, in December 1950, pictured the short, gray-haired thought reader staring up at the Empire State Building in New York. A small silver banknote clip had been stashed away somewhere in the 102-story structure. Another photograph showed the confident performer leading a woman, who knew where the clip had been hidden, through the lobby as she held one end of his pocket handkerchief. The final picture disclosed that Polgar had found the object of his search in a subbasement locksmith shop. It had been tucked in the lower drawer of a metal file case.

Polgar's first big publicity break came when journalism students at New York University acted out a murder pantomime, then called him into the classroom. In twenty seconds Polgar pointed out the victim. Fifteen seconds later he identified the killer. In another twenty seconds he held up a blackboard eraser that had been used as the weapon.

"There could have been no collusion," said the four-column wide, photo-illustrated story in the May 2, 1936, *World-Telegram*. "It was, the professors agreed, an undeniable demonstration that thought transference, a matter of unceasing debate, is possible."

Polgar was critical of "fake mind readers, mentalists and foretellers of the future" in his autobiography, *The Story of a Hypnotist*, which was published by Heritage House, Inc., in 1951. He said the credulous public was "being milked . . . to the tune of forty million dollars a year." These charlatans, he charged, produced "the most irresponsible literature." He called mind reading a racket, supported by people who "want to believe." Yet he claimed that his own brain was similar to a radio receiver—it picked up thought waves when he went into a "semi-trance." He boldly defied science to explain his uncanny talent; he said he himself did not know how or why it worked.

Most of Polgar's predecessors also professed not to understand the technique of thought reading. J. Randall Brown, "The Great! The Only! The Original! MIND READER," arrived in New York after successful demonstrations in Chicago, St. Louis, and Cincinnati in the summer of 1874. The twenty-two-year-old showman staged a press preview July 2 at the Sturtevant House hotel. He told a reporter to think of any object and its location, then pressed the open palm of the reporter's left hand to his forehead. Earlier the slender mentalist, whose long blond hair reached almost to his shoulders, had tied a handkerchief over his eyes. Now he walked through an open doorway. Two rooms away he found the object—a cup—under a desk. Then, in thirty seconds, he followed another man's unspoken directions and took him to the adjoining chamber where he pointed out the ornamental inkstand which the volunteer had pictured mentally.

The *Daily Graphic* reported: "Mr. Brown can even locate the birthplace of any stranger, or can tell you the name of any deceased friend or person upon whom you will concentrate your unspoken thoughts."

Before Brown became a professional, while he was still a reporter for a Chicago newspaper, he won a bet by finding the proverbial needle in a haystack. The needle in this case was a pin, the haystack was the downtown section of the city. He asked only that the pin be concealed within walking distance. When the challenger returned, the thought reader blindfolded himself, took the man's hand, and made his way through the crowded streets to the entrance of the Sherman House hotel. There he knelt, flipped up the rug by the door, and pulled the shiny bit of metal from its fibers. Pin finding was to be a feature of J. Randall Brown's performances in America and abroad.

An amateur mind reader in Dublin who thought he knew how the feat was done hired a theater. A pin was hidden and the ambitious performer was blindfolded and led to the center of the stage. He wandered uncertainly back and forth behind the footlights until his patience and the audience's had been exhausted. The pin hider suggested that the mentalist should rest. When the seat of his trousers touched the chair he jumped up with a howl. He had found the pin, which had been inserted point up in the cushion.

Washington Irving Bishop, whose showmanship as a thought reader has never been equaled, was born in New York, March 4, 1856. His mother, Eleanor, claimed his given names honored his godfather, the author of "The Legend of Sleepy Hollow" and "Rip Van Winkle." A former friend of the family disputed this statement. The boy, he said, had been baptized Wellington, not Washington.

Eleanor Fletcher Bishop's peculiar behavior was frequently noted in the press. At the family mansion on Fifth Avenue she held spirit séances which Cornelius Vanderbilt and other notables attended. The wealthy commodore, it seems, was more interested in tips on the stock market than the afterlife. When her husband died, the impetuous Eleanor charged he had been poisoned by his mistress. At the cemetery she shocked the other mourners by leaping into his grave after the coffin was lowered.

Young Irving was also high-strung and had a nervous temperament. At St. John's College in Fordham, New York, his principal recreations were writing music and poetry. He worked for a time with Hudnut, a chemist who had a shop in the Herald Building, and later at the Customs House. Then for two years he served as a "floor walker" for Anna Eva Fay, the leading American stage medium. He gathered pads after spectators had written and torn away their questions, then took the pads backstage where carbon-like impressions made via wax-coated second sheets were developed with a sprinkling of black powder. The powder adhered to the wax impressions of the words. These were quickly copied and dispatched to the medium, who astounded her audiences as she revealed the words on slips of paper which they still had folded in their hands.

Though tied with tape and secured to an upright wooden post, Anna Eva Fay caused bells to ring, tambourines to jangle, and mandolins to play after the cloth drapes of her cabinet were closed. A skeptical Chicago reporter suggested that a small child was hidden under her long, flowing skirt, that it was the child not the spirits who made the psychic sounds. The next day the medium gave her performance in a close-fitting gown under which it was impossible for the smallest midget to be concealed.

Bishop soon learned that, though tied, she could maneuver her body so that her hands could reach and manipulate the instruments. He explained in later years that he had worked with the famous medium at the suggestion of Dr. William A. Hammond, a former surgeon general of the United States, to learn the secrets of stage spiritualism and expose the fraud. There is no evidence however that he met Hammond until after he left the Fay act.

Bishop gave his first public performance as an "anti-Spiritualist" May 18, 1876, at Chickering Hall in New York. The hall was packed beyond comfort; people stood along the sides of the chamber and hundreds were turned away at the door. "The Spiritualists may as well give up," an editorial in the New York Times advised. He "has not only done all that the so-called spirits do, but he has beaten them at their own game. . . . This latest exposure leaves the spiritists without a leg to stand upon."

Bishop went on to repeat his success at the Brooklyn Academy of Music, the Boston Music Hall, and various church auditoriums in the northeast states.

Along with his news-making exposures of mediumistic marvels Bishop performed "Mindreading or Unconscious Cerebration." This, he asserted and continued to claim through later years, was not a fraud but a legitimate phenomenon.

In England he expanded his thought-reading repertoire. At a private performance, attended by British nobility, he suggested that a gold sovereign be hidden somewhere in the room while he waited outside. Someone had an amusing idea. The least likely place would be inside one of the Duchess of Kent's silk stockings.

Not a word was spoken during Robert-Houdin's improved version of "second-sight" in 1848. The French magician rang a bell, and his son, whose eyes were bandaged, immediately identified objects submitted by spectators and read words though they were written in foreign languages.

PHONE

82-0478

ADMISSION
ADULT $1, CHILD 50c
INCLUDING TAX

LADY WONDER
THE EDUCATED MIND READING HORSE
WILL ANSWER QUESTIONS
MRS. C. D. FONDA
PETERSBURG PIKE AND RUFFIN ROAD
OPEN EVERY AFTERNOON AND ~~EVENING~~
4TH HOUSE ON RIGHT

12 noon to 3 P.m

Calling card of America's most publicized "talking horse." Dr. J. B. Rhine believed Lady was gifted with extrasensory perception. She predicted the winners of national elections, ball games, and turf events.

The highlights of Bishop's demonstration in London in 1883 were the finding of a hidden pin and the writing of the serial number of a bank-note thought of by a volunteer from the audience.

Learned Pigs were great attractions at British and American fairs. They identified cards that had been selected and spelled out answers to questions by picking up alphabet cards.

VOL. 14 NO. 350   JUNE 30 1888   PRICE 10 CENTS

Judge

ENTERED AT THE POST OFFICE AT NEW YORK AS SECOND-CLASS MATTER.   COPYRIGHT 1887 BY THE JUDGE PUBLISHING CO.

GREAT
DEMOCRATIC
ENGLISH
CIRCUS

FREE TRADE

THE LEARNED P—RESIDENT.
Professor John Bull's very apt pupil.

Judge magazine in 1883 used the Learned Pig theme to show how British influence swayed an American President, Grover Cleveland, to espouse free trade.

MUNITO,

OR

THE LEARNED DOG.

To be seen every Day at Mr. LAXTON's Room,

No. 23, NEW BOND STREET,

AT THE HOURS OF THREE AND SEVEN PRECISELY.

THIS WONDERFUL DOG understands the Alphabet, can read, copy Words, and cast Accounts. He knows all the playing Cards, and will select out of a Pack the Cards which any of the Spectators may be pleased to ask for. He plays at Dominos: is acquainted with the Principles of Botany and Geography: and exhibits many other astonishing Performances.

☞ *Admittance One Shilling.*

Munito, the Learned Dog, was awarded a gold medal in England for saving a lady's life "in a most extraordinary manner." Aside from being a strong swimmer, Munito was well posted, it seems, in geography, botany, and natural history.

The Prodigious Goose, "the most Stupid and Insensate of the Feather'd Creation," read thoughts, spelled out "the Day of the Month, and the Month of the Year," and found selected cards, while blindfolded, in London in 1789.

John Banks exhibited Morocco, the most famous "talking horse" of the seventeenth century. Charged with "consorting with the devil" in France, the horse knelt before church inquisitors and saved his and his master's life.

Nostradamus, wand in hand, kneels in his magic circle as he conjures up a vision of the future in a mirror for Catherine de Medici. His verses of things to come were interpreted by later generations to fit specific events.

Evangeline Adams was the first American astrologer to have her own thrice weekly radio program. Mary Pickford, Enrico Caruso, and J. P. Morgan were among her clients. Though arrested in New York for fortune-telling, she was acquitted when she gave the magistrate an accurate analysis of his son's character.

The elderly duchess agreed. When the five-foot-five mentalist returned he took the Prince of Wales's hand and in seconds led him to the chair where the noblewoman was sitting. Bishop hesitated, his right hand extended, and went almost immediately to the area near her left ankle. Calmly he lifted the edge of her gown, removed the slipper, and, touching the bottom of her stockinged foot, pointed to the coin which was beneath her instep.

Henry du Pré Labouchère, member of Parliament and crusading editor of *Truth*, a journal dedicated to the revelation of corrupt practices and political deceptions, was sure that Bishop's thought reading was a trick based on the interpretation of subtle sensory cues, not occult brain force. He offered to wager £1,000 against the American's £100 that the mind reader could not reveal the serial number of a banknote sealed in an opaque envelope when it was held by a reputable gentleman who alone knew the number. The member of Parliament from Chelsea was his nominee for the post. Bishop declined this suggestion; he said he would not experiment with any man Labouchère proposed—whereupon the editor withdrew his offer. When a special challenge performance was given June 23, 1883, at St. James' Hall, Labouchère refused to attend.

That evening Bishop asked for the critical editor to come forward and take the chair though he knew Labouchère was not in the audience. Two other critics, Charles Russell and Professor E. Ray Lankester, challenged him to read the numbers of a five-pound note and an unidentified man threw a sealed envelope with a banknote inside to the stage, but these offers were not accepted. After a considerable hullabaloo a Mr. Statham concentrated on the numbers of a bill provided by a Colonel Trench.

Bishop drew a rectangle on a large blackboard and marked it off into five sections. With a handkerchief tied over his eyes, he took Statham's wrist with his left hand and circled his right hand, which held a piece of chalk, over the first square. After a few moments he wrote the figure 6, then with further effort he filled in another 6, and later 894. The number on the banknote was 66,894! There was a torrent of applause in the hall; a fire balloon was sent aloft in the street outside to inform the rest of London that the thought reader had succeeded.

Bishop's most outspoken critic in England was John Nevil Maskelyne, the great magician who, at his Egyptian Hall headquarters, had stated without equivocation that thought reading had nothing to do with the execution of the American's feats.

A few days after the banknote test Maskelyne learned that thousands of copies of a spurious edition of *Truth* had been distributed throughout London. In its pages Bishop said that Labouchère and Maskelyne had hatched a "dastard" plot to ruin his reputation; they had tried to bribe William Ladyman, a man in Liverpool for whom Bishop had found a concealed pin, "with a sum of money as small as the juggler's brains or morality to declare that he had been guilty of a fraud."

Bishop charged that Maskelyne was "devoid of honorable instincts." He said that "with the proofs of infamy in my possession" he could hold the magician "criminally liable and make Justice punish him for his villainous conduct."

Maskelyne promptly advised his lawyer to enter suit for libel. Long before the case was tried Washington Irving Bishop left the British Isles. His final statement in the press was: "It is my intention shortly to discontinue my public life, in order to resume my investigations of the mysteries of the East."

Maskelyne was awarded £10,000 in damages. He never collected nor did Bishop ever appear in England again. He did go east however. His performances in Europe were applauded by sovereigns and common folk alike. During the Christmas season of 1884 he was summoned by the Russian tsar to his St. Petersburg palace to entertain his friends and family.

On his return to America Bishop created a sensation with the most dramatic publicity exploit of his career—a blindfold carriage drive. A diamond brooch owned by Mrs. Frank Leslie, widow of the wealthy publisher of pictorial periodicals and editor and publisher of *Frank Leslie's Popular Monthly,* was hidden somewhere in Manhattan. Bishop, who had grown a beard and who wore the decorations he had received from continental royalty, blindfolded himself, mounted the driver's seat, and, holding the reins firmly, set off at a gallop. Passersby stared; other drivers turned their horses aside as the thought reader with bandaged eyes drove blithely through midtown traffic. Reporters who followed in other conveyances wrote that he eventually stopped in front of a tenement, then, holding the hands of the committeemen who were with him, went straight to a room where he found the jewel. Packed houses were the rule rather than the exception for his performances at Wallack's Theater.

At the Boston Music Hall, November 30, 1886, "The Enigma of the 19th Century" advertised "his only performance in Boston prior to his retirement from public life." A blindfold carriage drive and private demonstrations at the Press Club and the Vendome assured a standing-room-only attendance.

Charles Howard Montague, city editor of the *Boston Globe,* was so intrigued by the feats Bishop had performed at the Press Club that he decided to cover the show himself. He arrived long before curtain time and asked the mentalist what he could do to make the evening a success.

Bishop, who suffered from preshow jitters, took him by the arm, led him to a seat in the last row, then said he could just be quiet. Rankled by the rebuff, Montague watched the performer with a far more critical eye than he had at the private demonstration. His review was laudatory, there was no question about Bishop's talent and brilliant showmanship, but whether he had the "phenomenal power" he advertised was open to speculation.

Montague, who like Bishop was short and of a nervous disposition, wondered if he could duplicate at least one of the master mentalist's feats. He had a friend hide an object, was blindfolded, then told the man to direct him mentally as he held his hand. If he was going in the right direction, the friend should think "Straight ahead," or if not, the thought should be "To the right," "To the left," or "Turn Around." To his own amazement, the city editor found the object. Not as rapidly as Bishop had, and not without several false starts, but he found it.

With his hand on his friend's, with his mind as blank and receptive as possible, Montague was aware of a slight but perceptible pressure which indicated that he was not headed the right way. There seemed to be no noticeable tremor if he was approaching the object, but there was a slight throb if he veered from the direct course.

A long and detailed description of his discoveries was published in the December 19 *Globe* under the heading: "THE SECRET. How the Minds of Many Men Are Read. What The Globe Has Recently Discovered. The Riddle Told in All Its Diverse Phases." Montague admitted it was difficult to describe the sensory clues precisely. "I am a very busy man . . . I have spent more time upon it than I could really spare . . . I have no doubt that I have discovered the kernel of truth which underlies the whole matter. I propose to dismiss it with that."

Bishop, then in Washington, was asked for his reaction to the article. The thought reader that morning was even more agitated than usual. The night before at the National Theater Anna Eva Fay, the medium he had exposed years earlier, had said: "I will read Mr. Bishop's thoughts. He is thinking of what that girl in Peoria will say when she finds he has come back from Europe and married another girl."

The new Mrs. Bishop, the former Mrs. Helen Loud, had met the thought reader abroad, secured a divorce from her first husband, a wealthy Boston broker, and married Bishop on his return to the United States. A strikingly beautiful woman, she was with the mentalist at the Arlington Hotel when reporters came for an interview. Neither she nor the thought reader wished to comment on their private life, but Bishop had something to say about Montague's revelations: "The only fault I have to find now is that he does not share the credit with God Almighty . . . he asserts that it is simply a cunning physical accomplishment. The exposé is all very well in its way, but it is not the truth."

Scientific experimentation with a scalped monkey, he went on, had convinced some researchers that there was a better explanation for thought reading:

"They have shown, first, that every thought produces a disturbance of a brain molecule and each class of thoughts affects a different molecule. They would pinch the monkey's toes, and there would be a movement of a particular molecule of the brain, and when they squeezed his nose another would move. Next they made grimaces and frightened the animal, whereupon still another molecule was disturbed. From these experiments it was reasoned that it was possible for me to read the brain movements of a man. However they do not know that this is the secret, neither do I . . . ."

The Boston editor, Bishop concluded, may have pleased his friends with his attempt at thought reading but if he tried the feats in a theater filled with strangers he would soon find how ridiculous his so-called explanation was.

Montague decided to make the test. To gain experience he performed Bishop's feats at the Boston Press Club, made an appearance before the local Society for Psychical Research, entertained the Somerville Cycle Club, and gave a Sunday lecture-demonstration at Low's Opera House in Providence, Rhode Island. February 6, 1887, he faced a "theater filled with strangers" at the Globe in Boston. Test by test he repeated the marvels of Washington Irving Bishop and explained how he was guided by the physical pulsations of those who came up to assist him. The performance was a triumph. Even the rival papers admitted he had delighted the audience not only with his performance but with his explanation.

Montague could have embarked on a successful stage career but he was more interested in the newspaper and two novels he was writing. Still, an offer to appear at Dockstader's Theater in New York in March was too tempting to refuse; Bishop was performing at Wallack's playhouse a short distance away.

Montague wrote the New York *Daily Tribune:* "I understand that Mr. Washington Irving Bishop has been repeating the statement in New York that the newspaper exposures of his methods have been made by unscrupulous men who are simply seeking thereby to gain a little notoriety at his expense. I suppose this carries with it the inference that the exposures are not true. As the author of the first newspaper exposure of Mr. Bishop in this country I propose to show the people of your city who are interested in this matter, as I have already done in Boston, that these exposures are the truth. It has been suggested, it is true, that Mr. Bishop is not worth a great deal of powder, but the fact is that his occult claims, if true, would be of a very great scientific importance, and there is no doubt that he deceives intelligent persons . . . . I shall ask the New York press to name the charity to which the box-office receipts should be devoted."

The "rather good looking young man of about thirty-five—perhaps younger—instantly excited the admiration of all the young ladies in the house," the New York *Journal* reported. He had golden chin whiskers, wore his hair "à la Pompadour and looks very intellectual and refined, especially his mustache."

Anticipating Polgar's test at New York University, Montague found the dagger that had been used in a mock murder, and "stabbed" again the spectator who had played the part of the victim. He cut his own finger with the sharp edge, but bound it up and went on with the show. He wrote four figures, 9435, which had been thought of by a spectator on a blackboard and explained how the man's unconscious responses guided him. If he made a circular pattern with his hand and felt no resistance he knew the number would be a 0, 6, or 9. More test movements before he applied the chalk to the board indicated a 9. Similar exploratory gestures revealed the other figures and the same process was used when a spectator, whose hand he touched, thought of letters in a word. He didn't get the whole word at once, but if he went step by step he could apparently read thoughts. Basically the process depended upon the assistant concentrating so intensely that his unconscious tremors could be felt. It took long practice to perform the feats as swiftly and effectively as Bishop. Montague had been experimenting only a few months. When he had difficulty finding the coat pocket in which a knife had been hidden the concentrator admitted he hadn't known in which pocket it had been placed himself.

The response from the audience and the press was so over-whelming that Montague was booked for a repeat show the next Sunday. Bishop, at Wallack's Theater that night, told his audience that people should be wary of experimenting with thought transfer-ence. It often produced insanity or hysterics. He admitted he suf-fered hysteria after each performance. His doctor had advised him to retire.

Six days later the papers reported that Bishop's wife had fled from her home in Boston or been abducted. The night before the thought reader had received a wire from Detroit: "Can I meet you either in Buffalo or Albany? Have much to reveal. Helen."

He sent an answering telegram:

"The false information received by me in answer to urgent in-quiries to your family, concerning your whereabouts and your inexplicable conduct in Detroit, instead of coming to me your hus-band after you had been repeatedly advised by his physicians that he was at death's door, will tomorrow be criticized by the press throughout the country. If you wish to protect your honor it will be necessary for you to come to New York immediately. Otherwise you will give me and the world just grounds for believing that you have disregarded your marriage vows. Your heartless conduct and refusal to answer any of my communications have received the se-verest censure. Impossible for me to meet you en route. My mother will receive you at her residence. Telegraph me immediately your intentions."

There was no reply. He thought the Boston millionaire she had divorced was still in love with her and was trying to regain her affection. Her wealthy parents, he told a reporter, had never liked him; perhaps they were responsible for her strange actions. He had had a daughter by his first wife. Someone was trying to turn her against him, but she still had confidence in her father. If he didn't hear from his wife within another twenty-four hours he would engage a detective to find her.

In his dressing room at the Park Theatre in Brooklyn Bishop admitted that he had received two further messages from Detroit. One was on half a sheet of black-edged mourning paper, the other was scrawled on the back of one of his personal visiting cards. Both were incoherent. He thought his wife might be insane. Earlier in the week he had had an inflamed bladder; an operation was performed; he had been unconscious for two days. Only the great skill of the physicians had saved his life.

The cause of all his recent misfortunes, he now said, was Henry Labouchère, the editor of the British periodical *Truth*. Since he left England Labouchère and his friends had hounded him and tried to make his life miserable.

Meanwhile the editor of the Boston *Globe* received a letter from John Stanley Babson, who had known the Bishop family since Irving was a child:

> It is about time that all the nonsense about *Wellington* (not Washington) Irving Bishop was stopped . . . . His father was an old roué of bad repute who was a real estate operator . . . who left his wife—the greatest *vixen* that ever made a man's home *hell*. This woman—Wellington's mother, Eleanor Fletcher Bishop—has been mixed up in more ridiculous and notorious affairs than any ten women you can name. She wormed herself under the guise of religion and cant into the family of Bishop Southgate, a reputable Episcopal Bishop of the Church of England. When she made herself so obnoxious that her presence there could no longer be tolerated, she lied about them to such an extent that the venerable and good clergyman thought best to resign . . . . Then, she became a public lecturer, then she claimed the body of some unknown suicide 'for the sake of Jesus,' got her name into the papers as a philanthropist, got hundreds of dollars from wealthy sympathizers (toward the burial of the poor girl), ran in debt for the funeral expenses, appropriated the money for her own use and was almost kicked from the doors of those on whose sympathies she had worked. When the poor old fool of a husband died, she thought to become more notorious still and had his body exhumed, and after a long farce and having the stomach examined (and accusing an innocent boarding house keeper of his murder), Dr. Doremus pronounced his death to have resulted from natural causes . . . . At this time Wellington who had come from school was vibrating around and living on his wits . . . .

After a while Wellington went to England and came back as the agent of Miss Annie Eva Fay, a spiritualistic medium, so called; but learning her methods he demanded more money—in default of its being granted, he exposed her tricks. You see that the spirit of the mother had descended on the child.

Then he went back to England and buzzed like a gnat around great people . . . . I don't write these lines to have them published nor to blackmail anybody, but only to show you what a supreme fraud this fellow is. I read in a late paper that he had advised his wife to go to his mother's residence. God help the poor girl if she gets in the hand of that harpy . . . . *Wellington* Irving Bishop ought to get one or two good horsewhippings and it might prove a benefit to him."

The letter was not published. The editor of the *Globe* passed it on to Montague, his city editor; Montague pasted it in his scrap-book, and today the scrapbook, which covers the Bishop-Montague controversy, is in the author's collection.

Helen Bishop filed suit for divorce alleging the mind reader took cocaine, beat her, was not faithful, and had fits of insanity. The divorce was granted on March 27, 1888.

Bishop was performing in Minneapolis when he learned the verdict. He became so unnerved that he lost control of the horses he was driving during his blindfold carriage ride test. The horses crashed into a tree, but he managed to regain the reins and successfully found the hidden pin. Still the strain was too great to fight off. He collapsed in a cataleptic fit and was carried to his hotel.

A few days later he remarried his first wife in St. Paul. The mind reader made several appearances in California in the summer of 1888 with Harrison Millard, a popular singer. The combination of music and mentalism was a strong attraction. In August they decided to tour the southern part of the state and Mexico. From San Francisco they went by way of Los Angeles, San Diego, and El Paso to Mexico City. A private performance for President Porfirio Díaz and his family was staged a few days after their arrival in September. Flooded streets and poor drainage in Guadalajara were no obstacles for Bishop's find-the-hidden-brooch test. The committeemen who went with him returned thoroughly soaked, but the thought reader scarcely dampened his silk stockings and opera pumps. Audiences were enthusiastic in Guanajuato and Vera Cruz. Though he knew no Spanish and had to speak through an interpreter, he found this no barrier to the successful completion of his feats.

Bishop and Millard engaged the Tacon Theater in Havana for three nights. There they encountered the first major harassments of their Latin American tour. The manager was uncooperative; the audience was noisy; and the committee selected from the audience on opening night was skeptical. A physician charged that Bishop could see through his blindfold. Millard finally convinced the doubter that Bishop always rolled up his eyeballs when he was in a trancelike state and therefore could not peep down even if the handkerchief over his eyes permitted this to be done. Angered by shouted calls from the spectators in a language he did not understand, Bishop was only too happy to leave the stage when the time came for Millard's ten minutes of song. There were some hearty handclaps, but for the most part hootings and catcalls greeted the arias from *Di Provenza* and *La Traviata.*

Bishop returned to present musical thought reading. While a member of the committee concentrated, he played the tune on a piano. The audience was understandably annoyed when "Home Sweet Home" was the chosen melody. They had never heard the song. They shouted for Bishop to play a Cuban dance rhythm or an aria from a Spanish opera.

The mind reader was obstinate. He sat down and absolutely refused to comply with the audience's wishes. In Cuban theaters there was a censor who attended to insure that the program was moral, inoffensive to local taste, and presented exactly as advertised. After the mind reader refused to repeat the music test, pandemonium broke out. The censor called Bishop over to his box and explained that if the program were not carried out precisely as printed on the playbills, the receipts for the evening would be turned over to charity.

Bishop had no difficulty interpreting the censor's thoughts. He returned to the center of the stage and invited someone who was familiar with classical music to come forward. The volunteer was requested to go into an anteroom and write the name of an Italian opera. When the Cuban returned, he said he had written the name not of an Italian opera but of one in Spanish. Bishop trembled, quivered, then shouted through the interpreter that he knew no Spanish music, and therefore he could not play it. The audience became unruly again. They could not understand why a man who claimed to read thoughts was unable to carry out the test.

The censor quieted the tumult by announcing that a fine would be imposed; he ordered the curtain to be rung down. When Bishop and Millard left the theater, a hundred soldiers were outside ready to control any further outbreak. Permission was withdrawn by the government for the use of the theater for the next two nights, and they would not refund the rental money which had been paid in advance. Furthermore, a hundred dollars was demanded from the performers to meet the fine. This was never paid. Bishop and Millard went on to Mantanzas and other cities where they worked without incident, and early in December they returned to the United States by way of New Orleans.

During the tour Bishop convinced Millard that he was not only a thought reader but also a powerful spirit medium. Though he never exhibited the latter powers publicly, he could hold his own in any social circle. The ladies especially found him fascinating. His wavy dark hair, neatly trimmed beard, and blue-green eyes with an almost mystical gaze intrigued them, as did his stories of his friends at the British court and his pal the tsar of Russia.

An American socialite who met him at a party in Honolulu doubted that she could be hypnotized. She made such a point of this that Bishop borrowed a silver coin and asked her to stare at it intently. In a few moments she was under his control. She performed ridiculous antics at his suggestion, and when he left the party, she was still in a trance, seated with her right leg extended horizontally. Bishop told her that it was as rigid as an iron bar, and she would be unable to move it.

Later that night, after the mind reader had returned to his hotel, he received an urgent message. The woman was still holding her leg aloft and her friends could not awaken her. Bishop sent word that they should call a doctor who would bring her around with a shot of morphine.

There were rumors that Bishop was a drunkard. Millard said this was not true; liquor could not phase him. He had seen Bishop down a quart of strong wine with no aftereffects, though a single glass of it would intoxicate anyone else.

Saturday night, May 11, 1889, the famous thought reader, who had been visiting his mother and his wife in Philadelphia, checked in at the Hoffman House in New York. After he wrote his name in the register he added another word above it—"Kamilamilianalani." The clerk was puzzled. Later he said he thought this might be a Hawaiian version of the name. Bishop was in town to work out the final details of the fall tour he would make with Jules Levy, the famous cornettist.

Sunday evening Bishop went with his friend Henry E. Dixie, the noted actor, to the last Lambs Club Gambol of the season. Except during the summer the theatrical club, which then had its clubhouse at 34 West 26 Street, staged a gala party once each month. Dixie left about midnight, but the thought reader was enjoying himself and stayed on. Eventually he was asked to perform one of his feats. He readily acquiesced. Bishop said he would show how a mental detective solved a crime. After he left the room, someone was to act out a murder, then hide the weapon.

He returned, tied a handkerchief over his eyes, and took the hand of a man who had seen the pantomime. Swiftly he indicated the murderer, found the concealed knife, and used it to reenact the slaying. Bishop acknowledged the round of applause. "That's an easy one," he said. "Wait and I'll show you one you've never seen before, and I'll guarantee no one else can do it."

He instructed Clay M. Green, the club's secretary, to think of a word that was written in a Lamb's record or account book. Clay and Dr. John Henry Irwin went to the floor below, opened an old volume and chose the name Margaret Townsend, who was listed among the participants in a benefit performance. They fixed Townsend in their minds, remembered the page number and the place where the name had appeared, then hid the book and mounted the stairs. Again Bishop was blindfolded. He took Green's hand and led the group downstairs. He soon found the volume and began flipping the pages. Suddenly he stopped, began circling his finger on a page, then brought it to rest on Townsend.

"Is that right?" he asked eagerly. Assured that it was, still blindfolded, he led the group back up the stairway. Bishop was in a highly excitable state now. He was perspiring, and the veins stood out on that part of his forehead which was not covered by the bandage. He said he would prove conclusively that muscle reading was not the explanation for his performance. He would attempt to reveal the word without touching anyone.

He was swaying now, breathing quicker, and very tense. "I think it is a name. I think it is a man's name." No one interrupted to say it was the name of a woman.

"Give me something to write with." A scrap of paper was passed to Dr. Irwin, who gave it and a pencil to the thought reader. Without a moment's hesitation, Bishop wrote Townsend—not in the usual way, but reversed, so that the letters would appear in proper order if reflected in a mirror. There were gasps and applause. Bishop pulled off his blindfold, not with a showmanly smile but a contorted expression of pain. He stiffened and fell back unconscious. Dr. Irwin, who first met the mind reader in Liverpool and knew about his sudden attacks, allayed the alarm of those in the room by saying that Bishop was only suffering one of his periodic cataleptic fits. He knelt beside the prostrate body and began to massage it. Several minutes later Bishop's eyes opened. Though he had not fully recovered, he had heard everything that had been said. A few moments earlier the doctor had explained that the peculiar way the mind reader had written the name could be accounted for by the fact that everything the eye saw was inverted, as in a mirror, and that the image was turned right side by the optic lens on the way to the brain.

Bishop whispered in a weak voice that the doctor should stress that he wrote what the eye saw without the reversal correction. When Bishop sat up, his pulse was racing. Dr. Irwin insisted that he be put to bed in an upstairs room. There, though weak and trembling, the thought reader refused to rest. He insisted he must perform the feat again so that everyone could appreciate what an incredible accomplishment it was. To pacify him, the physician had the minute book brought to the bedroom. He opened the volume, put his finger on another name, Stewart. The mind reader with great effort tied the handkerchief around his eyes and reached for Irwin's hand. This time he found it extremely difficult to locate the proper page, but eventually he succeeded. Then with the book open, he took a pencil and moved it slowly above the page. Finally he slashed a line under a word. "Right?" It was. Now he wished to stand and write as the doctor concentrated, but he was too weak to rise and lapsed into a coma again. Irwin sent for Dr. Charles C. Lee, under whose care Bishop once had been.

Bishop became convulsive. He twitched, kicked, squirmed, and attempted to bite those who came near him. Through the morning hours Dr. Irwin attempted to calm him. Both John Ritchie, Bishop's manager, and Augustus Thomas, his advance agent, had been at the Lambs. Neither knew the Philadelphia address of his wife and mother. Thomas went to the Hoffman House and finally found it on a letter in the thought reader's satchel. He sent a telegram saying that Bishop was desperately ill.

When Dr. Lee arrived, the mind reader was unconscious but still breathing. Brandy injections with a hypodermic needle had been given. Irwin set up the Gaith induction coil that one of the Lambs had fetched from his home. A wet electrode was put on Bishop's heart; another was forced into his clenched hand. Electric shocks were sent through his system. Lee eventually left to attend to other patients. When he returned about noon Bishop's pulse had stopped beating. It seemed obvious he was dead.

The body was moved to an undertaking parlor at 8 Sixth Avenue. Dr. Irwin signed the certificate, attributing the death to hysterio-catalepsy. He arranged for Dr. Frank Ferguson, a pathologist from New York Hospital, to perform an autopsy. Dr. Irwin Hance made meticulous notes during the surgery. Ferguson sawed through the skull and removed the brain. It was larger than would be expected for a man of Bishop's size—about forty ounces. The gray matter was darker than usual but not malformed. There was an indication of disease in some of his other organs but nothing that could have caused his death. Dr. Irwin concluded that the great strain of the thought reader's final feat had killed him and said the case was "one of the most remarkable in medical history."

When Bishop's wife and mother arrived from Philadelphia, they were horrified to find that an autopsy had been done. Eleanor Fletcher Bishop screamed that her son had been murdered. Why hadn't the doctors heeded the letter her son always carried? It forbade an autopsy. He was, as everybody knew, a victim of cataleptic attacks. Sometimes the periods of coma were of long duration. In 1873, when he was seventeen, during one of these seizures two New York physicians, Dr. Ford and Dr. Leach, pronounced him dead, but a Dr. Briggs, despite the obvious evidences, remained unconvinced. The three medical men tried several tests on the inert body. All substantiated the contentions of Ford and Leach. Dr. Briggs, however, stayed at the boy's side for twelve hours. At the end of the twelfth hour, according to Dr. Briggs, Bishop "gave a convulsive shudder, and in forty minutes recovered."

The doctors who performed the autopsy, she charged, were ghouls who were only interested in discovering the secret of his thought-reading ability. They were vicious criminals and should be punished.

At the inquest, which started May 29, 1889, Ferdinand Levy, the coroner, and his jury agreed that Eleanor Fletcher Bishop's charges were without foundation. No trace of the letter she had mentioned was found. The physicians had acted in good faith. There was no evidence of criminal intent.

The mind reader's mother was not to be appeased. The medical Jack the Rippers were a menace to mankind, she ranted, and she would not rest until they were incarcerated and made to pay the supreme penalty for their wanton conduct. She made such a public furor that Delancey Nicoll, the district attorney, was forced to reopen the case. The three physicians who participated in the autopsy, Irwin, Ferguson, and Hance, were indicted by a grand jury in June for "unlawfully making and causing and procuring to be made, a dissection of the body of a human being."

Dr. Irwin was tried before Judge Fitzgerald of the General Sessions Court three years later. During a sensational two-day trial the jury, after deliberating five hours, could not reach a unanimous verdict. Nine thought he was guilty; three held out that he was innocent. The judge dismissed the jury; Irwin was not convicted. The charges against the other two physicians were dropped in 1893.

Newspapers of the time said that Eleanor Bishop intended to commemorate the doctors' butchery by having carved on the tombstone marking her son's grave in Greenwood Cemetery the inscription, "Murdered March 13, 1889." This was not done. Instead under his name is the date of his birth and "Died March 13, 1889."

Charles Garner, who had been Bishop's assistant in England, took the name Stuart Cumberland and achieved a notable success as a thought reader. Unlike his former employer, he made no claims for supernormal power. Two of his books, *A Thought-Reader's Thoughts* (London, Sampson Low, Marston, Searle & Rivington, 1888) and *People I Have Read* (London, C. Arthur Pearson, Ltd., 1905), describe his performances for kings, queens, sultans, and khedives. Another British specialist, Alfred Capper, mentions his own performances in *A Rambler's Recollections and Reflections,* which was published in 1915.

Eugene de Rubini was introduced by Houdini June 4, 1926, during the show which followed the annual Society of American Magicians banquet at the McAlpin Hotel in New York as the greatest thought reader who ever lived. The slender, dark-haired Czechoslovakian performed his first feats with his subjects holding one end of a thin metal watch chain. Later he carried out their thoughts without contact. At first the magicians had been entertained but as Rubini's act stretched to an hour and ten minutes many quietly adjourned to an anteroom to perform card tricks among themselves. Though Houdini had seen many thought readers, Rubini was the first he had met who could work without touching his subject.

Rolf Passer offered the most entertaining thought-reading demonstration I have seen. In 1941 he was featured at the Rainbow Room in New York, the Palmer House in Chicago, and the Fairmont Hotel in San Francisco. While he was performing in Baltimore, we frequently appeared on the same shows. For his theatrical dates Passer used his attractive wife, a brunette with long, flowing hair, as his medium. When he left the room the audience would suggest acts that he should carry out on his return. For example, a cigarette was to be taken from one man's pocket and placed on the head of another, or Passer was to find a woman's ring, which was hidden in a bowl of sugar, and return it to her finger. He worked equally swiftly when a member of the audience volunteered to be his subject.

My friend the late C. A. George Newmann of Minneapolis performed the blindfold carriage drive à la Bishop in his younger days. He was still adept at noncontact thought reading when I met him. He could read sensory cues though the subject stood several feet away.

I worked with Frederick Marion, whose act had perplexed European and American investigators, at a performance arranged by Clark H. Getts, who then handled our lecture tours. Marion was born Josef Kraus on October 15, 1892, in Prague. He claimed psychic powers but his methods were apparent to those who knew the technique. His work was baffling to audiences. Why not? Brilliant scientists and interested laymen who cannot detect how a magician produces a dove from an empty silk handkerchief or conjures an orange under an inverted teacup are not likely to discover the subtle secrets of a mentalist without prolonged study.

Dr. S. G. Soal wrote a ninety-six-page report on Marion,

Preliminary Studies of a Vaudeville Telepathist. Copiously illustrated with diagrams, photographs, and statistical tables, it was published by the University of London Council for Psychical Investigation in 1937. After analyzing the results of twenty-four test performances, Soal reached the conclusion that Marion "had the power" to locate objects in a room where he could observe the reactions of half a dozen or so people; that he didn't succeed when he was alone in the room or when his subject was concealed from view in a movable upright wooden box.

Soal said that Marion "probably derives" his information "from head movements and changes in facial expression when the agents are seated," and "from footsteps when a single subject follows him." These are only a few of the clues. The proficient thought reader, I might add, is acutely aware of changes in breathing, tensions and relaxations, and varying positions of the fingers, hands, and feet of his subject when he works without contact. No two people reveal their thoughts in precisely the same way.

Most people can learn contact thought reading if they are not phlegmatic and have a keen sense of awareness. With your fingers on a subject's wrist you can detect his unconscious signals to go in one direction or another. Once the basic skill is mastered the experimenter can progress to the link method. The subject holds one end of a diagonally folded handkerchief as you walk with him behind you. Stop occasionally and, with the cloth taut, move slightly in several directions. The way to go will be indicated by a lack of resistance at the far end of the handkerchief. You can write thought-of words, as Bishop did, if you peek down from your blindfold and sight the word in a book when your subject's pulse, as you hold his wrist, indicates that the pointing finger of your free hand is on the word.

Noncontact thought reading is more difficult, but the skill may be acquired. Some performers, such as the late C. A. George Newmann, after years of practice amaze even themselves with their ability. They almost believe they read minds.

JEANE DIXON & CO.

The trip from Athens to Delphi today takes less than four hours by car. By the side of Mount Parnassus are the ruins of the once magnificent temple of Apollo which marks the site of the most renowned oracle of the ancient world. The priestesses of other days were all past fifty to insure their chasteness. After bathing in sacred waters, a seeress clad in flowing robes would sit on a tripod, chew a laurel leaf, and inhale the fumes that arose from a crevice in the earth's surface beside the temple. When she lost consciousness and began to mumble, a priest interpreted her words. The prophecies were phrased cunningly.

Herodotus, the Greek historian who lived in the fifth century B.C., recorded the best-known Delphic foreboding. Croesus, the fabulously wealthy king of Lydia, had sent a messenger to ask if he should attack Cyrus, the king of Persia. The oracle answered that if Croesus went to war he would destroy "a great empire." Elated by what he thought was a good omen, he marched confidently off to do battle. His army was decimated and he was taken prisoner. Yet, in a way, the prophecy had been valid. He had destroyed an empire—his own, Lydia.

Cicero, the Roman orator who died in 43 B.C., made note of another prime example of oracular double-talk. King Pyrrhus had asked if he should fight the Roman legions. The Delphic reply was "Ajo to, Aeacide, Romanos vincere posse." The first part was perfectly clear "I say to you, Aeacide." The last could be taken two ways, either "you can conquer the Romans" or "the Romans can conquer you."

No one made a prophecy while I was at Delphi; the days of laurel-chewing and vapor-inhaling oracles are past. Modern seeresses however still use the Delphic approach.

Jeane Dixon is adept at the ancient art. She has predicted, in carefully chosen words, the destiny of nations, the rise and fall of national figures, and the start and cessation of major wars. Mrs. Dixon, who with her husband operates a successful real estate business in Washington, D.C., is a part-time prophet. Her annual forecasts regularly make the wire services, and many people believe she has a personal pipeline to the future.

Jeane Pinckert Dixon was born in Medford, Wisconsin, in 1918. After her family moved to Santa Rosa, California, she learned she had a gift for prophecy. A gypsy saw the signs in her palm and gave her a crystal ball. One of the eight-year-old's first readings was for novelist Elinor Glyn, whose *Three Weeks* was filmed in Hollywood. The crystal revealed that Miss Glyn wrote best by moonlight. It was not until Jeane married James Dixon and settled in the nation's capital that world affairs became a subject for her speculation. By then she was also interested in astrology, and sometimes she had visions unrelated either to horoscopes or to the crystal orb.

She has since explained that if she knows the astrological sign under which someone was born she can find the future in a special segment of her crystal. Some signs are tuned in better at the center of the sphere, others are read to the left, right, above, or below. Julius Zancig, an earlier user of the crystal ball, once said that a doorknob could be used just as effectively. The object merely serves as a focal point for concentration. If one has a lively imagination the scenes conjured up can be quite entertaining. Prolonged staring, however, produces headaches. If you really believe you can see the future in the transparent sphere, some psychiatrists warn, this may be a sign of trouble on your personal horizon.

Jeane Dixon has never, to my knowledge, performed in vaudeville theaters; she is not a working professional. Futurecasting is her hobby. Money is the least of her worries. She lives in an impressive house with marble floors and antique French furniture. She sleeps in a canopied bed once owned by the wife of Napoleon III and in which no doubt the Empress Eugénie rolled and tossed as she pondered the marvels of another psychic, Daniel Dunglas Home.

It has been written that she predicted John F. Kennedy would be shot seven years before he went to Dallas in November 1963. This story has been so widely circulated and accepted that today she is firmly established as a luminary in the great American psychic legend. Recently she complained during a television interview that many predictions had been attributed to her which she never made. Unless one saw her predictions in print, she continued, they should not be taken seriously.

Fair enough. Here's what appeared in print seven years before the Kennedy tragedy. In the May 13, 1956, issue of *Parade*, a nationally distributed Sunday newspaper magazine, were these words: "As to the 1960 election, Mrs. Dixon thinks it will be dominated by labor and won by a Democrat. But he will be assassinated or die in office, though not necessarily in his first term."

As we know now, the election was not "dominated by labor." She did not name the Democrat she said would win; no date was given for the president-to-be's end; and his announced demise was qualified with Delphic ingenuity "assassinated or die in office, though not necessarily in his first term." Thus if the president served a single term, it would be within four years; if he was reelected, there was an eight-year span.

Such a surmise was not illogical for anyone who has studied recent American history. William McKinley was assassinated a year after the turn of the century. Warren Gamaliel Harding and Franklin Delano Roosevelt died in office, and during Harry S. Truman's tenure an attempt was made on his life. Moreover, the nor-

mal burdens of the Presidency are such that it is commonly re-
garded as a man-killing office. Woodrow Wilson and Dwight
Eisenhower were critically ill during their terms. Unfortunately for
the nation, the odds against Mrs. Dixon's prophecy's being fulfilled
were not too great—7 to 3, based on twentieth-century experience.

In January 1960 Mrs. Dixon changed her mind. Kennedy, then
a contender for the Democratic nomination, would not be elected in
November, she said in Ruth Montgomery's syndicated column. In
June she stated that "the symbol of the presidency is directly over
the head of Vice-President Nixon" but "unless the Republican
party really gets out and puts forth every effort it will topple." Fire
enough shots, riflemen agree, and eventually you'll hit the bull's-
eye.

A study of other Dixon predictions is equally disillusioning. In
Mrs. Montgomery's January 1, 1953, column she foresaw that President Eisenhower would soon "appoint five-star General Douglas
MacArthur to an exceedingly important post, probably an ambas-
sadorship." The former commander of the United States's armed
forces in the Pacific must have been disappointed if he read this;
he was never to assume even a minor role in Washington. Nor did
"Russia move into Iran in the fall of 1953," as she forecast, or in-
vade Palestine four years later.

Not infrequently Mrs. Dixon will amend a prophecy. She said,
in Ruth Montgomery's October 23, 1954, column, that "in 1963, CIO
President Walter Reuther will make known to his Union followers
that he intends to run for President of the United States the following year." The following year she revised her prognostication. This
time she said Reuther would make his bid for the White House in
1960, "but will not win his heart's desire until 1964." He did not
announce his intention to run in either 1960 or 1964. He was killed
when his plane crashed in 1970.

In 1954 the Washington seeress was quoted in the Montgomery column as seeing Thomas E. Dewey, the former governor of
New York, in a "powerful new post at Ike's side." This, like her

prediction for General MacArthur, did not transpire. Nor did Senator William Knowland "become much more important and prominent" as a member of Eisenhower's official family.

Among Mrs. Dixon's notable clinkers was her statement in October 1958 that Red China "would plunge the world into war" because of Matsu and Quemoy. In the May 22, 1960, issue of *American Weekly* she said that China would use germ warfare against the United States. "Russia will be the first nation to put a man on the moon, probably in about three years' time," she predicted in Ruth Montgomery's best-selling story of her career, *A Gift of Prophecy,* which was published by William Morrow and Company, Inc., in 1965. The first *men* on the lunar surface were Americans, Neil A. Armstrong and Colonel Edwin E. Aldrin, Jr. They arrived July 20, 1969. Another American team landed four months later. She gave no hint of the coming six-day war between Egypt and Israel; instead she proclaimed, "Great wisdom will flow from certain decisions made by Gamal Abdel Nasser, President of the United Arab Republic, and because of some alliances he will forge." She warned Sargent Shriver to "guard against assassination attempts." None materialized.

In the spring of 1966 there were rumors of internal strife in Cuba. A reporter from the New York *Post* questioned Mrs. Dixon, who was in Manhattan promoting the Montgomery book, about Fidel Castro. "My vibrations tell me that he's nowhere around," the future teller answered. "He's either in China or dead." The story was printed May 17. It is doubtful that Castro was in China —at least no evidence has been offered that he had gone there— but certainly he wasn't dead.

There were cheers in the Hancock Auditorium of the University of Southern California May 7, 1966, when Jeane Dixon, crystal ball in hand, peered over the footlights and announced that the war in Vietnam "will be over in ninety days. Ended but not on our terms." Four years later it was continuing.

Brad Steiger who tried to assess Mrs. Dixon's predictions for 1969 in the January 1970 issue of *Fate* found this a difficult task.

Her forebodings were "more philosophical than pragmatic," and at least a third were "not predictions at all, but rather some kind of physical character sketch." Religion, she had said, would "play a big part" in Governor George Romney's life, which anyone who reads the papers knows. She compared Aristotle Onassis' "vibrations" to those of Pierre du Pont and found they were very alike. Both loved "art, literature . . . the theater and all beautiful things." She foresaw a "great future" for Senator Edward Kennedy of Massachusetts but not the tragic accident at Chappaquiddick that July or Mary Jo Kopechne's death by drowning in his car. She was still touting "spectacular space accomplishments" for the Russians, though by then the date had been postponed to 1969; her cloudy crystal ball had not yet given a hint of the two American landings on the moon.

More than forty years ago Gene Dennis, another seeress, was the rage. The superstitious will be quick to notice that, though her first name was spelled differently from Jeane Dixon's, it was pronounced the same, and her last name also began with a *D*.

Gene Dennis was a seventeen-year-old Kansas high school student when people first began to talk about her gift. David P. Abbott, an expert in detecting mediumistic fraud, invited her to his home in Omaha, Nebraska. He had written a popular book, *Behind the Scenes with the Mediums*, and he thought if she tried to use a trick to peep at questions written on a folded piece of paper or sealed in an envelope he could catch her. She surprised him. Unlike the mystics who were then appearing in American theaters, she worked alone. No questions were written; you simply asked her whatever you wanted to know, and she gave you an answer. She couldn't tell you the serial numbers on the bills in your wallet or the address of your Aunt Cynthia in Rhode Island, but she could score high when asked about love affairs, lost pocketbooks, or future plans. She was booked for a three-day engagement at the Omaha Rialto theater as an extra added attraction in addition to the usual movie, and Abbott, a portly gray-haired man, introduced her at every performance.

Not only was the theater packed, but she received a mound of mail, including offers to perform in vaudeville in the principal American cities. Abbott had no wish to travel. Chaperoned by her mother, Gene Dennis went on the road.

Though she frequently told theater patrons that a lost watch was in another suit hanging in their closet or that an earring could be found under the rug in their bedroom, her talent was of little help when she lost something herself. When she returned to play at the theater in Kansas City, she lost her wristwatch. Not until she ran an ad in the paper was it returned.

Like Jeane Dixon, Gene Dennis predicted the outcome of elections. During her first visit to New York in 1924, she said the next American president would be a Democrat. Though she didn't give his name, she described him as "a good talker," a man of medium height with a dark complexion and leathery skin. The incumbent, Calvin Coolidge, must have chuckled if this prediction came to his attention. He was reelected that year, and when finally he left office another Republican, Herbert Hoover, took his place.

Her first Manhattan appearance at the Aeolian Hall, under the direction of Hereward Carrington, a psychical researcher who was always willing to sponsor a mystic whose name was in the news, was not a success. One reporter wrote that she "seemed to have ability to lure the desired answers from the questioners themselves." Another commented: "The majority of the audience seemed as skeptical . . . as the reporter upon whom she hazarded the wrong guesses. Her cross-questioning act was ancient when Civic Virtue [a statue] was a mere block of uncarved marble."

To make matters worse the attractive eighteen-year-old brunette was arrested on a fortune-telling charge. An irate mother complained to the police that she had given the psychic twenty-five dollars to tell her where her runaway son could be found. Gene Dennis said he was in Los Angeles. When the boy returned home, he said he hadn't been farther west than Pittsburgh. A magistrate at the Washington Heights court fined the mystic twenty-five dollars and warned that if she turned up again on a similar charge he would give her the maximum fine allowed by law—two hundred dollars—and a six-month jail sentence.

It should be noted that Jeane Dixon, the Washington seeress, does not accept money for private readings. Even so a complaint was filed in Columbus, Ohio, in late 1969 that she was practicing astrology without a license during a personal appearance there. When she didn't appear in court to answer the charge, a bond that had been posted to guarantee her appearance was forfeited and a warrant was issued for her arrest if she returned to the city.

All mystics agree that it is ridiculous for cities to outlaw their work or demand license fees. They say they have a God-given talent and that they help the less gifted cope with the complexities of modern life.

Gene Dennis was performing at Loew's State Theater in Los Angeles in 1927 at the time of the Dempsey-Tunney fight for the heavyweight crown. Her prophecy in the sports section of the September 17 issue of *Evening Express* was a Delphic masterpiece: "The general opinion of the fight will be that Dempsey, from a strictly fighting standpoint, won the fight. But to those who are wagering heavily on Dempsey I want to give a word of advice: Don't wager too heavily, for the real winner is not always the AC-TUAL WINNER. Please think that last over."

Tunney, the ex-Marine, won; so did Gene Dennis. So many people stormed the theater to see her that the box-office gross was a mighty six thousand dollars more than it had been the previous week. She was held over for another seven days.

Gene Dennis attempted to explain her gift in 1928. She said that the questions people asked brought a series of pictures to her mind. The images were vivid, like scenes in a movie. Other people thought back, but she thought forward. Her inner movie projector was out of whack when a reporter questioned her on a train bound for New York in May 1930. She said the child the Charles A. Lindberghs were expecting would be a girl. She predicted that the United States would engage in a war with Great Britain about 1940 and added that France would join the battle against Uncle

Sam. She could not see Prohibition being repealed though the clamor to have liquor legalized was increasing. Finally she said the deposed German kaiser would regain his throne.

When the big story of the day was the disappearance of Judge Joseph Force Crater, the twenty-three-year-old predictor from the prairies said the missing jurist was alive and well and living with a blonde in a remote part of either Cuba or Honduras. To date he has not been found. When Gerard Croiset, the Dutch *paragost* (the word he prefers to psychic), was in the United States a few years ago the plot of ground he indicated as the burial place of the long-lost Crater was dug up, but no bones were found.

Typical of the predictions future tellers make was Gene Dennis' prophecy as Ruth Nichols prepared to fly across the Atlantic Ocean; she would make it "if she watches her oil line."

Still the public lined up at the box offices of theaters where the seeress from Kansas was headlining. They forgot her frequent misses. When a forecast came true, it was remembered. She was always willing to make a string of prophecies if a newspaper would print the story. The papers seldom embarrassed her by mentioning the ones that did not materialize. She was always a good human-interest feature. People like to read about mystics.

I had seen perhaps a dozen question-answering acts in vaudeville before I saw Gene Dennis perform. It was easy to see why David Abbott had been impressed in Omaha. She was an attractive woman with a trim figure and graceful movements. She had none of the exotic trappings associated with her craft. She wore a smart gown, not a spangled robe or a turban. There were no bowls of incense burning on the sides of the stage and no assistants in oriental garb distributing and collecting folded papers in the audience. She traveled alone. The managers of theaters and the regular ushers were her liaison with the audiences. Their only task was to see that one question at a time was asked and that the questions came from various parts of the theater.

Once a question had been propounded, Miss Dennis almost immediately began her answer. "Shall I change my job?" The reply was ingenious, satisfactory to the girl wearing glasses and a dark dress, who stood so Gene could see her. The psychic said the girl had been thinking of working elsewhere for some time. The people with whom she was now associated did not appreciate her worth. She should not however make a quick move. Yes, she would change her position, but the proper time would be several months in the future.

"Will I marry the man I am seeing now?" asked a plump woman who rose from a seat in the sixth row. "You are more interested in marriage than he is," Gene said. "He finds you attractive; he relaxes in your company; but there are complications in his personal life of which you are unaware. I would not press the matter. I see no wedding ceremony in the immediate future. You will meet another man—someone you do not know now—who can offer you more security. In April you will make perhaps the most important decision of your life."

A middle-aged man on the other side of the theater wanted to know who had taken his signet ring. Gene said the ring hadn't been stolen. It had fallen from the piece of furniture on which he had placed it. She advised an immediate search of the room. The ring, she added, was a gift. Was this true? The man said it was. As the next question was asked I could see him walking quickly to the back of the theater, obviously on his way home to search under tables and behind bureaus for the missing ring. No one would ever know how many of the answers Miss Dennis gave that afternoon came true.

When Gene Dennis went to England in 1934, she was as big an attraction in British theaters as she had been in the United States. Though many mentalists were playing the variety houses, none worked alone or matched her charm and emotional appeal. She was a quick thinker, a clever improviser, and—above all—she appeared completely sincere.

Gene Dennis lived well in her day—no theatrical digs for the girl who could see the future. She preferred and could well afford the finest suites in the best hotels. In London she stayed at the

Savoy. It was reported that Prince George consulted her on three occasions. Her friends included members of the peerage, prominent sportsmen, and distinguished men about town. A marvel of concentration when performing, she was always forgetting where she put her fur coat or handbag when off stage. One day she left her bulging purse on a chair in the lobby of the Savoy when she rushed to take a phone call from Paris. A friend who was there when she came to retrieve it asked if it contained anything of value. She shrugged, opened it, and took out a roll of bank notes. She didn't know precisely how many and asked him to count them. The total was a thousand pounds—five thousand dollars in American money.

Luck was with Gene when she predicted the results of important sporting events in Britain. In Brighton she had a vision of Colombo, the Derby favorite, being nosed out by Windsor Lad. Her friends who bet heavily on the longshot won. Queried as to how Jack Peterson, "the Walloper from Wales," would fare in his title match with Len Harvey, the British heavyweight champion, she became so excited that she started jabbing the air as she predicted Peterson would take the crown. Again those who bet on her insight were on the winning side.

When a torso was found in a trunk, she said the murder was linked with another killing. Not long afterward a second body was found in another trunk.

A reporter in New York was eager to question her about a $427,950 armed car robbery in Brooklyn. He interviewed her before the ship that brought her back from the British Isles was docked. She started concentrating. She had the impression that the leader of the gang was someone who knew his way around watery areas. She had a flash of a navy uniform. No, she amended the statement, it was Navy Street. The gang was headed north, near water. The man's name began with an O—perhaps it was Owen? She saw paper stacked in rolls—a warehouse on the waterfront?

The police said later the flow of words was of no help.

A few months after that, she offered her thoughts on the Bruno Richard Hauptmann trial. She said he would be convicted of mur-

dering the kidnapped Lindbergh baby, but that the child was still
alive, somewhere in New York or New Jersey. Of course, she was
right about the conviction, but not about the child's being alive.

On September 11, 1942, someone wrote to ask columnist E. V.
Durling of the New York *Journal-American* if he remembered the
famous psychic. He said that he did and that the last he had heard
of her was that she was happily married in Seattle, Washington.
She had made some remarkable predictions, he said, but six times
she had failed to pick the winner of the Kentucky Derby.

The clairvoyants who for a fee look into private futures, like
Gene Dennis and those who now perform publicly, are frequently
masters of what is known in the trade as instant analysis or cold
reading. A limp, cough, or skin condition is a readily observed ail-
ment. The cut and quality of a client's clothes and shoes will re-
flect his or her affluence, as will expensive finger rings and gold
cigarette lighters. Accents and patterns of speech indicate
backgrounds.

Even without visual clues, readings can be given which convince the customer that the psychic is in tune with his vibrations.
For instance,

> You are impulsive, quick thinking, ready to take an occasional
> risk, though your good judgment seldom allows you to make a seri-
> ous mistake. Yet you take chances and enjoy successes that would
> not be otherwise possible.
>
> Details bore you, but you force yourself, often at the last possible
> minute, to take care of them.
>
> Other people, especially those with insight, enjoy your company,
> but you are always conscious that you must control your reactions,
> not express views that may clash with other opinions. You know a
> misunderstood word or phrase can cause hard feelings, wounds to
> vanity. You are quick to anger, but generally hide your feelings,
> mask your emotions.
>
> About seven months from now you will start on a new venture.
> You may be thinking of it now. Don't rush into it without consider-
> able thought. Be sure you're right, then go ahead.
>
> I see the letter *D* or *J*. Does this ring a bell? Do you know such

a person now? It has to do with something important in your life. A woman will play a vital part in your success. Listen to her; you may think she doesn't understand you, but she has your best interests at heart.

You are planning a trip. It will work out better than you think, though you have occasional doubts. Within a year I see a decision arising that can change the course of your life. When this time comes, eight or ten months from now, you will have two alternatives. You will need further advice at this time.

Your health shouldn't worry you, but you should take it easier. Learn to relax. Don't try to cram thirty hours into a day. You must learn how to dismiss problems from your mind. Take it easier. You'll get what you want; don't work so hard to get it. I don't mean you should lessen your efforts. Learn how to apportion your time so you can have periods of relaxation. This is necessary so that you can build up energy for tomorrow.

Conditions in the world today depress you. Things are happening in this country that confuse you. You can't carry the weight of the world on your shoulders. Do what you think is right. Don't overly concern yourself with conditions that are beyond your control.

This will be, all in all, a good year for you. The best in many ways of the last five or six. Your mind is expanding; you are exploring new avenues of thought.

Read these words again. Do they apply to you? Who doesn't take an occasional risk, who isn't impulsive, who isn't bored with details? Who isn't thinking of a new venture? Note the future projects are not identified. If you can't think of someone you know whose name begins with the letter D or J, you are a rarity indeed. Note that neither first nor last name was specified.

In some ways the coming year will be memorable for you. Even a generalized analysis like this can have an influence on a person's life. People will read into it what they wish. One doesn't have to be a Gene Dennis or a Jeane Dixon to predict that people will never lose their desire to get a glimpse of the future.

FORTUNE-TELLING AND SEEKING

Styles in fortune-telling change with the times. Teacup readers are less popular at the moment than cocktail scanners. Phrenologists, specialists in analyzing the conformation of your skull are out; graphologists, who see your character and desires in your handwriting, are in. Numerology, interpreting names and words by the positions their letters occupy in the alphabet, a favorite system of the 1920's, is making a comeback though many of the oldest forms of divination are almost forgotten.

In ancient Athens alectryomancers drew a circle on the ground and marked it off in twenty-four segments—one for each letter of the Greek alphabet. Grains of wheat were scattered in the various areas. A hungry rooster was deposited in the center of the circle, and note was taken of the letter in each section as the fowl turned here and there to gobble up the grain.

If the smoke that arose from a fire was black and billowy, capnomancers said the future was dark. Thin, wispy, gray clouds were a good portent. Hydromancers saw visions in bowls of water. Dots made haphazardly on a piece of paper formed prophetic designs in the minds of the geomancers who studied them. Other prognosticators searched for the secrets of tomorrow in the entrails of dead animals, the flights of live birds, or the shapes of blobs of melted wax as they fell into water-filled goblets.

My future has been indicated by the slips of paper that trained birds plucked from trays in Hong Kong and Singapore, by roadside mystics in Japan who watched the order in which marked sticks fell from a cylinder. A bearded mendicant in Delphi predicted I would be a success because of the shape of my earlobes.

Shortly after I received my 1-A draft card—the printed invitation to World War II—I made the rounds of the fortune-tellers in Baltimore. I visited a gypsy palmist, a cocktail-bar martini reader, and a nightclub clairvoyant. None mentioned I would soon be in uniform; all predicted an evil end for Hitler; none guessed correctly when the war would end.

What harm, you may ask, is there in anyone's visiting a fortune-teller? They offer conversation to the lonely, solace to the worried, hope to the frustrated, amusement to the sophisticated.

Hundreds of police records could be cited to show how those who believed in the powers of such mystics have been swindled, but a single case, unusual only because of the amount of money involved, will illustrate the point.

In September 1956, Frances Friedman, a widow in her early forties, was attracted by a window display on Madison Avenue in New York which advertised psychic advice. Neither she nor her sister, who was with her, had previously been interested in fortune-tellers.

Mrs. Friedman asked for a horoscope. The gypsy woman who greeted them said that while she was not an astrologer, she could tell them the past, present, and future. Mrs. Friedman's sister was not impressed by the reading the dark-skinned brunette gave her. Frances Friedman, however, found the woman fascinating. She seemed to have an uncanny ability to reach into her mind and reveal her inner self. Mrs. Friedman returned frequently to the mystic she knew only as Lillian, and each visit increased her confidence in the gypsy's powers. Once the gypsy tore one of her dollar bills in half, balled the pieces together, and pushed the torn banknote in the front of the widow's dress. Later, at home, Frances took out the crumpled paper. Miraculously the dollar bill was again in one piece; there was no evidence that it had ever been ripped.

Mrs. Friedman lived alone. Once, her oldest daughter, the daughter's husband, and her granddaughter had shared the house. Now they lived in another city. Another daughter had her own apartment since returning from college.

After the death of her husband Mrs. Friedman had discovered that other men lacked his sterling qualities. "I felt almost not needed, and that's a bad thing for a woman." She wanted companionship but could not find it. She relied more than ever on the advice and sympathy that Lillian, the gypsy, gave her. She could not understand why her life had changed so much in recent years. The gypsy had a ready answer. Frances had an evil side to her nature that caused those who knew her unhappiness and trouble. There was an old gypsy test that would either verify or disprove this analysis. The widow was instructed to wrap an egg in one of her late husband's handkerchiefs, then tuck the package in the toe of one of her shoes—a left one. Frances was to bring the shoe with the egg in it to Lillian the next day. Mrs. Friedman followed the instructions precisely. When she arrived at the Madison Avenue establishment, Lillian told her to crack the egg. She did, and from it came not the normal yolk but a repulsive greenish-yellow mass that seemed to be the torso and head of a small-sized devil. The head had two horns, black eyebrows, and a goatee.

Money, the gypsy stated emphatically when the loathsome object dripped from the broken shell, was the cause of Mrs. Friedman's misfortunes. There was only one sure way to counteract its malevolent influence. The widow was to take $30,200 from six banks where she had accounts and redeem 93 bonds. The total amount, $108,273, was to be put in a safe-deposit box in the form of a cross.

Mrs. Friedman followed Lillian's directions to the point where she was to insert the bills in the safe-deposit box. She found it impossible, however, to form the cross. The bulk of the bills was too great for the box.

Lillian, when she learned of this dilemma, had a solution. Rent another safe-deposit box! Mrs. Friedman noticed that the number of one box was 1233 and the other 3123. Each had the same 123 pattern plus an additional 3. She thought this numerical similarity was an omen for the success of the evil-dispersing ritual.

Mrs. Friedman patiently waited for the pattern of her life to change. Now certainly she would meet a man who was understanding and admirable; now certainly those who knew her would find her even more attractive and companionable. But no changes came.

The gypsy was sympathetic; she seemed genuinely distressed that the bills had not exercised an influence for good on the widow's behalf. She had apparently underestimated the power of the money. This money was tainted; it must be destroyed. She could perform a mystic rite that would insure Mrs. Friedman's happiness. Frances was told to buy a live chicken and to bring it and the banknotes from the two safe-deposit boxes to the gypsy parlor.

The widow did not object to bringing the cash to Lillian, but she absolutely refused to be seen on a downtown Manhattan street with a live fowl under her arm. That was ridiculous. Lillian consoled her. She was not to worry about the chicken, one would be there when she arrived with the evil lucre.

Mrs. Friedman brought the contents of the two safe-deposit boxes to the gypsy parlor on Madison Avenue in a large paper bag. She was ushered into a back section of the quarters that was reserved for Lillian's very special clients.

The live chicken was there. It was to play a part in a final test to demonstrate the terrible power of the widow's money. Lillian put the fowl's head in the top of the cash-filled paper bag and squeezed it tightly around the creature's neck. At first the chicken put up a strenuous fight; then its movements gradually lessened until its feet hung limp. The bird was dead, Lillian proclaimed, killed by the evil odor of the money. The money must be destroyed. She tossed the bag into a trash can. Fire and flames reduced it to cinders as one of Lillian's gypsy friends stirred the smoldering ashes. Mrs. Friedman's $108,273 was gone, and gone too, she hoped, was the cause of her misery.

A year later Lillian phoned her client. Had the spell worked?

Was Mrs. Friedman happy now? Apparently there was still a trace of the bad influence affecting the widow for, on the gypsy's advice, she took another $10,000 to her. The gypsy's spells were once again ineffective. By the time Mrs. Friedman took her problem to the police the gypsy had vanished like the $118,273 invested to ward off evil.

"Devil eggs" and bill switches are still being used in New York City. According to my friend Detective James Stewart of the New York Police Department, the victims, more often than not, are foreign-born members of minority groups. The appearance of a small demonic form emerging from the shell of an egg that the fortune-teller's patron has brought to the mystic and that the client herself has cracked has a staggering effect on a superstitious person.

The dupe seldom remembers that before the egg was broken the mystic had it in her hands and returned it. The switch of the unprepared egg for the one in which the devil form has been sealed is covered by perfectly natural moves. "Did you bring the egg?" The victim displays it and the mystic, who has the "devil egg" palmed in her right hand, takes it with her left hand, brings both hands together as she examines it. She raises her eyes. "Did you follow my instructions?" The victim raises her eyes to the eyes of the charlatan as she answers. At that moment when attention is misdirected, the exchange is made. The customer's egg is palmed in the left hand, and the prepared egg is brought into view.

"I don't want to touch it," says the mystic as she returns the devil egg to the client. "Break it yourself." Later the patron remembers that the mystic said she preferred not to touch it and forgets that she did.

A similar sleight-of-hand movement brought about the restoration of Mrs. Friedman's torn dollar. After a bill is torn in half, the gypsy rolls the two pieces together to form a ball, and as she tucks the ball into the dress front of her client, she switches a balled, unripped bill for the packet that contains two pieces.

For less affluent customers the gypsy bill switch is used in another way. The client is asked for a bill, the largest the gypsy can get. This is rolled up and tied in a corner of the patron's handkerchief. "Don't untie the knot for seven days," the gypsy says, "and you will have good luck." When the knot is untied a wad of paper is found in place of the bill. By then the gypsy has moved on to another place. Few people report the loss of their money to the police. Some are ashamed to admit they have been taken in by a trick. Others, the more credulous, actually believe that the gypsy's miraculous power has been demonstrated by the conversion of legal tender to plain paper and wait hopefully for unseen influences to bring them good fortune.

When a bag of money is apparently set afire in a trash can and burned to a crisp, the flames never reach it. It is either switched for another bag filled with paper, while the victim's attention is diverted, or put in a hidden metal container in the can where it is shielded from the fire. The gullible patron who has seen the chicken die because of the money's "evil odor" is too overwrought emotionally to realize that when the top of the bag was closed around the fowl's head the gypsy's finger pressure, not the money, ended its life.

A wider range of gypsy deceptions was used in Kansas City, Missouri, when a palm reader conjured away seventeen thousand dollars and a diamond ring from Mrs. Eunice Elizabeth Caster.

Mrs. Caster, then visiting a sister in Kansas City, walked into the gypsy parlor in October 1966. Sister Helen sized her up immediately. Her clothes, shoes, and the glittering diamond on her ring suggested that she was a customer worth cultivating. As the gypsy studied her sixty-eight-year-old client's palm, she saw signs that someone was after Mrs. Caster's money, that she needed psychic protection. She advised the widow to bring a spool of white cotton and a pure white handkerchief on her next visit.

Two days later Mrs. Caster looked on as Sister Helen broke off a length of the thread, folded it, and tied three knots. At the gypsy's behest she added three more knots herself. When the knotted thread had been wrapped in a piece of paper, the palmist prayed. The paper was opened; the knots had vanished. Visible evidence that Sister Helen controlled invisible forces.

Two of Mrs. Caster's twenty dollar bills were dipped in water, then torn. The gypsy wadded up the pieces and tied them securely in the widow's handkerchief with three knots. Mrs. Caster was told to take the handkerchief to bed with her that night and in the morning she would see more proof of Sister Helen's power when she untied the knots. If the widow had any lingering doubts about the dark-haired woman's influence, this was dissipated when she found the two twenties were whole again.

Next visit, the fresh egg Mrs. Caster had brought was cracked and a black yolk spilled from the shell. Now the time had come to show Mrs. Caster that the gypsy could apply her talents to cash. Two of the widow's bank notes, both twenties, along with three ten-cent pieces, three dabs of salt, and nine crumbs of bread were sealed in an envelope. After a night of incubation in Mrs. Caster's bed, two more twenties and three more dimes were hatched inside the sealed container. Little wonder that Mrs. Caster was eager to comply when Sister Helen asked her for a hundred dollar bill. This was sewn in a small cloth bag. Overnight it became two.

Mrs. Caster now was $140.30 ahead of the game—and she was ripe for harvesting. Before returning to her home in Los Angeles, she gave the gypsy her phone number. She was eager to participate in any other money-making experiments Sister Helen could devise.

In a few days her phone rang. The gypsy told her to take seventeen thousand dollars from her bank and have it ready in thousand-dollar bills for her arrival November 1. That night, Sister Helen purified the banknotes for Mrs. Caster, using a ritual that involved water, earth, prayer, and spitting three times in the toilet bowl. Sister Helen sealed the bills in a large manila envelope, instructing the widow to deposit it under lock and key in her safe-deposit box. Before leaving, Sister Helen noticed that Mrs. Caster's diamond ring also had an evil quality. She took it, explaining that she would bury it in a deep hole. Once the evil had been removed, it would join the bills in the locked box.

For the first time Mrs. Caster became suspicious and, unlike most dupes, went immediately to the police. Detective Sergeants Richard McCann and Robert McIntosh listened, asked questions, then decided the gypsy would make a play for more money. If she did, they would be ready.

A tape machine was attached to Mrs. Caster's telephone. It recorded Sister Helen's voice each time she called from Kansas City. On November 14 the gypsy brought the conversation around to some stocks the widow owned. She said she would call back a week later. A study of the recorded conversations indicated that Sister Helen had used a pay phone for her calls. Seven days later when the gypsy left her home, she was followed by two officers. They arrested her in a booth after she had put through her call to California. In her hand was tangible evidence that could be presented in a court, Mrs. Caster's name and number.

A Kansas City jury found Diana Marks, alias Sister Helen, guilty of using an interstate telephone with intent to defraud. United States District Court Judge Elmo B. Hunter sentenced her to a three-year prison term, then ruled that if the money and ring were returned to their rightful owner the gypsy would be released after three months.

Fortune-telling is illegal in many cities, but seldom is it the target of a special crusade by the police; they are too busy coping with major violations of the law. Those who tell fortunes today very rarely use cards, signs, or advertisements that mention fortune-telling. They skirt the law by calling themselves psychic advisers or spiritualists.

A single November 1969 issue of the New York *Amsterdam News,* whose readers live for the most part in Harlem, carried five columns of advertisements under the "Spiritualists" heading. To quote from one:

DON'T GIVE UP!! Guaranteed Results in 24 Hours . . . . He tells you all before you utter a word . . . . He reveals to you all of the hidden secrets, evil eyes and lurking dangers. If you really want something done about the matter. Here is the man who will do it for you in a hurry. Don't tell him let him tell you. See him in the morning. BE HAPPY AT NIGHT.

The appeal of a mystic who advertised that he is from Columbia, South Carolina, is even stronger:

Do you know you are supposed to have everything you want. Regardless what it may be. There is a special way to get it. Do you read between lines? The old Fashion remedy is still the best way. All it takes is one visit and your troubles are over. If you have tried everybody and everything and nothing seems to work, then see this great man . . . . Confidential. Guaranteed.

While a few of the women who advertise have a simple Mrs. before their name, others preface it with Madam, Rev., or Sister. Most of the men use Rev., though Bishop, Prof., Dr., or Voodoo Witch Doctor is added by some.

Competition is keen and "I will do what others claim to do" is a not infrequent boast. A "free answer to one question" by telephone is a come-on, calculated to attract the cautious. Once a prospective client is on the wire, the caller learns that a personal interview will produce hoped-for results more quickly and effectively.

A Louisiana man, "chosen by God," makes the most all-encompassing claims in his advertisement. He states that he has aided those with pains in their backs, legs, feet, ankles, navel, and near the heart. He states unequivocally that he has stopped scalps from itching and grown hair through prayer; that he can cause his clients either to gain or to lose weight, and dispel "crazy spells from your home and body." No problem seems to be too complex for him. He promises to

Stop that woman from messing around with your boyfriend or husband, make your boyfriend or husband bring his pay to you . . . . Make you lucky in games, store business, beauty parlor business. Make your father-in-law or mother-in-law like you and treat you right . . . . Bring your husband or boyfriend back to you if they have left you—no matter how long they have been gone. Give your husband his man power back, give wife or woman her woman power back so her boyfriend or husband won't tell her she's cold.

This miracle man's address is not given in his advertisement but two phone numbers are. One is for use from 6 A.M. to 2:30 P.M.; the other is for midnight calls. Why waste time asking questions when this marvel worker avows he can change the future?

The Better Business Bureau investigates misleading advertisements of manufacturers and retailers when complaints are received from the public. No one seems to care that people who can ill afford to pay for services that are not as advertised are being taken in by a con game older than the Pyramids.

ASTROLOGY

This, the era of scientific exploration of outer space, moon walks, and planet probes is also the age of Aquarius, the most felicitous period for astrology since its heyday in Babylonia. More horoscopes are being erected; more forecasts are being made; more popular guides are being printed and sold than ever before.

Modern astrologers predict the rise and fall of stocks, analyze the influence of the stars on cats and dogs, and chart the destinies of companies, institutions, and countries. Advertisers employ the signs of the zodiac to pique public interest in cosmetics, motor cars, clothes, insurance policies, cheeses, and soft drinks. Artists paint new and colorful versions of the ram, the bull, the crab, and other symbols of astral dominance.

Personal astrological forecasts are more avidly studied in the daily press than comics or crossword puzzles. Monthly magazines detail how the stars have impelled celebrities to their present eminence. A giant computer with flashing, multicolored lights spews out personal profiles and six-month guides for the future in New York's Grand Central Station. Like its forerunner on the Champs Elysées in Paris, it was programmed by André Barbault and offers readings in Spanish and French, as well as English. A new elevator tower on the Canadian side of Niagara Falls offers a panoramic view of the breath-taking natural wonder. The top money-making concession at the base of the tower is another computerized horoscope machine which, for a price, gives tourists an insight on the subject that interests them most—themselves.

Ptolemy, Claudius Ptolemaeus, a Greek scholar who lived in Egypt in the second century A.D., wrote the books upon which modern astrology is based. His *Almagest* was a compilation of ancient astronomical lore; the earth, as he visualized it, was the center of the universe. His *Tetrabiblos* was based on the belief of Babylonian astrologer-priests that the planets, which were given the names of gods, controlled the destinies of mankind.

The Chaldean mythology was replaced by the Greek (and thence Roman) equivalent. Nergal, the war god, became Ares (Mars); Ninurta, the storm raiser, became Kronos (Saturn). These were evil influences. Ishtar, goddess of love and fertility, was replaced by Aphrodite (Venus), and Marduk, the all-powerful, by Zeus (Jupiter). Venus and Jupiter were forces for good.

Forecasts are based today not on the actual movements of the planets in our twentieth-century sky but as they appeared in the heavens at the time of Ptolemy. The position of the earth in relation to the planets has changed considerably since then. Aries has moved into the area Ptolemy ascribed to Taurus, and the other divisions of the ancient zodiac have changed accordingly. Few modern astrologers are interested in the current movements of heavenly bodies and though the planets are at different distances from the earth, astrologers accept their influences as uniform.

Only five planets and the sun and the moon could be seen when Ptolemy formulated his system. The three planets discovered since were given their own special characteristics by later theorists. Astrology now is more symbol-interpreting than planet study and the symbols relate to the sky of almost two thousand years ago.

In the Orient the view was held that the control of the planets was absolute; in the Occident it was believed that the stars impelled, not compelled; that man, forewarned, could change his fate. The influences were there, but once they were known a cautious person could protect himself, at least to some degree.

Anyone with sufficient intelligence to carry out the necessary calculations can erect a horoscope with the aid of an ephemeris, which converts clock time to sidereal time—the time it actually takes the planets to make a circuit of the heavens—and a table of houses. The latter indicates the planet that was ascending in the skies at the time of the birth and the positions of the other planets and the sun and moon.

It is another matter to interpret a chart, as Dr. C. W. Roback, a Swedish-born astrologer, noted in his book *The Mysteries of Astrology*. For an accurate reading, Roback said, a person must be "favored with that peculiar supernatural gift of judgment and of prescience which seldom belongs to more than one family in a nation." Roback claimed to be "the seventh son of a seventh son in a family thus rarely endowed."

Those in the past who predicted when the world would come to an end obviously misread the portents. Waters from the seas were to wipe out mankind in 1186, but 1187 arrived on schedule without the catastrophe. Agostina Nifo read the signs of a mighty deluge coming in 1500, as he studied his charts in Italy. Twenty years later Johann Virdun, an Austrian, specified the year 1524; Sebastian Constantinus, in Rome, also warned of the impending calamity. Johan Stoefler in Germany was positive that the rush of turbulent waters would engulf the earth. Terrorized peasants fled from their fields and sought havens in the mountains. The year passed without more than seasonal floods here and there in Europe.

Destructive winds forecast half a century later didn't ravage Europe; astrologers alibied that the storms they had predicted were political and had come to pass.

When a sixteenth-century astrologer's prediction sent Britishers scurrying from the cities even the abbot of St. Bartholomew's Church in Smithfield, London, built himself a stronghold at Harrow-on-the-Hill and stocked it with provisions so he could survive the expected flood. Later the astrologer admitted he had made a slight mathematical error. The event, his corrected calculations indicated, was scheduled for the same day a hundred years hence.

William Winston was a distinguished eighteenth-century astronomer, as well as an enthusiastic astrologer. At Cambridge University, he held the academic post once graced by Sir Isaac Newton. His scientific observations as an astronomer led him to announce that there would be an eclipse of the moon and that a mighty comet would streak across the sky in 1736. His studies in astrology indicated that the comet heralded an event of incredible importance. As he interpreted the symbols, the Saviour would manifest himself on earth after the comet appeared, and the world would be destroyed by earthquakes and flame.

At five A.M. on the Thursday that Winston predicted, a ball of fire appeared in the heavens. Pandemonium reigned in London. Friday, the day Winston said buildings would be reduced to cinders and rubble and that life would cease to exist, was an anticlimax. The sky, the earth, and the water remained in their accepted places. Repentant sinners who had rushed to churches, drinkers who had sworn off alcohol, returned to their normal ways of life.

A paper that was sold on the streets of Paris less than a hundred years ago carried a gory illustration of future destruction and an Italian astrologer's prediction that the world would end November 15, 1881. Leonardo Aretino, the prophet of doom, stated emphatically it would take just two weeks to complete the havoc. First the ocean would cover the land. Fish would die on the third day, animals on the fourth, and birds on the fifth. The last houses would crumble on the sixth day; rocks would disintegrate on the seventh. The remaining people would lose their speech on the tenth day, and all humans would die on the thirteenth. The world would end on the fourteenth day. The fifteenth would be the Resurrection.

Indian astrologers in Delhi were certain as they read the omens for the future that the world would end on February 5, 1962. They gathered with their followers to await the holocaust; but the sun rose as usual the next morning, and the Red Fort still stood where Shah Jehan had built it, and soon the noise of traffic and the sounds of commerce dispelled the clammy feeling brought on by the night air.

On the same date in the United States, members of Understanding, Inc., met in a mountain town in Arizona to see the old world out from a high vantage point. They too lived to tell the tale.

Gerolamo Cardano was a distinguished sixteenth-century physician, mathematician, and prolific writer on many subjects, including the occult. Like many of his contemporaries in Italy during the Renaissance, he was firmly convinced that man's destiny was written in the stars. The horoscope he erected for his son Aldo revealed that the boy had remarkable talents which would bring him wide acclaim and great wealth. Aldo's will, it seems, was greater than planetary influences; he was a source of constant trouble to his father and achieved a reputation for being a rascal. In London, Cardano visited the court of Edward VI, the boy who sat on the throne of England. The Milanese astrologer drew up a chart, at the request of Edward's followers, that showed the king would have a long, though not altogether healthy, life. He specified the illnesses that would affect the lad when he was twenty-three, thirty-four, and fifty-five; Edward died at sixteen.

Among Cardano's comments on astral influences, as translated by William Lilly, are: "When Venus is with Saturn, and beholds the Lord of the Ascendant, the Native [the person born under these conditions] is inclined to Sodomy, or at least shall love old hard-flavoured Women. Make no new Clothes, nor first put them on when the Moon is in Scorpio, especially if she be full of light and beheld of Mars, for they will be apt to be torn and quickly worn out. If a Comet appear whilst a Woman goes with Child, if it be either in the fourth, fifth or eighth month, such Child will prove very prone to anger and quarrels, and if he be of quality, to sedition."

Had not Mercury counteracted the threat of Mars at the time he was born "I could easily have been a monster," Cardano admitted. He died in 1576, fulfilling the prediction in the forecast made for his own future; critics say he killed himself at the age of seventy-five to make it come true.

Ercole dalla Rovere, an astrologer and mathematician from Bologna, wrote his forecast for Francesco de Medici, the grand duke of Tuscany, in Florence on April 8, 1575. The vellum-bound manuscript is even more interesting to read today than when it was first produced. The future that Rovere wrote about is now the past. Though Rovere, in customarily cautious phraseology, noted that "the angelic Intelligence of the Omnipotent Creator," which controlled "the influences of the stars" could also alter the destinies of humans, he foresaw that Francesco would have a life span of sixty-seven years, that he would father three boys and eighteen girls and that six of his children would be living at the time of his death. Actually the grand duke died in 1587 when he was forty-six. Hellmut Schumann, the Zurich antiquarian, noted that not more than three of Francesco's brood survived him.

Michel de Notredame, Nostradamus, was a physician, astrologer, and practitioner of occult magic. In the first half of the sixteenth century his reputed ability to conjure up angels and produce visions in mirrors must have been more awesome than his divinations. No prophet's predictions have been interpreted in more ways. The same words in different periods have been explained to forebode unrelated events. Certainly no one wrote more teasing similies. "The King-King will be no more, of the Gentle one destroyed," begins one of his quatrains. This is said to mean that Henry the Third, the king of Poland, later king of France (King King), would be killed by a man named Clement (synonym of gentle), which he was. This explanation was made after, not before, the slaying.

Nostradamus predicted troublesome times for Paris in the distant future. In 1999, Paris will be invaded from the air by a great king who will come from the east. The attacker will use reindeer in the battle; how is not indicated. Perhaps in 1999, or after, someone will explain that the word "reindeer" has a secret meaning. Paris, it seems, will survive this onslaught, for elsewhere in the astrologer's verses the city is pictured as a blazing inferno in the thirty-fifth century.

How any purely astrological calculation could produce Nostradamus' strange similies and provocative phrases is impossible to imagine, unless one credits him with clairvoyance. Many of the popular modern astrologers annoy more serious students of the stars by claiming this ability when they make predictions.

Few foes of celestial prophecies had as much fun as Jonathan Swift, the British satirist. Distressed because so many people accepted the prophecies in John Partridge's popular almanac, Swift issued his own, using for the purpose an assumed name—Isaac Bickerstaff. The title page promised: "Predictions for the year 1708. Wherein the Month and Day of the Month are set down, the Persons named and the Great Actions and Events of Next Year peculiarly related . . . . Written to prevent the People of England from being further impos'd upon by vulgar Almanackmakers."

Professing to be an astrologer who was outraged by "sottish pretenders," Swift directed his first prediction to Partridge: "I have consulted the star of his nativity by my own rules and find he will infallibly die on the 29th of March next, about eleven at night, of a raging fever." He advised Partridge to put his affairs in order while there was time.

Then, to stir up more trouble, Swift attacked his own prophecies, using the name of his target as a pseudonym. Complaining about the vexation the false forebodings had caused him to suffer, the spurious "Partridge" wrote: "I could not stir out of doors for the space of three months after this, but presently one comes up to me in the street. Mr. Partridge, that coffin you was last buried in, I have not yet been paid for . . . ."

Obviously enjoying the commotion his two assumed roles caused, Swift produced another Bickerstaff almanac, which carried as its subtitle: "A Vindication of the Stars, from all the False Imputations and Erroneous Assertions of the late John Partridge . . . ."

The "late" John Partridge, despite Swift's efforts to kill him off in print, did not die until 1715. His almanac had a longer life; it was still being published in the early years of the nineteenth century. Ironically, many people did not get Swift's joke and accepted the Bickerstaff predictions as true forecasts. At least one copy was even burned by the Inquisition in Portugal.

The first monthly periodical with a regular astrology section was *The Conjuror's Magazine, or Magical and Physiognomical Mirror*, which appeared in London in August 1791. In two years the astrological material had become so dominant that the title was changed to *The Astrologer's Magazine; and Philosophical Miscellany*. No one was more critical of the way horoscopes were interpreted than the readers whose letters were printed. The correspondents didn't disavow the art, they objected to the mistakes and conjectures of those who professed to be authorities. The controversies were "extended to a painful length," said an editorial note in the final January 1794 issue.

Robert Cross Smith edited *The Straggling Astrologer*, a weekly publication which ran from June 3 to October 30, 1824. He was more successful with *The Prophetic Messenger*, an almanac, and a new name—Raphael. Smith died in 1832; the almanac continued for years as a succession of other Raphaels carried on.

The Fortune-Teller's Own Book: A Manual of the Occult Sciences . . . By Raphael, the Astrologer of the Nineteenth Century was published by Fisher and Brother in Philadelphia in 1841. In its pages, the reader learned that while it was safe to put on a new suit on Sunday, the same action on other days was extremely hazardous. "If on a Monday, his clothes will tear. If on a Tuesday, even if he stand in water, his clothes will catch fire . . . . If on a Saturday he will be taken ill." Even on a good day, the hour of adornment was not to be overlooked. Morning or noon were propitious times, but to dress after sunset made one "wretched" and in the evening "ill."

Sunday was not the day to take a bath unless one wished to "experience affliction." Only four days of the week were recommended for shaving—Monday, Wednesday, Thursday, and Friday; "the other three are evil and inauspicious."

Evangeline Adams advised her clients on more important matters: love, health, business, and finance. The prophet from Andover, Massachusetts, who said she was a descendant of John Quincy Adams, the sixth President of the United States, arrived in New York in 1899. She made a forecast for Warren E. Leland, the owner of the Windsor Hotel on Fifth Avenue, where she checked in, before she unpacked her luggage. Danger, she said, was imminent; "it might overtake him on the morrow." A speculator in the stock market, Leland was unimpressed: "Oh, tomorrow's a holiday. Stocks can't go down." The next day the hotel was destroyed by fire. Her own chart hadn't indicated that she was to lose some of her possessions in the fire.

She was arrested on fortune-telling charges in 1914 and arrived in court with a stack of astrological volumes. She told the judge that she practiced an ancient and honorable art based on the principles established by Claudius Ptolemy in Alexandria, Egypt. Her readings were given after a study of the positions of the planets at the time of a client's birth and of data that had accumulated through the centuries. The judge was interested in how a chart was made. He gave her the date, time, and place of his son's birth, though he didn't say the man was his son. She consulted her ephemeris and table of houses, filled in the blank areas of a chart, and began her analysis. The judge listened attentively. When she had finished, he confessed that Evangeline Adams understood his child better than he did. The case was dismissed.

Those who had never heard of the astrologer before the story of her acquittal was published rushed to her Carnegie Hall studios to have horoscopes cast. It became the vogue to consult "America's female Nostradamus." Mary Pickford and other cinema luminaries visited her. Enrico Caruso, the great tenor, brought opera stars who were curious about their theatrical futures. The client who most intrigued the public was J. Pierpont Morgan, the financier. It was rumored he never made an important move on Wall Street unless it was sanctioned by the stars.

Almost inevitably Evangeline Adams, along with the other

much-discussed people of her time, faced the microphone. Through radio she became known to thousands who had never had the money or opportunity for personal readings. She began this new career in April 1930 and was an instant success with a thrice weekly program. In a month she had received 150,000 letters and postcards asking for horoscopes. Offers for lecture tours and personal appearances poured in. She demonstrated that there was money to be made with astrology—and on a scale never dreamed of by the showmen who pitched horoscopes in dime stores or in boardwalk star parlors by the sea. She died November 10, 1932, before the Federal Radio Commission, the forerunner of the Federal Communications Commission, forced astrology and other future-predicting practices from the nation's air waves. Thousands of complaints had been received from those who sent questions—and money—to the radio mystics. Crystal gazers, clairvoyants, and assorted swamis, as well as astrologers, had reaped a rich harvest from the gullible public. At one time five future tellers were on the air in New York. With American microphones denied them, some of the more persistent questers for easy money moved below the border. Their voices via high-powered Mexican transmitters reached listeners in several states, but none achieved the popularity of Evangeline Adams in her heyday.

The prophecies of Tomas Menes, a Spanish seer who had "an unbroken record for making predictions that came true," were noted in a *New York Times* report from Madrid October 7, 1934. On May 23, Menes had foreseen that Chancellor Engelbert Dollfuss of Austria would lose his life by violence before three months had passed; Dollfuss was killed by Austrian Nazis on July 25. Menes also successfully predicted the results of the November 1933 Spanish elections and the deaths of the president of the Catalan Generalidad, Francisco Macia, and Miguel Primo de Rivera, the Spanish premier of Morocco. Looking into the future, Menes said Fascism would fail in Spain, Hitler would be deposed by a German civil war, and Mussolini would be overthrown in 1937—none of which came to pass. Nor did the Labour Party win the elections in Britain in 1935, as he foresaw, nor Britain "lose India" before that election. And Russia did not "fight, but eventually . . . win a frightful *chemical* war with Japan."

War and the rumors of war always stimulate great interest in prognostications. A dispatch from Holland in 1939 said that a new and effective form of propaganda was being used to undermine German morale. Ominous predictions of the downfall of Adolph Hitler, who was said to be interested in astrology, were being widely circulated in Nazi territories. The most impressive were the sixteenth-century forebodings of Nostradamus who saw a near-pagan regime in Germany. It would be controlled by a sect that cared nothing for "death, gold, honor and riches" and it "should dread the hour, the northern naval power will too deeply involve it." As World War II progressed, the Germans too used astrological predictions as weapons in their psychological attack, and Nostradamus and lesser prophets were quoted to forward their own cause.

H. R. Trevor-Roper noted in his book *The Last Days of Hitler* that in the middle of April 1945 Hitler and Dr. Joseph Goebbels, his propaganda expert, studied a horoscope that had been made for the German Republic on November 9, 1918, and the Führer's personal chart, dated January 30, 1933. After crushing defeats early that year, a major victory was indicated for late April and peace in August. There was no hint in the stars that Hitler would take his own life on April 30 or that the German Army would surrender on May 7.

War of another sort was declared seven years later in the United States.

The television code of the National Association of Broadcasters, which became effective March 1, 1952, included this paragraph: "Exhibitions of fortune-telling, astrology, phrenology, palm-reading and numerology are acceptable only when required by a plot or theme of a program, and then the presentation should be developed in a manner designed not to foster superstition or excite interest or belief in these subjects." All stations do not subscribe to the code.

Yet in January 1969 David Susskind, who through the years has offered astrologers and clairvoyants an opportunity to promote their arts on his syndicated television program, sought to capitalize on the current revival of interest in astrology in America by producing "Maurice Woodruff Predicts." The show featured the short, mild-mannered, bespectacled British clairvoyant-astrologer who had appeared previously on video in England.

Variety reviewed the first presentation on WNEW-TV, New York: "For those incorrigible doubters who are dubious of Woodruff's psychic talents, this hour did little to allay their skepticism . . . he displayed a capacity for blandness and generalization that made his mind-reading somewhat less than fascinating." Noting that the studio audience was impressed by the personal readings, the review went on to say: "Woodruff displayed a gracious modesty concerning misreadings and erroneous predictions (which he conceded do occasionally occur)."

Those who wished to check the clairvoyant-astrologer's accuracy had an unusual opportunity in his *You and Your World (October 1968 to September 1969)*, published by the New American Library in September 1968.

While Woodruff wrote that Nixon "should, by all the portents" be the next American President, he also saw British Prime Minister Harold Wilson losing his position, but October 1969 passed with Wilson still on the job.

"One of the weddings of the year," in which the ceremony would be performed twice, once on each side of the Atlantic, with its participants "a titled Britisher" and "an American lady," did not occur.

Nor did Barbra Streisand give birth to another son, Senator Javits of New York "come very much into the foreground," President Nasser leave office, Castro disappear from the Cuban scene, Grace Kelly make a "thriller" film, canes and spats regain their one-time popularity, or China succeed in orbiting a moon shot. Certainly there is no controversy, as Woodruff predicted there would be, about whether the United States or Russia put the first man on the moon.

Woodruff's second book for the New American Library, published in May 1969, was entitled *The Secrets of Foretelling Your Own Future.* In ancient China, it has been written, astrologers who made false forecasts lost their lives. The penalty is not nearly so severe in the modern world. Mr. Woodruff is still prophesying for his clients though his weekly WNEW-TV show has vanished from the New York screen.

Why has astrology surged in popularity? It offers an appealing system that permits people (who may not be especially interested or knowledgeable in the system's basic foundation) to find not only their own traits under the proper sign, but also the characteristics of their friends and associates. Aries (the ram) men, for example, are viewed as adventuresome, quick on the trigger, easily moved to passion, masculine, and commanding. Those born under the sign of Taurus (the bull) are slower to arouse, but, once moved, sometimes violent. They are creatures of the earth, not the clouds, interested in the material side of life. Gemini's influence promotes changes of mind, fickleness, inquisitiveness. The head rather than the heart is the source of Gemini decisions.

Astrology provides a way for people to find out more about themselves with a minimum of exertion. It also may be a ploy to stimulate conversation with casual acquaintances or an excuse for eccentric behavior. As Shakespeare put it in *King Lear*: "as if we were villains by necessity, fools by heavenly compulsion, knaves, thieves and treachers by spherical predominance, drunkards, liars and adulterers by an enforced obedience of planetary influence." How convenient to "make guilty of our disasters the sun, the moon, and the stars."

Bypass the many objections astronomers and other scientists make to the movements of the planets as fixed for astrological calculations. Why is someone born at a certain time, on a certain day,

in a certain part of the world of a certain nature? Did the origi-
nators of astrology study the traits of millions of people and discover that all those born at a specific time had identical characteristics and futures? No! Nor has it been proven since that the early
fictions are fact.

The ancient horoscope makers understood the nature of humans. We all have the same basic problems, disappointments, and
hopes. Read the revelations under the other signs in your horoscope book. You will find that they too apply to facets of your
character.

Some people say they do not take astrology seriously, that
they read the forecasts in their daily paper for amusement. Others
subscribe to astrological journals and have personal charts made
hoping to stave off invisible planetary influences that might have
an adverse effect on their lives.

In the spring of 1969 on the day before it had been predicted
that California would slide into the sea, I flew by jet from San
Diego to San Francisco. The college sophomore who sat beside me
was tense during the trip. She said she was changing planes in the
city by the Golden Gate for the East. She didn't really believe the
state would disappear under the water the next day, she said, but
she wasn't taking any chances.

TILTING TABLES

Tables are tilting across America again. A phenomenon that once was an international sensation has been revived by a new generation which is intrigued by the occult. In the past few weeks tables have tipped on television news reports and on panel shows, and those who saw the furniture behave strangely were as puzzled as savants and scientists were when they first observed the uncanny actions of the inanimate objects a hundred and twenty years ago.

In the early 1850's, only a few years after the Fox sisters rapped out their spirit messages in upper New York State, table turning became a national pastime. No special equipment was needed; everyone had a table, and almost any sort of table could be used. When a group of people sat around a table, touched their fingers to its surface and concentrated on the movement the table should make, it was rare indeed that their thoughts were not carried out. Tables with a single central support tilted back and forth and turned. Those on four legs rocked so that two legs rose from the floor, then banged back. When questions were asked, answering knocks were received. One bang was affirmative; two indicated no. It was amazing how well informed the tables were about those who sat around them. They told the number of children present or indicated how many rings a woman had on her finger with uncanny accuracy. It was more fun than a quilting party. Not infrequently a table would wobble rapidly across the room, dragging those who touched it in its wake.

A woman in Bremen wrote a sarcastic letter to her brother in New York ridiculing the current American rage in March 1853. He replied that it was unfair for her to be critical until she had tried it herself. Her first test was so successful that in a few days furniture was acting up in hundreds of homes in the German city. Dr. Karl Andrée, the editor of the Bremen *Zeitung*, sent an account of the "fantastic locomotion" to the prestigious Augsburg *Gazette*; it was "no cock-and-bull story, no American joke, no Yankee extravagance." He called on scientists to explain "how it is that the fluid emanating from the hand of man has sufficient influence on the wood of a table to set it in motion, without producing an effect on surrounding objects."

Dr. H. Schauenburg, a professor at the University of Bonn, affirmed the phenomenon. At the home of Jean Neusser he made notes as two men, between the ages of thirty and forty, seven women, the youngest twenty, the oldest forty, and several boys and girls, from eight to twelve, participated in the tests. At half past four in the afternoon, the professor noted, there was a wind from the northwest and the sky was clear. Three hours earlier the barometer "had registered 187 degrees above the level of the northern ocean."

The table was made of smooth cherry wood. It had an eighteen-inch one-piece top and rested on three legs on a deal floor. Those who gathered around the table put their hands on its top with their thumbs overlapping and their little fingers touching. A table had been in motion earlier in the day, so the professor was not too surprised when in a mere thirty seconds tremors were observed. He reasoned that the necessary heat and electricity had already charged it. He felt "shudderings and shootings" from his fingertips to his elbows. The table moved jerkily and "the boards seemed to be snapping under some mysterious influence."

One of the ladies commanded: "Table, turn upon thyself, and go to the right." Balanced on a single leg, it whirled so fast that those around it were forced to run to keep up with its pace and the person-to-person finger link was broken. Despite this the table still wheeled dizzily until "halt" was called and the action abruptly terminated. Then, on order, the table revolved to the left equally as fast. It also turned with all legs on the floor, though much slower than before.

"March," it was directed, toward the stove, or the window, or the writing desk, or down the corridor to the kitchen. The table obeyed, jerking forward, first on one leg, then another.

The longer the experiments continued the more readily the table responded. It was as obedient as a trained dog or an automaton, the professor observed. It would bow to anyone named, often so low that it would have toppled over had not the fingers on the top restrained it.

Now the real fun began. The table replied to questions. When asked the hour, it banged five times; this was verified when a clock in a nearby church tower tolled. The table answered simple mathematical queries and rapped ages. When it banged out that one of the women present was thirty-seven, the professor gallantly noted that this was true, but "nobody would have suspected it." Questions were limited to those not likely to upset the participants. In Cologne a woman had asked the number of years in her future; the single answering rap had caused her to faint. She was still ill according to the last report he had heard.

When a mahogany table with an oval top four feet long was used, it answered questions equally well. An antique chest of drawers that weighed more than sixty pounds and had iron casters on its bottom corners spun in a circle as fast as the light table had.

Table turning, Professor Schauenburg concluded in capital letters, was "A FACT." He thought that a lukewarm room was best for the experiments, that the hands of the experimenters should be moist. He observed that after prolonged participation his hands were swollen.

A Professor Weidkoffen from Cologne gave exhibitions in Hamburg of the "galvanic, electro-magnetic" influence. Tables danced merrily to musical accompaniment. After a table had two-stepped for forty minutes, it waltzed across the room and out the door with the operators scampering after it.

Later in April the contagion reached Paris. It was said that the chief of the French police was responsible for the lengthy stories that appeared in the press. The emperor, Napoleon III, had summoned him to the Tuileries. There was so much gossip about family affairs at the palace that the police official was charged to create a new topic of conversation: anything that would divert the public's attention. That night he read in the *Journal des Débats* how table turning had captivated the imagination of the people in Bremen. The next morning he instructed every Parisian newspaper to print an article on the subject, and his agents were sent through the capital to discuss the phenomenon in cafés, restaurants, and salons. Moving tables became the topic of the hour.

Some people were skeptical. The Academy of Sciences had tested Angélique Cottin, a teen-age girl from La Perrière, Normandy, in March 1846. François Arago, the physicist, and a Dr. Tanchou had claimed that a flow of current from her body made tables vibrate and attracted and repelled pith balls and feathers tied to the ends of silken threads.

Even heavy pieces of furniture trembled when the bottom of her petticoats touched them. It seemed apparent to the two men that electricity accounted for the phenomenon; why, the former glovemaker could identify the positive and negative poles of a magnet by merely touching them! The negative produced no reaction but the contact of her fingers with the positive gave her what she described as a shock. Magnetic needles trembled when she approached; no compass was to be relied upon when she was near.

The experiments carried out by the six-man commission from the academy with the "electric girl" under close scrutiny allowed her little opportunity for trickery. The official report stated that Angélique did not affect the magnetic needle and she had failed to differentiate between the two poles of a magnet. The only unusual movement seen was the sudden, vigorous shaking of the chair on which she sat. When the investigators suggested that she could do this by muscular power and asked for the feat to be repeated Angélique's manager had a ready out. The girl's electrical current had been used up, he said, at least for the time being. This brought an end to the probing. The manager avoided further confrontations with scientists, though he continued to exhibit her before the public.

Those who had heard about the "human battery" could not duplicate her alleged phenomena, but almost everyone could make tables turn. Dr. Felix Rouband, a Parisian physician, wrote that he was fathoming the "new and illimitable ocean which has suddenly appeared on the scientific horizon." A month's study led him to conclude that men had more and faster-acting motivating powers than women.

Only one death was attributed to the popular fad. A gout sufferer named Benaris in Roth, Germany, was frustrated by his attempts to influence the movements of a table. When it danced with others touching it, he was stricken with apoplexy. Dr. Rouband observed that when tables revolved rapidly the operators became dizzy and experienced "twistings of the head." Fatigue, sore arms and elbow joints were frequent aftereffects. When headaches developed, the doctor counseled, a few drops of ether would ease them.

A lively evening with the tables at a countess' residence in Paris left two of her guests physically exhausted. In addition to having excessive heart palpitations, they were trembling hours afterward. In Vienna two ladies were so affected by the "mysterious fluid" as they sat at a table that they felt pains in their arms and unusual heat in their heads. When the table spun swiftly, one of them collapsed, with tears streaming from her eyes, in a cataleptic fit. The other fell too. For ten minutes they writhed on the floor. A doctor in Leipzig warned that the electric fluid that passed through the fingertips from one person to another could transmit bodily ailments, particularly gout.

Stories of swoonings, vertigo, and swollen muscles didn't

lessen the appeal of table turning. The fanatics who experimented for five and six hours each evening enjoyed the pastime to a greater degree when they learned there was an element of danger present.

In England tables tilted and turned with less reckless abandon than on the Continent. The daughter of the editor of the *Family Herald* told about the perverse table she used: "It is a shocking liar, and has no conscience whatever, and contradicts itself without any scruple; but it is very funny. It tells them about their sweethearts; and having been asked what sort of husband the housemaid would have, it nodded out by means of an alphabet that she would marry a pieman."

Three theories were advanced to explain table turning: intervention by spirits, an electrical fluid that emanated from the body, and muscular pressure. Each had strong supporters. The spiritualists naturally accepted the first. Researchers who tested the second found that instruments didn't indicate the presence of an electrical current during even the most violent agitation.

The third theory seemed reasonable to the Reverend Hiram Mattison, professor of natural philosophy and astronomy and a member of the American Association for the Promotion of Science, though at first he thought a mysterious new force might be charging the tables. In January 1853 he sat with a fellow clergyman and several acquaintances around a "magnetized" table in West Winstead, Connecticut. For more than fifteen minutes there was not even the slightest tremor. When a group of believers took the chairs the skeptics had occupied, the table tipped. He observed almost at once that the hands of one of the participants were applying pressure to tilt it.

In Burlington, Vermont, Mattison used muscular force himself on a table with a single center support and casters at its base. Though seven other sitters had their hands on the top, he easily made it revolve in any direction he wished and no one was aware of his control. Later when the table turned without his help, he set about to discover the mover. Again the eight men touched it. Mattison kept his hands passive, his eyes alert. As the revolving began, he asked one man after another to leave the circle. When only a single other person remained, Mattison asked the man to put his hands over his own. He felt pressure from above as the table spun. He charged the man with deception. The New Englander answered innocently that if he had caused the movement he was not aware of it.

The library hall of the Manchester Athenaeum was the scene of the first public probe of table turning in England on June 9, 1853. Volunteers from the audience sat around seven tables; all but three were active during the evening. A round table that stood on three legs spun like a top five minutes after ladies touched its leather surface. The rapid movement, which had the women running to keep up with it, made them dizzy, and two stepped away for fear they might fall. The Reverend H. H. Jones, chairman of the investigating committee, asked the ladies to repeat the test, this time with pieces of tissue paper under their hands. Three tried to make the table move without success. Two more joined the circle, and in three minutes the table was revolving. When it stopped, the investigators found that the tissues, soaked with perspiration, were sticking to the surface.

There was a twenty-five-minute wait before a heavier table, with eight men around it, moved sluggishly. Eventually it turned so fast that the men had to sprint to match its speed.

Dr. James Braid said he was convinced that the action was due to what Dr. William Benjamin Carpenter had called ideomotor power. When the mind concentrated on a movement, it was carried out by the muscular system. This was not a conscious act; it might be in opposition to a person's wishes.

Other experiments were tried. A table on which a thin wire circle had been placed, with loops for the ladies' hands, didn't respond when their fingers touched only the wire and not the table top. Olive oil was spread in a circular band on the top of a round table from its edge five inches inward. Six people pressed on the oiled area for twenty-five minutes before there was any movement.

It was found that when fingers were put on a table top near the center, which was far away from the experimenters, the edge of the table remained motionless.

Michael Faraday, the British physicist, ended scientific conjecture about table turning in 1853. He demonstrated dramatically that tables tilted or spun because people pushed them. He sandwiched pencil-thin glass rods between two small flat boards and held the rods in place by winding rubber bands around the boards. An indicator attached to the device revealed the slightest displacement of the upper surface. The device set on the table, the participant put his fingers on it rather than the wooden top. Each time the table moved, the indicator showed that the top board had been pushed in that direction. When the subjects were aware that the movements of their fingers were being signaled, the table remained motionless. If the indicator was hidden from their view, pressures were again observed. It was proved that many people were not consciously aware that their hands had followed their thoughts.

Should you wish to experiment with table tilting, use one that is solidly put together. The closer the legs are to the center, the quicker you'll get action. A table with a single center support and a wide top is best for beginners. Put your hands flat on the surface (you need not bother to have little fingers and thumbs touching). Will the table to move, tell it out loud the direction you wish it to take. Visualize it following your commands. You must play the game all the way to get good results. The more those who sit around the table with you get in the spirit the livelier its actions will be. Years ago people sometimes sat for thirty minutes or an hour before anything happened. I doubt that you will have to wait more than five or ten minutes if everyone cooperates. Once hands are on the surface, don't lift them—just press down.

Two or four people are sufficient for a light table. A large one may take eight or ten. If a table isn't handy, use a stool, a taboret, or even a chair. Folding bridge tables, the sturdier the better, may be employed, but don't cover them with a cloth. A word of caution. Don't waste time with the heavy four-legged tables hotels use as service stands. George Kreskin, the mentalist, appeared at a press party once to promote a record that gave instructions for table turning. I attended with John Kobler, then an associate editor of *The Saturday Evening Post*. Kreskin knew that *almost* any table could be used, but he didn't know the room at the Americana Hotel in New York would be filled with the boxlike serving tables just mentioned. The tables were covered with white tablecloths that reached to the floor. Kreskin instructed us to put our hands flat on the cloths and listen to a recording of his voice.

Forty people obediently pressed their hands on the tops of ten covered tables. "For 10 tedious minutes and then some, the recorded voice kept exhorting the assembled reporters to will the tables in motion. Everybody willed until they were blue in the wrists, but not a table stirred. Not even a tablecloth," reported Joseph Cassidy in the *Daily News* the next day.

Though Cassidy didn't mention it, there was one startling side effect. A girl became so enrapt that she had hysterics. She screamed, mumbled, and groaned, then fell face down on her table.

The press party was held October 30, 1967—the day before the forty-first anniversary of Houdini's death. Tilting tables were logical for an amusing Halloween newspaper feature.

There was no mention of involuntary muscular action as Kreskin's recorded voice kept insisting that the tables would move. If you believe in ghosts it is easy to account for those stubborn tables: the spirit of the master magician came back that afternoon and—as was his custom—stopped the show.

THE OUIJA BOARD

The secretary of a New York advertising executive was upset. She called me one morning to explain her plight. She and her sister had been amusing themselves with a Ouija board the night before. Questions they asked had been answered with an amazing accuracy; then the indicator had spelled out future events so horrible that she could not sleep. How did the board know so much about their lives? Would its ominous predictions come true? How did it work? Was a psychic force directing its replies?

The American Ouija board was preceded by an earlier French device, the planchette, which came in vogue as interest in table tipping waned. To get a word message from a table, the whole alphabet was called. A tilt indicated a letter. The alphabet was repeated, and another tilt produced another letter. The process was time-consuming and laborious.

The planchette sped up the action. It was a miniature table, usually shaped like a heart, less than eight inches long. Two easy-rolling wheels supported it at one end, and a pencil was fastened in a hole at the other so that the top was level. This was placed on a large sheet of paper. Two sitters touched the wood over the wheels. As they concentrated on a question the planchette wrote an answer. Professional mediums used planchettes in their séances, and when the gadgets, beautifully made of polished hardwood, appeared in the shops another parlor amusement captured the public's fancy.

Isaac Fuld, a cabinetmaker who owned a small toy factory in Baltimore, carried the idea a step further. He painted the alphabet, ten numerals, and the words "yes," "no," and "good-bye" on a board and built a small planchettelike indicator that could slide easily on the board. Now two sitters could place their fingertips on the indicator and quickly get a yes or no or, if a longer reply was required, watch the marker as it indicated letters or numbers. Fuld patented this creation in 1892 as the Ouija board. The combination of the French and German affirmatives, *oui* and *ja,* was far more appealing than a prosaic yes, yes. The Fuld instrument was self-sustaining; it eliminated the need for sheets of paper and the occasional sharpening of a pencil.

The Ouija process was described in the patent application: "A question is asked and by the involuntary muscular actions of the players, or through some other agency, the frame will commence to move across the table." The "some other agency" was the explanation preferred by spiritualists who insisted that forces from the Great Beyond were moving the sliding indicator to communicate messages to their loved ones on earth. If naughty words or slanderous accusations were spelled out, they said an evil spirit was responsible.

The First World War stimulated a wide revival of interest in spiritualism. Distressed mothers, wives, and lovers yearned for messages of consolation from those who had died or been lost in action overseas. Ouija-board profits zoomed to a new high. Isaac Fuld and his brother William were incensed when the government levied a ten-percent war tax on their product. The authorities classified it as a game. Game indeed! They took the case to court to prove their contention that the Ouija board was a scientific device. Despite statements from professors, who were studying the instrument as a means of revealing subconscious thoughts, jurors were not convinced. When the case reached the Supreme Court, it was suggested that the nine judges put the question directly to the Ouija board. They relied instead on the evidence that had been presented to the lower courts. The solemn verdict of the country's

highest tribunal was that Ouija was a toy—nothing more. Ten percent of the Fuld profits were duly siphoned off by the tax collec-
tors.

What was a game by law was a source of psychic information
for those who believed in spirits. Mrs. Nellie Hurd used her Ouija
board in Kansas City in 1935 when she suspected her seventy-sev-
en-year-old husband was in love with another woman. The moving
finger of the indicator confirmed her opinion. She went into a
trance to gain additional information from the spirits. Her suspicions were confirmed, at least in her own mind. She also learned
from her occult sources that the old gentleman had buried fifteen
thousand dollars in the ground, but the uncooperative spirits
would not tell her where the money was hidden. Nor would they
spell out when and where to catch her husband in an illicit act.

She hired a private investigator, then refused to believe his report that Herbert B. Hurd was faithful. Finally, according to Mr.
Hurd, she tried a new tactic. His slumbers were disturbed when
his jealous wife struck him on the head with a pistol. When he revived, he found she had lashed him to the bed and was ready to ex-
tract a confession from him with the aid of a sharp knife, a red-hot
iron, or beatings with a thick rope whip. She forced him to sign a
document admitting he had given the fifteen thousand dollars to
her imaginary rival, the wife of a man who lived nearby.

All this Herbert B. Hurd testified when he was on trial for killing the woman who had tortured him because of the messages that
came through on her Ouija board.

This was not an isolated instance.

E. J. Turley, a former sailor who lived on a ranch in Arizona,
was shot in the back with two bullets from a double-barreled shotgun. His teen-age daughter, Mattie, explained that she had been
walking behind him, had tripped, and the gun had fired as she fell.
Investigation proved that the bullets would have been in align-
ment with the barrels of the weapon only if the fifteen-year-old girl
had held it supported by her shoulder while in a standing position.

Confronted by this scientific evidence, she told a different story to Justice of the Peace Frank Whiting and the local sheriff.

Mattie said her mother had consulted a Ouija board to learn if she should stay with her husband or live with a romantic cowhand. The Ouija board offered a solution that terrified the child. She was told to kill her father.

Her mother took the answer calmly and asked other questions as to how this should be carried out. A shotgun was indicated; five thousand dollars would be paid by her husband's insurance company and the law would not punish the girl for her action.

Twice Mattie tried to carry out the instructions the Ouija board had given her; twice her finger on the trigger failed to pull at the crucial moment. The third time she fired. The spirit advice was wrong on two counts. Her mother did not get the insurance money, and the child did not escape legal consequences for the crime.

Not all Ouija advice was bad. The world would not have heard Robert Schumann's "lost concerto" until 1956 had not Yelly D'Aranyi, the violinist, owned a Ouija board. The composer had given the manuscript to Joseph Joachim, Yelly's grandfather. Joachim's will stipulated that the music was not to be released until a hundred years after Schumann's death. The Ouija board told her to share the composition with the world as soon as she could. She found it in the State Library in Berlin, and long before the restricted period was up it was played in concert.

By means of the Ouija board, those who believe in its mystical powers say Shakespeare, Shelley, and other literary figures of the past have produced new works. William Hawley Smith conjured up a poem that he said James Whitcomb Riley had transmitted to him via the "Mystifying Oracle." His wife's ability to see visions permitted an even more interesting collaboration with a bygone great. James McNeill Whistler permitted her to glimpse a painting he had completed in the afterlife, then directed her brush as she painted a replica in her Peoria, Illinois, home.

Artist's impression of a stage séance in the late nineteenth century. Although the performer was tied to a chair, bells rang and musical instruments played.

Another artist's concept of a stage séance and the turmoil created in the dark. A frightened spectator, whose coat has been whisked away, runs from the stage.

Most mediums gave parlor performances. "Spirit hands" tugged on ladies dresses, rapped, tapped, and appeared in the dim light.

Daniel Dunglas Home, "the medium who was never exposed," also never appeared for the public. His séances were given while he was a guest of friends or noted patrons. Napoleon III and Empress Eugénie were amazed at his manifestations in France.

The first step in releasing a medium's hand in the dark. A little finger to little finger link is made. Then the lights are extinguished. In the dark the medium moves his hands closer together until the fingers of the spectators are a hand's span apart.

The medium lifts his right hand, uses his left thumb to touch the finger of the man on his right. With his free hand he can bang the tambourine, manipulate the bell, or bring the horn to his lips.

With the gaslights low, spectators see a pale spirit hand "materialize" above the edge of the table.

The "spirit hand" is a false hand fitted on the end of the medium's foot. It is on an elastic, so it will fly up the trouser leg when it is released. Most adept performers took off a shoe and used their foot to simulate a hand.

To create the illusion that he is floating in a dark room, the medium removes his shoes, puts them on his hands, and touches the heels to the heads of believers in a dark room.

Eusapia Palladino's hand release. This is only one of several methods detected during her séances.

Another way to make one hand play the part of two in the dark is shown by Mrs. Benninghofer to Houdini. The reformed medium revealed her methods to the public to aid him in his campaign against psychic fraud.

PROGRAMME

ILLUSORY MIRACLES   ..   .. PROF. ALEX FAY

MISS ANNIE FAY'S
MARVELLOUS LIGHT SEANCE.

STRANGE MANIFESTATIONS!
MOST BEWILDERING RESULTS!
MID-AIR EXTRAVAGANZAS!
AND STARTLING PHENOMENA

Miss Fay's hands, feet, and neck will be fastened to solid iron staples by a committee selected from the audience.

FLOATING EXTRAORDINARY.   THE LIFE-LIKE GUITAR.   THE MYSTERIOUS BELL RINGING.
THE SPIRIT CARPENTER.   THE ANIMATED VIOLIN.
[THE GREAT GOBLET AND WATER MYSTERY.
(A Puzzle to the Scientist.)
THE TAMBOURINE FLIGHT.   THE WORKING SCISSORS.   THE MOUTH [ORGAN IN ITS TRAVELS.
THE HUNTER'S HORN.   THE SPIRIT DRUMMER.
THE MOST THRILLING SPECTRAL PHENOMENA,

THE GREAT PAIL SENSATION.   THE SELF-ACTING KNIFE.

Remarkable Materialised Forms and Weird Spirits of Katie and Cissie King
ARE NIGHTLY PRODUCED AT EACH SEANCE, IN THE IMMEDIATE PRESENCE OF THE COMMITTEE.

Program of a stage medium in Limerick, Ireland, November 15, 1886.
This was not the original Annie Eva Fay, but one of her many imitators.

Houdini and Anna (she was called Annie when she was younger) Eva Fay in her garden in Massachusetts. A "crystal ball" pedestal was one of the outdoor decorations.

Houdini and his wife Beatrice demonstrate how slates may be switched under a table during a séance. An assistant reaches through a secret opening in the wall to exchange them. Though this method has been used by mediums, sleight-of-hand techniques are more effective since they can be used in clients' homes.

The most prolific ghost-writer of the twentieth century has been Patience Worth, who, though reticent to give details about her life on earth, admitted she had been born in southern England in 1649 and had never married. Later she crossed the ocean to America where at the age of forty-five she was murdered by hostile redskins.

She began her literary career 216 years after death, introducing herself to the woman who was to be her amanuensis in St. Louis, Missouri, July 8, 1913. Mrs. Pearl Lenore Curran and a writer friend were whiling away the summer evening with their fingers on the indicator of a Ouija board. The pointer swung to the letter *M* and a message followed quickly:

> Many moons ago I lived. Again I come—
> Patience Worth, my name—

It was Pearl Curran and not the literary lady who, as the intermediary of the long-dead author, gave the quaint prose and poetry in book form to that portion of the American public which was eager to read volumes dictated by a spirit. *The Sorry Tale, Hope Trueblood,* and *The Pot upon the Wheel* were followed by *Light from Beyond* and *Telka.* The latter two also appeared in German. In 1918 the phantom author was so popular that ten issues of a *Patience Worth Magazine* were published. Newspapers noted that the author had a vivid imagination and could express herself with great feeling. A *New York Times* critic analyzed her style: "Notwithstanding the serious quality and the many pitifulnesses and tragedies . . . much humor of a quaint, demure kind . . . the plot is contrived with such skill, deftness, and ingenuity as many a novelist in the flesh might well envy."

Until the invisible Patience introduced herself, Mrs. Curran had lived a quiet life. As a girl she had taken piano lessons in Chicago, and at one time for several weeks she had provided the musical accompaniment for the hymns in an uncle's spiritualistic church. She had been a professional musician and had worked at a department store before her marriage at twenty-four to John H.

Curran, who had been an emigration commissioner in Missouri.

Her formal education ended in the eighth grade. There had been no compulsion to write until she sat at the Ouija board. There the words from Patience Worth flowed easily:

"Go ye to the lighted hall to search for learning? Nay, 'tis a piddle, not a stream, ye search. Mayhap thou sendest thy men for barleycorn. 'Twould then surprise thee should the asses eat it."

The production of a novel by Ouija board is an extremely long and wearying procedure. Not surprisingly Mrs. Curran discovered that Patience Worth could speak through her own voice as her mother or a friend transcribed the messages and that Patience Worth could control her fingers as she typed.

Patience's archaic words and unusual sentence structures provoked considerable speculation among both literary critics and psychical researchers. Psychologist Joseph Jastrow asked his friend Professor Shelling, a specialist in the Elizabethan period, for his opinion. Shelling replied:

> The language employed is not that of any historical age or period; but, where it is not the current English of the part of the United States in which Mrs. Curran lives, it is a distortion born of superficial acquaintance with poetry and a species of would-be Scottish dialect . . . the borrowing of some dialect words and the clear misuse, misunderstanding and even invention of many others . . . . There is an easy facility of phrase almost wholly in our contemporary idiom and showing nowhere the qualities of the language of Elizabeth's or any previous age.

There is no evidence that a Patience Worth lived in England or America during the time she gave as her life span. I believe that Mrs. Curran that July evening discovered not a spirit but a way to express herself.

To many people the Ouija board is a fascinating pastime. It allows them to spell out their secret thoughts and astonish themselves when the board reveals so much about their lives. To others it is a crutch for decision making. Rather than make a conscious choice of possible alternatives they consult the Mystifying Oracle. If the selection turns out to be unsound, they blame Ouija, not themselves. Two clippings in Houdini's files stress dangers. One is undated:

> A serious warning comes from Dr. Curry, medical director of the State Insane Asylum of New Jersey, with regard to the use of 'Ouija board' which he declares is a 'dangerous factor' in unbalancing the mind. The 'Ouija board,' he says, is especially serious because it is adopted mainly by persons of high-strung neurotic tendency who become victims of actual illusions of sight, hearing, and touch at spiritualistic séances. He predicts that the insane asylums will be flooded with patients if popular taste does not soon swing to more wholesome diversions.

The other was printed in the March 25, 1920, London *Daily Express*:

> At the village of Cerrito, across San Francisco Bay, the craze for séances with Ouija boards, with which it is claimed that spirit messages can be received, has reached such a pitch that five people have been driven mad and taken to the lunatic asylum. There is a strong demand for the examination of all the 1,200 inhabitants of the village by mental specialists.

The current popularity of the Ouija board was heralded by *Time* in 1966. The newsmagazine reported that three times as many were then being sold as ever before. Parker Brothers, Inc., the game manufacturer, launched a campaign to acquaint this generation of mystically inclined searchers for truth with the seventy-two-year-old oracle. An advertisement was designed to appeal to the venturesome young: "You can ask it questions about love, school, money, travel, careers, the future, other people . . . anything! The indicator may spell out surprising messages. How or why is the great mystery, involving mental telepathy, ESP, and the subconscious." The *Wall Street Journal* estimated that two million boards were purchased in 1969.

The Ouija indicator moves as tables and planchettes move—

by conscious or subconscious muscular pressure from the finger-tips. When I have seen it in action, the direction was often more conscious than unconscious.

The operator's attention was riveted on the alphabet, the pointer slid from letter to letter with little effort on the part of those participating.

Should you wish to make a simple test to establish whether it is the brain of the operator or the intelligence of a spirit at work, use a board on which you paint the letters not in their usual posi-tions, but at random. Hide the surface of the board so that the par-ticipants can't see the sequence of the letters. Don't blindfold them —it is easy to peek when the eyes are covered. In an informal test, seat the people at a table with the special board upside down. Ask them to look at the ceiling of the room and keep their eyes fo-cused there. Turn the board face up, place the indicator on it, and lift their fingers so that they touch the top of the indicator.

Two observers should control the experiment. One makes sure that the operators never glance down; the other takes note of the letters the pointer indicates. Pure gibberish will be spelled out under these conditions.

For a more scientific test a board with the letters in a haphaz-ard arrangement is also used. A fourteen-inch-square box is pre-pared so that it opens at the back. A neck-size slot is cut in the bottom, and large air holes are made in the top. The back is opened; the head of a participant, eyes front, is inserted so that the neck fits in the slot in the bottom; then the back is closed. Only then is the board with its rearranged letters brought into the room, face down. It is turned right side up on the table.

Under these circumstances not only would the novels of Pa-tience Worth never have been written, but the supposed spirit would have found it impossible to spell out her own name.

DOWSING RODS
AND PENDULUMS

Diving sticks made from coat-hanger wire were being used by marines in Vietnam to ferret out buried land mines, hidden weapons, and tunnels, Hanson W. Baldwin, *The New York Times* specialist in military affairs, reported on October 13, 1967. He had seen Major Nelson Hardacker, commander of the Thirteenth Engineer Battalion, Fifth Marine Division, at Camp Pendleton, California, demonstrate the procedure for men soon to be shipped overseas for duty in the combat area.

Hardacker held the L-shaped wire indicators so the long ends, each approximately twenty-six inches, were horizontal and pointed forward as he grasped the eight-inch handles lightly in his fists. As he walked the rods remained parallel until he reached a position above a subterranean passage. Promptly, with no apparent guidance on his part, the extended wires swung suddenly, one left, the other right, to mark the presence of the tunnel. Baldwin followed the major's instructions and found that he too could locate the direction of secret passages in the terrain.

The technique had been used a year earlier by Louis J. Matacia while he served with the Ninth Marine Regiment, Third Marine Division, in the war zone. On his return to the training center at Quantico, Virginia, the "operations analyst" demonstrated the sensitive wires there and at Camp Lejeune, North Carolina. Neither Matacia nor the military physicists, college professors, or intelligence officers he approached could explain how two pieces of bent metal could perform the work of complicated mine detectors —and find tunnels as well.

The method received no official sanction but some officers and men were sold on its practicability.

For centuries European dowsers have used similar devices. Holding the ends of a forked stick, they paced the countryside until a sharp downward pull signaled ore deposits or an underground stream beneath the surface. Georgius Agricola described the action in his *De re metallica* in 1556:

> It is said that the moment they place their feet on a vein the twig immediately turns and twists, and so by its action discloses the vein . . . they assert, the movement of the twig is caused by the power of the veins, and sometimes this is so great that the branches of trees growing near a vein are deflected toward it.

He noted there were critics:

> Those who say, the twig is of no use to good and serious men, also deny that the motion is due to the power of the veins, because the twigs will not move for everybody, but only for those who employ incantations and craft.

Martin Luther denounced divining rods and later churchmen shared his view that they were tools of the devil. Cautious dowsers, rather than risk condemnation, used pious words to replace the occult spells:

> In the name of the Father, and of the Son and of the Holy Ghost, I adjure thee, Augusta Carolina [the rods in the sixteenth century sometimes were given the names of recently baptized infants], that thou tell me, so pure and true as Mary the Virgin was, who bore our Lord Jesus Christ, how many fathoms is it from here to the ore.

Each downward thrust of the sticks signaled a fathom.

The first known dowser-detective was called in to help French police solve a vicious double murder in 1692. Jacques Aymar went to the house in Lyons where a wine merchant and his wife had been slain. He followed the trail indicated by his divining stick and tracked down a hunchback who confessed his part in the atrocity and admitted two other men were involved. By then, however, the other fugitives were far beyond the reach of Aymar's criminal finder.

Peasants, priests, and the nobility were adept as dowsers. Count and Countess Beausoleil discovered 150 mineral deposits in France early in the seventeenth century, though their divining rods gave no hint that they would be imprisoned for practicing sorcery.

Pendulums were as sensitive as forked twigs in the hands of dedicated dowsers; they were also employed to predict future events. A group of conspirators met in the fourth century to determine who would succeed Emperor Flavius Valens. According to Ammianus Marcellinus, the Roman historian, a small table made of laurel from Delphi was placed on a large metal disk which bore letters of the alphabet around its edge. "A priest, linen-clad, bowed himself over the table, balancing a ring tied to a thin thread." The swinging ring indicated that "Theo" would be the next sovereign.

Hilarius, one of the men charged with plotting against Valens, admitted he had been at the séance, after sufficient torture had been applied to make him talk. He and several fellow conspirators were slain; Theophilus, Theodore, and others whose names began with Theo were put to death by imperial command. Theodosius was overlooked; he made the pendulum's prophecy come true.

As a detector of bodily ailments the pendulum was less reliable. French dowsers claimed they could diagnose from photographs. Physician Auguste Lumière set up a test. Rhabdomancers and cryptesthesiasts—two more exotic terms for diviners—were first invited to tell the sex of the infants who were shown in a series of pictures. The youngsters were wards of foundling homes in Lyons. The dowsers reported that 44 percent of the children were boys. Actually all were girls.

Then a radiesthesiast, whose specialty was to pinpoint diseases with his pendulum, was given four photographs of older subjects. They were a sad lot, his divining weight revealed. Tuberculosis, heart disease, syphilis, liver trouble, and other ailments were spotted. No evidence of these ailments had been found by doctors who examined the people in the flesh.

Another French medical man, E. Pascal, investigated a Bordeaux diviner who claimed his instrument worked as well over a few hairs as over a patient's body. Pascal brought him several black strands and watched his procedure. Suspending the pendulum with one hand, the rhabdomancer moved a pencil in the other hand over an anatomy chart. When the weight traveled in a circle, he said this indicated the organ was sound. A straight back-and-forth swing denoted illnesses. His final diagnosis was that the hairs belonged to a young man who was in a feverish condition. His pharynx was weak; his blood was infected by coli bacilli; and he had carcinoma of the pancreas. The hairs, however, were not from a human; they had been plucked from a healthy bulldog.

Pity the trusting sufferer who first has his organic disturbance located by a pendulum, then takes a medicine prescribed by a swinging weight.

Searchers for buried silver or gold will be interested in the results of a contest sponsored by *La Vie Catholique* in 1935. A thousand-franc prize was offered to anyone who could find a packet of fifty-six silver medals, eight tries out of ten. The treasure container was hidden successively in various parts of an old house. Almost half of the contenders used pendulums or divining rods. In 860 tries there were 86 successes; no one found the silver more than four times. The rhabdomancers did no better than those who depended on intuition or luck. Ten priests who participated were no more accurate than their worldly rivals.

Abbé Mermet, a Catholic priest, the head of the Association Française et Internationale des Amis de la Rhabdoesthésie, supervised the arrangements. He must have been disappointed, for he, like his father, was a noted dowser. Mermet firmly believed he could locate water from a map just as well as he could walking along the ground.

Henry Gross, the most famous water witcher of modern times,

was also convinced that divining was practical from a distance. Kenneth Roberts, the novelist, wrote three books about the man from Maine and his adventures. One, *Henry Gross and His Dowsing Rod,* which was published by Doubleday & Co. in 1951, was a best seller.

Studying the movements of his magic rod over maps, Gross marked sources of water supply in Ireland, Nigeria, and Bermuda. On the spot his talents led to the recovery of a lost gold pocket watch, the submerged motor from a boat, and ball ammunition that had once been used for old-fashioned muskets.

Gross, when dowsing for oil or water, would attempt to predict the depth at which the liquid would be found and estimate its quantity.

It is important to remember that Henry Gross was no stranger to the soil. He was a naturalist, and most of his life had earned his living as a game warden. He believed his rod tapped a divine source of wisdom and was pleased when the answers it indicated to questions he asked it so frequently agreed with his conscious reasoning.

The first dowser I ever met seldom made an important decision without consulting either his watch and chain, which he used as a pendulum, or his pocket-size dowsing sticks. He was a fellow traveler on the S.S. *Brazil,* bound for Rio and Buenos Aires. At mealtime he would suspend his watch over the menu. If it remained motionless above an item, he would never include it in his order. If it swung, he was certain the food would agree with him. He found by this means that casaba melons could be eaten without fear, that papayas were to be avoided.

He was an American engineer who had spent most of his years overseas. In England he watched a retired British colonel, who had served in India, locate a well for his company with divining sticks. He tried them himself and found they worked. He gave me a demonstration one night on deck as we stood by the rail near the swimming pool.

His rods were L-shaped, like those used more recently by the marines, but smaller—only eight inches long, with three-inch handles. He held them loosely with the long ends extending over his fists and forward.

He touched the tips to the green paint of the boat rail to "magnetize" them. Then he walked back about four feet and approached the rail. When the parallel rods were over the green, they immediately formed an X. I tried them, and they crossed for me. He said he did not know why they acted as they did, but he thought electromagnetic forces were responsible.

I asked if he could find hidden metal with the rods. He said he could, so I proposed a test. We sat at a table, and I took a coin from my pocket. He touched the tips of the rods to it, then turned his back as I hid the coin under the cloth on the surface of the table.

When I said I was ready, he moved his hands holding the metal rods up, down, and across the area. Suddenly they crossed. I lifted the cloth. He had missed by a good ten inches. We tried again, and once more the rods gave false information.

When the operator knows where the object of his search is to be found, the rods never fail. A geologist, though not aware that the appearance of the surface of the ground has influenced him, will locate with his divining instrument precisely the spot his brain has chosen.

How do pendulums and divining rods work? Michel Eugène Chevreul, the French chemist, read that an iron ring suspended at the end of a string would swing over mercury. He tried the experiment; it worked. This did not seem reasonable to him as mercury was not magnetic. He also found that the movement of the ring was more pronounced when his arm was held free; if he rested his elbow on a table, the action, though still observable, diminished.

Further tests revealed that if a sheet of glass covered the top of the bowl of mercury, the ring remained motionless. When the glass shield was removed, the ring began swinging as before. Then he was blindfolded, and an assistant periodically covered the mercury with the glass barrier. It had no effect. Unless he knew the glass was there, it did not stop the apparent pull of the mercury on the iron. This proved conclusively that muscular action, not magnetism, made the pendulum swing.

Chevreul's open letter to André Marie Ampère, a fellow scientist whose researches in magnetism and electricity were monumental, in the *Revue des deux mondes* in 1833 explained the fundamental principle of the pendulum. Twenty-one years later, in a book on the divining rod, pendulum, and table turning, Chevreul showed that the mind, in every instance, was the motivating force.

I was familiar with the concept before I saw the dowser on shipboard demonstrate his rods. When I held them, a very slight inward turn of the fists caused the ends to swing and overlap, and a similar imperceptible reverse action made them return to their parallel positions. I was conscious I made the movements, but I am sure the engineer controlled the stick subconsciously.

Since then on numerous occasions I have given people similar rods and told them the ends would cross over a specific metal or color. Almost invariably this was all that was needed to activate them.

In experimenting with forked twigs, I found a slight twist brought about a quick, more violent action, for the ends are grasped with the twigs bent and under strain. The hand can hold a straight stick or rod so that its movement too is under control. Once you know why the pendulum or rods move it is difficult to activate them with thought alone. As Chevreul noted: "So long as I believed the movement possible, it took place: but after discovering the cause, I could not reproduce it."

In a recent issue of a popular magazine devoted to the occult was an advertisement for Abbé Mermet's "famous invention." For a mere $7.50 it offered "a patented dowsing instrument created by the Abbé." If you have a length of thread or string and a small fishing weight or a finger ring, you can make your own pendulum.

Tie the metal to one end of a string. Eight inches is a good starting length. Hold the other end between your index finger and thumb. Suspend the pendulum three inches above a friend's hand.

If the friend is male, the weight will swing back and forth; if female, it will gyrate in a circle That is, it will unless someone has told you that the circle marks the male and the straight swing indicates the female. Whichever you believe, the proper action will soon occur.

An even more intriguing experiment involves three pendulums. Tie them to a long ruler or rod with strings of varying length and rest the ends of the crosspiece on two candlestick holders or bottles so that the weights hang in three glasses spaced two inches apart. The weights must not touch the sides of the glasses. The equipment should be on a small table—a card table will do. Sit with three friends at the sides of the table. All hands should be flat on its surface. Chose one of the pendulums; you and your friends must visualize it swinging. When the weight strikes the sides of the glass, switch your concentration to one of the other weights. The first will lose momentum and the second will soon be swinging far enough to bang against the interior of its glass.

The differences in the length of the strings make each pendulum respond individually. When attention is centered on any pendulum, the subconscious pulsations are directed to it and regulate its swing. When another is chosen, it becomes the recipient of the force imparted by the pulsations of the hands. As the spectators concentrate on it, they see it begin to swing and without conscious effort they vary their pulsations to make it move. Meanwhile the action of the first pendulum gradually ceases.

Mediums at the turn of the century offered this pendulum test as an example of their occult power. They deliberately gave the pulsations that would start the swings. The necessary pressure on the table is so slight that it is not noticeable.

Granted that the mind, not a psychic force, activates pendulums or divining rods, how do dowsers find subterranean streams? The best dowsers are people who are familiar with the soil on which they walk, or who have through experience a knowledge of how the earth appears over areas beneath which there is water. Early researchers thought rising vapors or the lushness of vegetation offered visual cues, though the diviners did not agree. They said they had a gift that enabled them to find the proper spots for wells. They were not conscious of external surfaces; the water, they insisted, pulled the indicators.

P. A. Ongley reported in the *New Zealand Journal of Science and Technology* in 1948 that fifty-eight dowsers participated in tests devised to determine their ability to mark the same spots they had indicated with their eyes open when their eyes were closed, to tell if buried bottles contained water, and otherwise give evidence of their purported powers. Their scores were on pure-chance levels. Seventeen other diviners who specialized in diverse fields were observed. As in the earlier experiments in France, seven illness detectors found twenty-five diseases in a patient who doctors said was healthy, and one diviner, whose eyes were bandaged, said the leg over which he worked had varicose veins. Actually it was an artificial wooden limb.

The American Society for Psychical Research sponsored a series of tests in late August 1949. Twenty-seven dowsers and two scientists attempted to locate underground water in a field in Maine. First the diviners marked positions for wells; then they attempted to return to these spots while blindfolded. Each estimated the depth of the water and its quantity. An engineer and a geologist used scientific knowledge to make their calculations. Shafts were sunk at the points indicated. The scientists fared far better than the dowsers. "Not one of our diviners could for a moment be mistaken for an 'expert,' " said the report published two years later in the *Journal* of the A.S.P.R. "We saw nothing to challenge the prevailing view that we are dealing with unconscious muscular activity, or what Frederic Myers called 'motor automatism.' "

James A. Coleman, professor of physics at the American International College in Springfield, Massachusetts, offered a hundred-dollar prize to any dowser who could succeed in any divining test seven out of ten tries.

Five contestants experimented on the baseball field of the college the morning of May 2, 1964. Before the formal tests began, two diviners, Lancel H. Foote, of Bristol, Connecticut, and Josephine Smith, a junior at Smith College, paced the area and reported there was no underground water which would adversely affect their dowsing instruments.

Verne Spooner, of Claremont, New Hampshire, had brought a plastic container that held approximately a pint of water with him. It was buried somewhere in a trench a hundred feet long and a foot deep and wide. Neither he nor the spectators knew where. He walked along the trench, holding two upright metal pipes parallel. Each had a horizontal wire extending from its upper end. These were to cross when he reached the place where the water flask was buried. Twice the wires crossed; twice they failed to locate the water.

He then suggested that a capsule of pills, which he offered, be buried instead of the water bottle. This was done while he was away from the field. For this experiment he used another instrument, a U-shaped piece of thick wire, which he held in the manner generally used for forked sticks. It was to dip over the hidden capsule. Two times it dipped—but not over the right spot. Spooner said that underground water, which had not been detected by the two dowsers earlier, had affected his instruments.

Ten fifty-foot lengths of garden hose were placed on the ground a few feet apart; the ends were brought together and covered with pieces of canvas. One hose was attached to a water source. The problem was to discover the tube through which the water ran. Josephine Smith, with a forked twig, failed four times and admitted defeat. Lancel H. Foote also missed four times and withdrew from the contest. John Lenahan, who came from Northampton, Maine, like the previous two contenders used a forked stick; twice he located the right hose; then he failed four times.

"Dowsing," said Professor Coleman, who still had his hundred dollars when the day was over, "is nothing but self-delusion." Self-delusion or not, diviners are still being hired in areas where water is difficult to find.

POLTERGEISTS

Heavy objects crashed to the floor of an Oakland, California, office in 1964. A water cooler was found overturned with the tap open and water gushing from it. A hanging electric bulb "unscrewed itself from its socket," shot through space, and smashed in a thousand pieces. Police questioned a boy who worked for the firm. Their suspicions mounted when he refused to take a lie-detector test. Finally he confessed. He said he had carried out the unexplained actions when no one was looking. He had removed the light bulb from an overhead fixture, taken it into an adjoining room, then, with the door slightly open, hurled the bulb down the hall and immediately closed the door.

The boy later retracted his confession. He claimed he had been forced to make statements that were not true.

No phase of psychic phenomena is more disruptive to property or peace of mind than that attributed to the poltergeist. Poltergeist is the German word for "noisy spirit," an unseen destructive force, which breaks chinaware, shatters windows and furniture, and propels objects ranging from stones to stew pans across rooms, sometimes to land intact, often to "explode."

Usually, but not always, children are present during the outbreaks. Some parapsychologists have explained that youngsters, especially those at the age of puberty or in their early teens, attract rampaging spirits. Others insist that the humans at the center of the psychic maelstroms have split personalities or suppressed tensions that are relieved by violent actions.

An elderly woman in Massachusetts had another solution for the turbulence that invaded her Cape Cod cottage. Mrs. Maude Connolly, a widow who lived with two adopted daughters in Revere, was watching television with her family one evening in April 1957. For no apparent reason, papers in the living room began whirling in the air, and ornaments fell from a knickknack shelf and crashed to the floor. The seventy-four-year-old New Englander was baffled but not overly concerned. She cleaned up the debris and prepared for bed. A heavy mirror dropped from the bedroom wall, and an ash tray that had been resting on a table with a glass top slammed against the surface with such force that the glass was shattered.

By morning the strange sounds that had troubled her sleep had ceased. She found that during the night the imitation fireplace in the living room had been overturned and the upholstered chairs that had been in their proper places when she had last seen them were now scattered about upside down. Mrs. Connolly promptly called the police.

A thorough search of the premises was made. There was no evidence that doors or windows had been forced open, no trace of a human intruder. After the police had gone an ash tray struck her head. For four days unseen forces menaced the four-and-a-half-room structure. A building inspector tested the walls, thumped the floors, checked the electric lines and water pipes. Possibly, he said, the chimney was the source of her trouble. Mrs. Connolly phoned a man in Malden who came and climbed to the roof where he installed a protective covering over the chimney top. From that moment on, objects stayed put.

Mrs. Connolly offered what was to her a perfectly reasonable explanation for cavorting chairs, flying ash trays, air-borne papers, and falling ornaments. She said that powerful drafts must have swirled down the chimney and formed odorless gases that spun the objects in an invisible whirlpool.

Chimney drafts could not account for the showers of rocks and stones that rained on the roof and walls and broke the windows of a small white frame house in Clayton, California, three months later. During the three terrifying weeks that followed the initial assault, pots, pans, onions, dishes, bottles, ash trays, a salt shaker, and a fountain pen took flight inside the house. No visible force directed their trajectory.

Peter Gomez, a retired Portugese workman who lived with his wife, two children, and two young grandsons near Mount Diablo, may have suspected that the devil had descended from the mountaintop to taunt him, but he hoped for a more logical explanation.

Neighbors who saw the stones fall on the outside of the house reported the rocks were warm when they picked them up. Other observers, inside the house, testified that stones dropped apparently from the ceiling. Mr. Gomez' married daughter, Mrs. Lorraine McClean, gathered up sixteen stones from the kitchen floor in a single day.

It was hinted by outsiders that the grandsons were responsible for the phenomena, but no one saw either Bobby, who was ten years old, or Tommy, who was thirteen, toss as much as a pebble. Hundreds who had heard about the poltergeist drove out to see the house. Dr. Remi Cadoret, an associate of Dr. J. B. Rhine, who was then director of the Parapsychology Laboratory at Duke University, stayed four days with the Gomez family in an endeavor to witness the manifestations himself. While he was there, nothing unusual occurred. The psychic storm had passed.

Also in the summer of 1957 in Resthaven, a town sixteen miles south of Joliet, Illinois, a bar of soap jumped from its dish and slid across the floor of the Wall farmhouse. A pot of coffee bubbling on the stove tilted up as though a ghost were about to pour itself a cup of the brew. Furniture became animated, toppled, and crashed. Everyone in Will County seemed to have heard about the disturbances. Two friends of the family who came to console the Walls were attacked by flying fruit. The woman received an orange from nowhere on her back; the man was struck on the rear of his head by an apple.

When fourteen-year-old Susan Wall was not in the farmhouse, all was quiet. If, however, she crossed the road to visit her grandparents, the Mikuleckys, the poltergeist seemed to follow her. Bangs and squeaks were heard in unoccupied rooms, and there were rumbling noises in the walls.

Deputy Sheriff Chester Moberly was satisfied that there was nothing supernatural about the things that happened when Susan was around. He told the Walls flatly that if he heard one more report about weird events in their vicinity he would subject them all to a lie-detector test. Nothing more was heard about poltergeists in Resthaven.

Betty Ward was the focal point of another poltergeist outbreak that summer in Hartsville, Missouri. One night, she said, a comb flew from under a lamp on the bedroom dresser when the bulb burned out. Buckets of water took on life and upset periodically. The nine-year-old girl's father was not amused when a pail overturned on a shelf and doused him with an unexpected shower. Laundry baskets acquired the shakes, and tin cans careened across rooms. Neighbor Snowden Floyd was almost hit by one; Finis Delcour, Betty's uncle, was a better target. The can of coffee that shot in his direction from a shelf whacked him on a shin.

Stones fell mysteriously in the automobile in which Shirley Delcour, Betty's eleven-year-old cousin, sat with her baby sister. Betty confessed to reporters that the odd events frightened her. She was not half so terrified however as those who spent time in her company. A magician investigating the case attested that he saw Betty drop a can opener which she had concealed under her arm. No one had a ready explanation when a lantern fell with considerable impact on a chair.

Meanwhile in Berryhill, a suburb of Tulsa, Oklahoma, C. A. Wilkinson, an employee of an oil company, was being harassed in his home. Six times an electric clock fell for no apparent reason from the wall. Twice the motor of his electric refrigerator blew out. The mechanism of a thirteen-hundred-dollar electric organ broke down in a inexplicable manner. Plugs seemingly detached themselves from sockets in the wall. Most astonishing, an electric carpet sweeper moved mysteriously across the floor—though it wasn't connected.

Mr. Wilkinson thought that "wild electricity" might account for his misfortunes. There was a wire-mesh fence around his house. He reasoned that the wire must in some way be picking up a current and diverting it inside. He took down the fence. Still the house was plagued. Next he dug up the water pipes in his backyard. Perhaps they were attracting an "underground radiation"? The fantastic events continued.

Even objects that were not operated by electricity took on sudden motion. Chairs and tables seemed to vibrate. Pots leaped into the air. One night the commotion was so great that Wilkinson, his wife, and his twelve-year-old adopted daughter bedded down outside in the family automobile.

As usual the disruptions drew curiosity seekers, reporters, and investigators. A trap was laid for a possible human culprit. A light coating of powder was dusted over potential flying objects. The Tulsa *Tribune* duly noted that after the disturbance that followed telltale marks were found on the girl's hands. She confessed that she was the cause of hitherto mysterious turmoil.

Generally the news of a poltergeist outbreak is printed days or even weeks after the most baffling episodes. Occasionally the circumstances are so provocative that the story reaches a nationwide audience. The "Case of the Jitterbug Coal" was as exciting as a murder mystery. There seemed to be no possible explanation for the weird phenomena that took place in a rural schoolroom near the Dakota badlands.

Eight children in their early teens, or younger, were in the white one-room schoolhouse in Wild Plum, Stark County, North Dakota, March 28, 1944, when a strange, stirring sound emanated from a coal bucket. Mrs. Pauline Rebel, the twenty-two-year-old teacher, adjusted her glasses and stared at the bucket. There was no one near it. When her attention returned to her work the metal bucket tipped over. Lumps of smoldering lignite coal began bombarding the walls. Wisps of smoke curled up from the bottoms of the nine shades on the windows of the room. Tongues of fire and charred spots appeared on the curtains and the wall map, and papers caught fire on the pupils' desks. The class dictionary moved uncannily as though tugged by an invisible hand. Fire broke out in the bookcase.

When George Steiner, whose young son had been struck by a piece of coal, arrived on the scene and heard what had happened, he cautiously picked up a lump and reported it "trembled and jumped from my hand."

Some residents of the community said the schoolhouse was "bewitched" and insisted that their children stay at home out of reach of demonic forces.

The local school authorities were utterly baffled. R. L. Swenson, Stark County superintendent, phoned Charles Schwartz, the state fire marshal, for help. Schwartz admitted he had never heard of a spontaneous combustion of coal that could produce such fantastic effects.

Samples of the lignite were dispatched to chemical laboratories at the University of North Dakota at Grand Forks and the Dickinson State College. Analysis revealed no substance in the coal that would cause internal fires or self-propelled flights in the air. Fire Marshal Schwartz announced he would send lumps of the lignite, the coal bucket, and the dictionary that seemed to have moved by itself to the Federal Bureau of Investigation in Washington, D.C.

"At first we were convinced that the whole thing was a hoax and suspected arson," he told an Associated Press reporter in Bismarck on April 13, "but after we used the lie detector with negative results we are of the opinion that witnesses were telling the truth. To put it mildly, we are puzzled."

Two days later Edmund D'Moch, a United Press correspondent, reported some new developments. Mrs. Rebel, the attractive blonde teacher, was more worried about threats on her life than the cavorting coal in her classroom. During the seven months she had been teaching in Wild Plum, she had found more than a dozen abusive notes tacked to the schoolhouse door. Crudely lettered on tablet paper, they had warned her to leave town "or be shot." Neither she nor her husband, a farm worker with whom she lived near the school, had ever seen anyone fastening the warnings in place. Ismarie Steiner, a fourteen-year-old pupil whose brother had been struck by a piece of falling coal, said she thought she had seen a strange man, who appeared to be six feet tall and who seemed to be wearing a mask, in the schoolyard. Or, she qualified her first remark: "Maybe it was a shadow."

J. F. Hoff, the clerk of the school board, didn't share the opinion of some of the townsfolk that supernatural forces were at play: "I think we'll find that the whole thing was caused by a crank who threatened the life of Mrs. Rebel."

In another three days the Associated Press carried a story that the mystery had been solved. Neither self-igniting lignite nor a six-foot stranger had caused the commotion. Four pupils confessed, in the presence of Special Assistant Attorney General H. J. Austin, Fire Marshal Schwartz, and their parents, that they and other students had planned and carried out the exercise in terror.

When Mrs. Rebel was not wearing her glasses, or when she was out of the room, they had used long rulers and blackboard pointers to stir up the coal and tip the scuttle. While their teacher was not looking their way, they had hurled the coal at the walls, and they had used matches to ignite the lumps, set fire to the blinds, curtains, wall map, the bookcase, and papers on their desks. They had thrown the coal with underhand tosses so that no arm movements would be seen if the teacher happened to glance their way. They had shoved the dictionary so that it appeared to move on its own. Two of the older girls—one twelve, the other fifteen—had written the harassing, and at times obscene, notes that they then fastened to the door.

The youngsters had played their parts so convincingly, creating such an atmosphere of tension, that when George Steiner scrutinized a lump of the lignite he believed that the coal itself, not his hands, was trembling.

Why had they been up to such devilment? They admitted that when they had found their teacher and their parents so gullible, so easy to mystify, they thoroughly enjoyed the excitement and the publicity their pranks had provoked.

Press coverage often increases the frenzy of a poltergeist attack. Sunday, December 30, 1951, boxes, bottle caps, and Christmas cards began acting oddly in one room of the Henry Thatchers' home in Louisville, Kentucky. Neither he, his wife, nor the three Saunders girls who lived with them could explain why or how the objects whirled over their heads. Until then, it had been a sad Christmas season for the children. They were wards of the county Children's Home, which paid their board with the Thatchers. Their mother was in a hospital, suffering the ravages of cancer. Their father long before had deserted her. Joyce Saunders, an eleven-year-old student in the fifth grade, gave visitors to the house, in the days that followed, a vivid word picture of the phenomena. Sometimes objects flew when newspaper reporters were present, though they were always in flight by the time they were noticed. Joyce and her sisters posed for cameramen and appeared on television. Nothing so exciting had ever happened to them. Joyce, two policemen noticed, was the magnet that seemed to attract soaring pins, cans, and table knives. She finally confessed to officers Russell McDaniel and Jack Fischer that she had caused the disturbances to attract attention. Not all the phenomena reported had actually occurred. The child admitted: "I didn't throw all those things. People just imagined some of them."

The best-publicized poltergeist case of recent times erupted about 3:30 P.M., Monday, February 3, 1958. Bottles popped and spilled their contents in four rooms of a green and white ranch-style house at 1648 Redwood Path in Seaford, Long Island, New York. This phenomenon and others equally mysterious continued intermittently for more than a month. Before the last unexplained noise had faded away, the rampages of "the Seaford poltergeist" were familiar to Americans from coast to coast and to millions of people around the world. Countless newspaper stories, radio and television broadcasts, and innumerable magazine articles in many languages made this the most discussed poltergeist case of the twentieth century.

As a study of human response to the unexplained, it is without parallel. What does an average family do when strange events, apparently of supernormal origin, upset their normal pattern of living? What solutions are offered? How does the public at large react?

Only Mrs. Lucille Herrmann, thirty-eight, and her two children—James, Jr., twelve, and Lucille, thirteen—were in the house in Seaford when the first peculiar sounds were heard. They went from room to room to investigate. In the master bedroom they found an open bottle of holy water lying on the bureau. The liquid was seeping out. Its cap was some distance away. In the bathroom two more bottles were discovered, open and pouring. A bottle of liquid starch on its side was dribbling in the kitchen, and a container of liquid bleach in a similar state was in the basement.

The sight of the spilled holy water was enough to upset Mrs. Herrmann, a devout Catholic, but the children accepted that and the other spilled fluids calmly. Mrs. Herrmann, a registered nurse, was also a practical woman. She phoned her husband, who worked as a liaison airlines representative at the offices of Air France in New York.

James M. Herrmann, forty-two, listened to the strange story attentively. His first thought was of his family. Had anyone been injured? He learned that neither the children nor his wife had been harmed. He breathed easier. The Long Island Rail Road took him the thirty-five miles to Seaford that evening after work as usual. If he had surmised that carbonation or fermentation had forced off the bottle caps, this was soon to be disproved. Corks might be popped by confined gases, but all of the containers had metal or plastic screw caps. A turn or two to the left was necessary to dislodge them.

There were no popping noises that night in the one-story structure on Redwood Path or during the three days that followed. On the afternoon of February 7, however, when Mrs. Herrmann and the two children, who had returned from their classes at the Seaford Junior-Senior High School, were in the house, the manifestations again occurred.

Sunday morning, February 9, when Mr. Herrmann was exposed to the phenomena, he saw something that no one in the family had experienced before. He was in the doorway of the bathroom, chatting with his son, as Jimmy vigorously brushed his teeth. He stopped in midsentence when two bottles moved on the Formica surface above the drain. One, a bottle of medicine—Kaopectate—went "in a southerly direction for about 18 inches" and dropped in the bowl of the sink; the other, containing shampoo, slid "in a westerly direction" and clattered to the floor.

Mr. Herrmann, a law-school graduate and an ex-marine, took quick action. He phoned the Nassau County police. Patrolman James Hughes was sent to examine the premises and take statements from the witnesses. He worked with some detachment until he heard a noise in the bathroom. Sure enough, a bottle with the cap off was found on its side on the Formica adjacent to the sink.

A police force is normally concerned with violations of the law. Unexplained disturbances in a private home may seem far afield of their interest, but the circumstances were so unusual that Detective James Tozzi, thirty-two, who lived nearby, was assigned to the case.

Once the story broke in the newspapers, he answered telephone queries from the press and calls from people who thought they could clear up the mystery. Mail addressed to the Herrmanns concerning the phenomena was given to him for study and possible action. The letters approached the problem from angles he had never considered. One claimed that if a white handkerchief was waved in every room the spirits would flee. Another directed that a pad and pencil be put in the various rooms. Each pad was to have the words "Who are you?" at the top. This, the writer said, would give the ghost a chance to identify itself.

A Texan said that he had tried for four years to open an old bottle. He offered to send it on, perhaps the spirits could pop it? Another correspondent claimed that the tops of bottles of Canadian whiskey he had purchased in Washington, D.C., had jumped off untouched by human hands. What caused this, he inquired? Detective Tozzi didn't know, neither did the Herrmanns. If they knew, he wouldn't be on the case.

In the earliest stages the poltergeist activity in Seaford centered on bottles. The third week in February a more typical spirit manifestation took place. Miss Marie Murtha, a middle-aged relative, and the two children were watching television in the living room. Miss Murtha said she saw a white porcelain figurine, which had been on the end table by the sofa on which Jimmy was sitting with his arms folded, take off, fly about two feet across the room, and land with a loud noise some six inches away from the TV set.

Young Lucille was by the side of Miss Murtha, who was seated in a chair. The visitor stated unequivocally: "No one in the room . . . was close enough to touch the figurine or propel it in any way."

Several nights later, while Mr. Herrmann was in New York to tell Jack Paar and a nationwide television audience about the fantastic things that had happened in Seaford, the porcelain figure took off again and hit a desk across the room with enough force to break one of the arms. Mrs. Herrmann and her children said they heard the noise about fifteen minutes before ten P.M. "At this time," the police report notes, "the only appliance running was the oil burner and no one was again in the room."

Appliances were suspect as they had been earlier in the Wilkinson case near Tulsa, Oklahoma. High-frequency radio signals were suggested as a possible answer to the mystery early in February. A known ham radio operator nearby was questioned. It had been years, he said, since he had sent messages from his transmitter. The Long Island Lighting Company was cooperative with the police. It installed an oscillograph in the basement. The machine recorded no special shocks though three incidents took place while it was in operation. The company also checked the lighting fixtures, fuse boxes, and intakes. All were in normal condition.

The arrival of Robert E. Zider raised Mr. Herrmann's hopes. He had asked for scientists to take a serious interest in his bedeviled house. Mr. Zider was a technician associated with the builders of a 35-billion-volt synchrotron at the Brookhaven Laboratory of the Atomic Energy Commission. He came not with a complex mechanical instrument but with a forked twig from a willow tree. His hobby was dowsing—locating subterranean sources of water. Grasping his willow wand, he paced through the house and made notes of the points where the pull of his dowsing stick indicated underground streams. His calculations showed that the trajectories of the flying objects were directly over the waters which he believed ran far beneath the house. North about a mile, he said, there was a reservoir that might be sending out waves of energy generated by the supersonic impacts from jet aircraft.

However, maps at the Hempstead Engineers' Office showed no subterranean streams in the Seaford area.

Hi-Fi Phonograph Is Newest Woe
In Home of Beleaguered L. I. Family

This was the heading in William Michelfelder's February 26 story in the New York *World-Telegram & Sun.* The day before Jimmy had been alone in the basement recreation room when his portable record player "took off like a jet plane, hurtled twelve feet through the air and crashed against the cellar stairway."

The article reported that on the morning of the twenty-sixth a mobile RCA transmitter unit from Rocky Point had arrived at the Herrmann home. The ultra-high-frequency receivers could detect any impulse between 15 kilocycles and 220 megacycles that might be centered on the house. If, as the physicist with the willow wand had said, there was a possibility of magnetic fields emanating from water beneath the ground, the RCA team thought it would find them.

That evening Dr. J. Gaither Pratt, then Dr. J. B. Rhine's assistant at the Parapsychology Laboratory of Duke University, arrived for an investigation of another sort. The next morning's *New York Times* carried four Seaford photographs on the first page of its second section. One showed the RCA men and their equipment, and the story noted that no trace of vagrant radio waves had been found. Another pictured a globe of the world which was "said to have flown—a distance of fifteen feet." Mrs. Herrmann posed by the spot where Jimmy's phonograph had hit after its flight, and she was pictured holding a bottle and a cap as the parapsychologist from the South looked on.

Pratt admitted that such phenomena in the past had never been proven to the satisfaction of scientists. He had not witnessed the movement of an object by mental influence. Yet, he continued, tests at Duke "led to the definite conclusion that there is some sort of influence of mind over matter."

No bottle popped during the period Pratt was on the scene in February, but other manifestations did occur. The night of the parapsychologist's arrival he had been in the basement talking with Police Sergeant McConnell and David Kahn of *Newsday*. The sound of confusion overhead brought him up to the master bedroom. There the Herrmanns told him that a dresser lamp, which had been upright only moments before, had overturned. The children said they had not been in the room. While Pratt was in the bedroom, Lucille brought her brother's dinner to the table in the dining area. She was putting a plate of bread on the table as the doorbell rang. She answered it. When Lucille returned the plate was on the floor, the slices strewn about. Jimmy solemnly asserted he had not seen it fall. Pratt decided these two incidents, neither of which he had witnessed, were well within the realm of childish pranks.

The following day the presence of reporters in the house interfered with Pratt's investigations; he went to the Nassau police headquarters to study the official records of the case. When newsmen found him there two days later, he returned to Duke.

Later in March he came to Seaford again with William G. Roll, Jr., a fellow researcher in the Durham, North Carolina, laboratory. If he had hoped to observe objects traveling in the air or bottles expelling their caps, he was disappointed. However, Pratt did hear what he first termed "a series of explosive sounds" and "a loud explosion which literally shook the house." Later, in the pages of his book, *Parapsychology: An Insider's View of ESP*, these noises are described as "dull thumps," which came from the direction of Jimmy's bedroom. The house-shaking "explosion" was pinpointed as the "explosive removal" of the top of a bottle of bleaching liquid, which was found open and aslant in the basement.

I followed the Seaford saga with great interest. After hearing Mr. Herrmann, during a television interview, make a moving plea for someone to solve the family dilemma, I phoned Detective Tozzi, identifying myself as the president of the Society of American Magicians. I thought it highly unlikely that a supernormal force was involved. I could duplicate the phenomena by perfectly natural means, and thought it might ease the mind of Mr. Herrmann if I could meet him and tell him this. The detective was cordial. He said he would be happy to get the matter cleared up. He relayed my message to the troubled father. The next day the detective phoned me. Mr. Herrmann had said in no uncertain terms that he did not want a magician in the house.

By then a priest from the nearby Church of Saint William the Abbot had blessed the Herrmann home. An uninvited visitor, "a holy man from Center Moriches," also had prayed in the dining area. Sound technicians, electrical experts, and a dowser had failed to locate the source of the trouble. After Mrs. Connolly in Revere, Massachusetts, had sent her theory to the Herrmanns that downdrafts could lift heavy objects, a chimney cap was installed on the roof. An anonymous phone call from a girl on Long Island propounded an even farther-out theory. Her pet leprechaun had disappeared about the time the disturbances had started. Perhaps O'Leary was raising the rumpus?

Mr. Herrmann made another of his, by then, frequent television appearances on Channel 5's "Night Beat." When host John Wingate asked why he hadn't accepted my offer, Mr. Herrmann brusquely replied that he wanted the government or scientists to help him, not "charlatans, mystics, mediums, or magicians." I could understand his objection to the first three categories, but not the fourth.

The program was scarcely over when my telephone rang. Jack D. Fox, of the New York *Post*, who had been at the studio, asked if it was true that I could reproduce the phenomena. When I replied I could, he said he'd be right over.

The story the next day was headed, "The Magician and the Seaford Spooks." It began:

> Milbourne Christopher sat back in an easy chair, offered a wave of his hand and said that house in Seaford, L.I. was no more haunted than his place. Just then the tops of several bottles unscrewed themselves in the bathroom, and an object went flying from a pile of magazines to the floor several feet away.

In the days that followed I repeated the demonstration six times for other writers and photographers. There is an interesting photograph of a white vase zooming across my living room in the September 1958 issue of *Cavalier*.

I never heard from Mr. Herrmann, but Dr. Pratt visited me that June. As we talked about poltergeists, a china figurine leapt from a bookcase shelf and landed some eight feet away by a television set. I was now about to see a parapsychologist from Duke in action. Pratt is an affable, soft-spoken man. He asked if he might look around. I gave him permission. He went to the bookcase and examined it thoroughly, moving volumes so he could be sure that no mechanism was concealed in the books or the case itself. Next he peered behind the bookcase. Could he see the room behind this wall? I led him into the bedroom. He scanned the wall, moved oil paintings aside. There was no tiny hole in the wall through which a slender rod could be pushed to send the figurine on its journey. It was evening, and the lights were on in the living room. He asked for the bedroom to be darkened. If there was even a minute opening, perhaps it would admit light from the room beyond the wall. There was not even the faintest glimmer in the dark.

A few days later I received a letter from Pratt, who was then in Andover, Massachusetts, with his wife for their son's graduation. He invited me to write him at Duke and explain what a visit by me to the Seaford house "would accomplish." He said he could understand why the Herrmanns would be apprehensive about people who "prejudged the issue."

Later I heard him on the Long John Nebel radio show. He dismissed the demonstration I had given as "magic." I noted with amusement he didn't offer an explanation of how it was done. Nor did his book offer a conclusion as to how the objects had taken on life in Seaford.

Dr. Pratt asks in his book how "skilled magic," if such was employed, could have been used to produce the Seaford phenomena. He says that "mechanical devices" could have brought about all the effects, but if they were used, why weren't they detected when they were put in place or set off?

In my opinion no complicated contrivances were used. A study of the record and a close examination of the floor plan of the house indicate that it was possible for the incidents to have occurred without either mechanical devices or supernormal forces.

It should be stressed that Mr. Herrmann refused to allow lie-detector tests to be made on his family and that the police and the investigators from Duke accepted Jimmy's statements. Let us suppose that what the boy said was not true, that he was in one room when he said he was in another in some instances. Also let us suppose that what people thought they saw and what actually happened were not precisely the same. It has been shown that the police notes record that the boy and his mother "actually saw" the bleach bottle leave a box and crash on the floor. Yet Dr. Pratt discovered during his interviews that neither witnessed the out-of-the-carton action. Any trial lawyer will testify that witnesses often believe that they have seen things that did not occur. For example, a woman hears a loud noise, then sees a pistol. She may be confident she heard the pistol fire, though the noise came from another source—the backfire of an automobile or an exploded firecracker.

Take the single instance where an outsider, Miss Murtha, saw a statuette take off and land. A television set was on at the time. It is logical to suppose her attention was there. A quick movement by the occupant of the sofa could have jarred the small end table with enough impact to send the upright figurine falling to the floor the mere two feet away.

Jimmy spoke to Miss Murtha, as Pratt's interview with her indicates, just before she saw the figurine move. She turned in his direction to answer. At *that* moment the falling motion began.

That is the *only* time anyone saw the takeoff of a flying object. In every other case, the object could have been thrown.

I mentioned earlier that no one *saw* a cap pop from a bottle. Noises were heard, then bottles were found open on their sides. People assumed the noises were made by the bottles. Could the bottles have been opened and overturned *before* the noise was made? Can this simple strategy fool anyone?

Yes, it can. This is exactly the system I used to baffle the writers and investigators who came to my apartment.

How were the Seaford noises made? As Mr. Herrmann did not invite me to his home to witness the phenomena, I cannot say precisely. I do know that hearing is the easiest of the five senses to deceive. A simple test you can try is this: Have someone sit in a chair with his eyes closed. Walk around the chair, then reach over his head and click two coins together. Ask him to point immediately in the direction of the sound. You'll be intrigued with the result.

If a sound is heard in a house and someone says "That came from the bedroom" and starts in that direction, others will follow and accept the location. If a disturbance is expected in a specific room when a noise is heard, attention focuses on that room.

I varied the sounds that preceded my "bottle-popping" demonstrations. On one occasion I leaned against the doorframe of my living room with my hands behind my back. When someone else was speaking I made a quick rap with the knuckles of my right hand against the frame and *immediately turned my head toward the hall.* This is what magicians call misdirection—diverting attention from the place where the secret action takes place. Another time my wife was in the bedroom with the door almost closed. She held a large china bowl in one hand, two marbles in the other. She threw the marbles inside the bowl, then quickly stopped their motion with her free hand. When this sound was heard in the living room, the investigators sped down the hall, past the bedroom, and into the bathroom where, a few moments earlier, she had turned two bottles on their sides so the liquid would seep out and put their caps in the sink. The observers were convinced that they had heard these caps strike the sink as the bottles fell.

What about the two bottles that moved in different directions in the Seaford bathroom while Mr. Herrmann was standing in the doorway? I offer two possible nonsupernormal solutions. While the father was talking to his son, he may have turned his head to speak with his wife or daughter. If so, it would have been possible for the boy, who was brushing his teeth, to use his free hand to start the bottles sliding.

Another tactic that requires no "mechanical devices" employs a single heavy thread. Hold a bottle in your left hand near its base. With your left thumb press the end of the thread firmly to the side of the bottle near its bottom and wind the thread around the bottle several times until, by friction, the end is held firmly. Place this bottle upright on a shelf close to the wall with the thread extending horizontally so that you can pull it taut. Take the second bottle, put it upright between the first container and yourself. Move it to the left so that it carries the thread with it. Drop your end of the thread until you are ready for action. To send the two bottles in different directions grasp the end of the thread and give a quick sharp yank. The second bottle will be sent to the right, the first will come forward. As the thread is not tied, it will come free.

If you were brushing your teeth, you would be looking in the mirror and there you would see the reflection of the man in the doorway. At the moment he turned his head away, you would yank the thread with your left hand. The second bottle would crash in the bowl; the first would fall on the floor.

Of course, one waits for the right moment to dispose of the string. If the man in the doorway is startled and rushes to tell someone else about the phenomenon, the string is pocketed immediately. If not, the free end is dropped and the almost invisible thread is picked up later.

Remember, the man in the doorway doesn't know what to expect in advance: the surprise element is all in favor of the "poltergeist!"

The use of a thread or a horsehair to move objects in this fashion is the sort of thing that someone who wished to cause a disturbance in a house would think of. As a matter of fact, someone did think of it almost two hundred years ago, and she employed it for precisely that purpose.

A pamphlet published at the time tells of "The most surprising and unaccountable Events that Ever happened," which occurred January 6 and 7, 1772, in Stockton, Surrey.

Mrs. Mary Golding, an elderly widow, and Ann Robinson, her twenty-year-old maid, were alone in the house when the nerve-shattering incidents began. Two hours before noon a great clatter came from the kitchen. The maid entered the parlor to tell her mistress that a row of plates had dropped for no apparent reason from their shelf to the floor. Mrs. Golding went to see the broken crockery, and while she was there, dishes from another shelf fell. Later that day a clock fell, a staircase lantern dropped, and an earthenware platter crashed, scattering the salt beef it held in many directions.

The commotion attracted attention from the neighbors. A carpenter theorized that the addition of a new room to the house had weakened the foundation of the building; a downward thrust of the structure might have caused the rumpus.

This did not seem reasonable to Mrs. Golding, for the havoc seemed to follow the maid and herself wherever they went in the house. When she could bear the strain no longer, she fled across the lawn to the neighboring Greshams. There, overcome by agitation, she fainted. Her niece, Mrs. Mary Pain, was summoned. By the time she arrived, her aunt had revived but was still shaky. To relieve her tensions, a surgeon named Gardner bled her—this was a standard treatment for many ailments at the time. Soon afterward, the basin containing her congealed blood fell to the floor along with a bottle of Mr. Gresham's rum.

While Mrs. Golding was at the Gresham house, some of her more fragile possessions were being removed from her home for safety. This, it developed, was an unwise procedure. As a neighbor put her large mirror on the lawn, its frame fell apart. A sudden rain caused Mrs. Golding to insist that the objects be brought inside the Gresham house to shelter them from the downpour. The large mirror and a smaller one were stowed beneath a sideboard. Soon goblets and chinaware tumbled from this piece of furniture and broke the mirrors. When it was suggested that a drink might soothe everyone's nerves, two bottles crashed before one could be poured.

Mrs. Golding ran now to another neighbor. Her maid stayed behind to sweep up the glass fragments. While she was at her work a jar of raspberry jam crashed, a pickle jar was found topsy-turvy, and a wooden box was smashed.

Mrs. Pain invited her aunt to spend the rest of the day and the night across town with her husband and family. The Greshams came for dinner. Ann Robinson, Mrs. Golding's maid, was sent back to her house to see if any further damage had been done there. All was quiet, she said on her return. About 8 P.M. in the Pain house pewter dishes began falling in the kitchen. The ghost or whatever it was seemed to be following Mrs. Golding.

In the Pain house the disturbances took on a more violent nature. An egg flew across the kitchen and cracked on the head of a cat. A mortar and pestle, brassware, and candlesticks jumped from

their places. To protect the glass and chinaware, Mrs. Pain had her maid and Ann Robinson place them flat on the floor. Despite this they were soon breaking in pieces.

Later it was difficult for the witnesses to recall exactly what happened. A kettle, a tray, and a silver tankard were as active as the glasses and plates. Two hams dropped from their hooks by the side of the chimney, a side of bacon followed.

While all this was happening, Ann Robinson was "walking backwards and forwards" through the rooms, seemingly perfectly calm even when the others were most upset.

At one A.M. Mrs. Pain went upstairs to see how her youngest child was resting and to escape from the fury below. She was asleep four hours later when her distraught aunt roused her. Mrs. Golding said she could no longer stay in the house as the destruction was too great. Mrs. Pain returned to the parlor and could scarcely believe what she saw. The room was a bedlam. Tables, chairs, and drawers were strewn about.

Mrs. Golding's maid took her to another house, the home of Richard Fowler, then returned to help Mrs. Pain dress her child in the barn. Mrs. Pain said she thought the house might collapse at any moment. While Fowler and Mrs. Golding were alone, it was quiet. After Ann Robinson came back, two candlesticks clanged together and fell, and a lantern dropped from the wall and splashed oil on the floor. Then a coal scuttle overturned and sent its contents rolling.

Fowler asked Mrs. Golding bluntly if she had committed a terrible crime for which Providence was punishing her. The old lady said she had a clear conscience, but if Providence was looking for her it would find her in her own home. Mr. Pain took her and the maid there. A nine-gallon cask of beer was found overturned in the cellar; a box of candles jumped from a kitchen shelf; a mahogany table fell over in the parlor; and water in a pail on the kitchen floor began boiling though it was not close to the fire.

Mr. Pain asked Mrs. Golding to send her maid for his wife. While she was gone, he pointed out that only when Ann Robinson was present did the strange things happen. Shortly before seven A.M. the maid returned with Mrs. Pain. Mrs. Golding discharged the girl on the spot.

In less than twenty-four hours an incredible amount of damage had been done in four houses. The broken china and glassware at Mrs. Golding's house alone filled three pails. Once Ann Robinson was away, the disturbances ended.

Not until almost a half century later did the public learn how the "strange transactions" came about. William Hone, the editor of *The Every-Day Book,* heard the details from the Reverend J. Brayfield, who lived on Southampton Street in Camberwell. Ann Robinson had confessed to the clergyman that she had thrown some of the objects whose movements were attributed to "an unseen agency." She had pelted the cat with an egg, hung the hams and bacon so they would fall when their weight caused the hooks to tear through their skins. She had dropped a chemical in the pail of water to make it bubble. Rows of plates were dislodged when she yanked a wire she had earlier arranged behind them. Long horsehairs were attached to other objects to give them sudden life. They seemed to jump or fall when she pulled the ends.

Harry Price, in his book *Poltergeist over England,* ridiculed Hone's account. Price claimed that not even the greatest magician could have staged the Stockton disturbances "surrounded by people who were on the look-out for tricks." As a professional conjurer I must disagree. If a magician were surrounded by people who were watching for tricks, it would be difficult but not impossible to create the same effects. Ann Robinson, however, was not a conjurer; she was not surrounded and she was not suspected. There was no reason for those present to keep a sharp watch on her actions. The attention of the startled witnesses was on the objects *as* they smashed, not on the maid before they smashed. The practicability of her deceptive technique is evident—it is still being used today in some homes where poltergeists are said to be on the rampage.

HAUNTED HOUSES

For centuries strange sights and sounds have been reported in houses that were said to be haunted. Some of the phenomena were of the sort now attributed to poltergeists, but ghosts and unearthly creatures were also frequently seen. Night, superstition, and lively imaginations conjured up menacing terrors that faded with the dawn.

In October 1649, when a rebellious Parliament sent a commission to strip the royal trappings from Charles I's manor house in Woodstock, Oxfordshire, and survey the property, the king's bedchamber was used as a kitchen, while the palatial dining hall became a storage area for firewood. The first day the members of the commission sat in what had been the king's audience chamber, their deliberations were disturbed by a howling black dog that knocked over furniture and crawled under a bed in the room. Giles Sharp, the commission's secretary, probed beneath the bedstead and reported that the space was empty. He doubted that a dog had been there as some meat that a servant had hidden on a plate had been untouched.

The next evening while the commissioners were at dinner, they heard footsteps in the upper rooms though the doors had been locked. Violent noises in the room where they had been working earlier, which also was locked, led to the discovery that their reports had been ripped in pieces, wood had been hurled about, chairs were overturned, and the inkpot was smashed. That night some beds were lifted so high that the occupants had their heads cracked against the boards as they were upended. On succeeding nights candles extinguished themselves, leaving sulphurous fumes in the air, pewter dishes and wooden trenchers flew about, sometimes bruising the commoners who had invaded the sanctity of a royal house. Windows were shattered, and bricks from the top of the chimney rumbled down to break inside. Great booming noises were heard as if "forty cannons discharged together." Buckets of "green stinking water" drenched the unwelcome intruders as they tried to sleep. One of the men called out "in the name of God" for the force, whatever it was, to identify itself and explain why it was taunting them. There was no answer.

The disturbances continued. All the window glass of an upper room was broken, tiling fell; explosive noises rocked other rooms, and someone swore he saw the hoof of an animal—or was it a demon?—descend on a lighted candle and, with three strokes on the wick, snuff it out.

The man who saw the hoof tried to unsheathe his sword, but something took it from him and whacked him so hard on the head that he fell senseless to the floor. This action was accompanied by a boom "like the discharge of a broadside of a ship of war" somewhere in the house. A minute or so later nineteen other explosive sounds were heard in other parts of the building. The din was so great that people who lived nearby rushed to the manor house, knelt, prayed, and sang psalms. Booms as loud as any before continued.

After the British civil war was over and tranquillity had been restored at the manor house, Joseph Collins, known to his friends in Oxford as "Funny Joe," claimed that he had been the "good devil of Woodstock." A royalist, he had taken a job with the commission under an assumed name—Giles Sharp. With two friends who worked in the house and a pound of gunpowder, he had terrorized the interlopers. There was a trap door in the ceiling that no one suspected; through this his friends entered and left. They had broken glass, smashed furniture, and thrown the foul-smelling water. Collins had claimed to see the hoof that wasn't there and, to lend conviction to his acting, had struck himself on the head with his sword. The booming explosions were produced by pouring white gunpowder over burning charcoals in tin plates. The powder detonated when it melted and caught fire. The candles that extinguished themselves had been prepared with gunpowder in the wicks. When the flame reached the charge the powder exploded, put out the flame, and left behind "sulphurous" odor.

The black dog that created the first uproar had given birth to a litter a day before. Giles hid the pups, and the dog, anxious to find her brood, had upset the furniture. Collins had taken her from under the bed secretly, then announced he could find no trace of an animal.

A building at Aix-la-Chapelle, France, went untenanted in the nineteenth century when ghostly raps were heard reverberating through its corridors. The knocks were not limited to the hours after dark. Sometimes they came in the early morning or in the afternoon. The source of the sound was traced to a chamber on an upper floor. Not only was this house unoccupied for five years, but the people who lived in the neighboring structures, frightened by the ominous sounds, moved to quieter areas of the city. As often happens with houses reputed to be haunted, other phenomena were reported. Some said weird lights flashed in the building, others claimed to have seen specters glide by the windows, or they heard groaning sounds. Holy water was sprinkled by a priest, but his prayers were ineffectual.

Eventually the house was sold for a fraction of its value to a hardheaded citizen, who believed in nothing he could not see. The new owner discovered the origin of the haunting by chance. A door flew shut with a loud bang behind his back. As he was alone in the room, he could not understand why this had happened. He walked calmly to the entranceway, but before he reached it the door opened slightly. This too puzzled him. Soon the portal slammed again and, as before, opened a few inches. The Frenchman looked closely at the door latch; he saw that it was broken, and he found that the upper hinge was loose. The lower hinge took the weight of the panel and caused it to open after it was closed. Glass was missing from a window across the room. When a strong wind came through the cracked pane, it blew the door shut; then, because the latch did not hold and the door was angled inward on the bottom hinge, it came open, ready for the next gust of air to produce another "rap."

There are sounds in old houses that are not made by human hands or human voices. They are heard during storms or at certain seasons of the year or in some cases on specific days and at specific times. When the sounds persist, rumors spread that houses are haunted, and they are difficult to sell or rent.

An undated clipping, preserved by Houdini, reports such a story. In Union, New York, seven miles from Binghamton, a once attractive two-story cottage was deteriorating. Paint peeled and cracked from its clapboards, grime clouded its remaining windows. Hinges, long unoiled, creaked, and the floors squeaked if a young-ster, intrigued by the empty building, forced open a door and ran through the rooms. The neglected frame cottage was owned by J. W. McAdam of New York City. For two and a half years a man named Hakes had rented it. Neither he, his wife, nor his two chil-dren noticed anything peculiar during their occupancy.

Edgar Williams was the next tenant. He and his wife were the first to report that something unusual was taking place. It did not happen often, Williams told the real estate agent, but whenever a high wind swept across the property, bending the branches of trees, a wailing cry would echo through the upper floor. It was im-possible to sleep then, he went on; his wife became so agitated that he thought her terror might affect her mind.

The agent went through the house, but could find nothing that might produce the weird sound. Shortly after this, the Williamses moved out. The next tenant had not been told of the strange noise. Less than a month later, he too was in to see the real estate man. He asked if anything odd had ever happened in the house. A mur-

der, perhaps? The agent assured him that to the best of his knowledge nothing of this nature had ever taken place within the four
walls. Then the tenant admitted that his wife too had heard the
shrill shriek in the night; she thought it came from the garret. The
agent made another trip to the house. This time he thoroughly examined the garret on the pretext that the roof might need repair.
Again his search for a clue to the mystery was unsuccessful. In less
than a week the house was vacant.

Three more families lived briefly in the cottage, all heard the
strange, wailing cries. By now the story had spread through the
area. It was impossible to rent the haunted house. Uncared for, it
gradually took on an appearance that only a ghost would relish.

Early in December a man visited the real estate office and
asked if the place which he had heard was haunted could be
rented for a short period. The agent, delighted that interest was
being expressed in a piece of property he had thought would never
produce another penny, answered warily. Yes, the house was available, but as to the haunting stories, they were sheer nonsense. The
stranger put him straight. He was interested in a haunted house;
he was investigating spiritualism and would like a week to study
the sounds the people in that part of the state attributed to a ghost.
The agency gave him access to the cottage for seven days without
charge. When the man returned to the real estate office again, the
rental agent was expecting the same old story of cries in the night.
He asked: "Have you laid the ghost?" His visitor replied: "I have,
and here it is." The man reached in his pocket and took out a
small metal object he had found in the garret. He displayed it on
the palm of his hand. It was a toy—a child's whistle, round, with a
hole in the side.

"This had been fastened in a knothole," he said, "and was directly opposite a broken pane of glass. When the wind blew hard, it
caused a draft, and the wild shrieks your tenants heard were the
natural result."

Who would have guessed that one of the Hakes children,
while playing in the garret, had plugged a hole with the whistle,

or that a blast of wind would make it sound? Yet there are many accounts of how strange sounds in old houses have been made in the past. The whistle in Union, New York, was something new, but currents of air have accounted for other mysterious noises throughout the years.

Windows partially raised have been instrumental in causing paper to rustle or light objects to fall. The strangest air-induced action I have seen was when a child's rocking chair moved back and forth by itself, until the slightly opened window directly behind it was closed. The chair was on an uncarpeted floor, and there was a heavy wind at the time.

Seasonal scratching noises have been produced by low-hanging branches of a tree as they brushed on a roof, and boughs bearing fruit have caused bumping sounds when the wind swayed them. Woodwork affected by a change of temperature has frightened superstitious occupants of both old and new houses.

Disturbances for which there seemed to be no possible explanation have been traced to sources far below the earth. A Glasgow house was so regularly visited by a racketing spirit that no Scot would live in it. The walls at periodic intervals trembled violently, and doors were set ajar when no one was touching them. Hubert Miles solved the enigma in 1938. Beneath the building was a railroad tunnel. The passage of most trains through it had no effect on the house. When, however, heavily loaded freight trains rumbled along the tracks, the added impact sent heavy jolts through the structure, by way of its foundation. These were strong enough to open an unlocked door, shake the walls, and rattle the fixtures.

Underground passages have carried the clatter caused by wagons and automobiles crossing bridges to houses from which the bridges could not be seen. Trevor H. Hall, the noted British investigator of psychical phenomena, traced disturbances in Ousedale, England, to an even odder source—underground tides. His comparison, in 1956, of the dates noises were heard in a house on Grove Place with the records of high tides in the Ouse River solved the problem. Later he dispelled stories of another haunting in Yorkshire by matching the disturbances with the unusually heavy flows of subterranean water.

Mine explosions and earthquake tremors have shaken structures and caused pictures to fall from walls in instances where those who lived in the houses were unaware of these natural disturbances until the circumstances were explained. It is more difficult to find the elusive disturber of the peace when humans cause mysterious noises. I heard raps on my apartment door in New York for five days. There was never anyone there when I opened it. Neighbors reported the same experience. Purely by accident on the sixth day I opened the door as a small girl from an upper floor raced down the hall banging on every portal as she ran, then darted down the stairs. She was wearing tennis shoes and on her way to play in the park.

When I was a boy in Baltimore, there was a youngster in my neighborhood who caused families lost sleep. In the middle of the night they would hear knocks on their windows. When they looked out, though the noises had sounded only moments before, there was never anyone in sight. The "ghost" used a simple but extremely effective device to annoy families to which, for one reason or another, he had taken a dislike. He had cut a two-inch disk from the inner tube of an automobile tire, then punched a small hole in the center. Through the hole he forced a metal screw until its head was flush with the rubber. To the other end of the screw he attached a long piece of fishline. Several large knots were spaced a few inches apart near the free end of the line. On those nights when the mischievous youngster was in the mood, he would stealthily approach a window, wet the side of the rubber disk through which the head of the screw protruded, then press it firmly against the glass. Suction held it fast. He played out the fishline until he was hidden some distance away. Then he would pull the line taut and slide his tightly pressed index finger and thumb along the cord over the knots. Each time a knot was passed it produced a rap as the distant screwhead hit the windowpane. Soon he would hear the window open and the sound of agitated voices. The furor he caused gave him great satisfaction. Of course he attached his device on the upper section of a window, not the lower. I doubt if any of the irate parents ever discovered his secret.

At least I never heard that they did. He boasted to the other boys about his ingenuity, and most of us made up similar devices to see if they worked. They did. A simple prank, but carried out by a clever twelve-year-old boy, it had a fantastic effect on some of the older people who attributed the sounds to a supernatural force.

One of the strangest sounds-in-the-night stories I have ever heard was told by the late magician Julien J. Proskauer. A man on the night shift in a World War II armament plant in New Jersey thought he must be losing his mind. Each night when he returned to his room on the second floor of an old row house, he was conscious of the noise he made climbing the stairs. As he opened the door to his room, he always heard the echo of his footsteps *descending* the stairs and the sound of the door to the street opening and closing. Night after night he heard the phantom footsteps, and though he looked down the stairs while they were sounding, no human could be seen.

Can you offer a solution without reading further?

In the adjacent house was another man, on a later shift. Through the wall he could hear the returning worker mount the stairs. This was his signal that it was time for him to start for the plant himself. It was the sound of his footsteps and the door opening and closing behind him that plagued the man next door.

There are normal explanations for unlikely sounds.

Objects left on unused radiators in the summer have caused uncanny noises when heat reached them in the winter. The ghost that sometimes thumped in a Pennsylvania house was not a ghost at all. The thumps were made when books precariously stacked in a locked closet were jiggled by the vibrations from a power tool in the cellar until they fell.

An electric clock in New York lost approximately ten minutes daily, except on the weekend. The clock was in perfect working order. No one could understand why it would lose time on a Monday or a Wednesday but not on a Sunday. When the mystery was solved, it developed that not even the person responsible had been aware that her actions had stopped the timepiece. The cleaning woman pulled out the connection of what she thought was one of the lamps when she plugged in her vacuum cleaner. When her work was done, she replaced the connection in its socket, and the stopped clock started again.

There have been instances where people have deliberately spread rumors that houses were haunted so that they could buy choice property at bargain prices. Before the turn of the century Andrew Oehler, a traveling tailor, was housed, with reluctance, in a building that his employer and other people in the town had said was haunted. He was awakened by loud rumbling noises on the stairs. In his haste to get to the street, Oehler was almost hit by the cause of the racket—a huge barrel that was rolling down the steps. He returned to talk with his employer and found a "thunder-making device" had been installed on the upper floor. He was offered a large sum not to tell what he had learned. When shortly afterward his employer bought the haunted property at a public auction for a very small amount, Oehler received his payoff.

People expect to hear strange noises and see stranger sights in buildings where ghosts are said to walk. The sound of an unseen rat as it scampers across a corridor becomes the scratches of a phantom, a billowing curtain becomes a shrouded woman, a shadow becomes a menacing intruder to those with vivid imaginations.

Reflections from the moon or a street lamp on the windows of an old house give rise to stories that ghostly figures have been seen inside carrying lamps or lighted candles. Edward Saint, who was Mrs. Harry Houdini's manager during her last years in Hollywood, was intrigued by the tale that a specter had been observed moving from room to room in a deserted suburban house; the lantern it carried was visible through the windows. The ghost always walked one route from a room at the right end of the house to the left; it never went in the opposite direction. Saint discovered that the moving light so many people had reported was not in the house. It was the reflection from the headlights of an automobile as it approached the house. As a car came up the road the reflected beams went, as the car progressed, from window to window—the path the ghost always traveled.

I have met people who took pride in family ghosts. Every strange noise or odd incident was attributed to their personal haunt. Some could talk endlessly about the uncanny things that happened in their houses. They wished no rational explanations; they accepted the occurrences without question. The surety that the shade of a Revolutionary War soldier or a long-dead witch lived with them brought them pleasure and gave them an almost inexhaustible fund of anecdotes.

As Hulbert Footner, an author who lived in an eighteenth-century house in southern Maryland once told me, a friendly ghost is company during the long nights when one is working on a novel.

"What would you do if the spirit turned hostile, set fire to your books, kept you awake with its banging, and tossed lamps around your den?"

"Make notes immediately," he answered with a smile. "There's a great audience for accounts of unexplained phenomena."

THE MEDIUM WHO WAS NEVER EXPOSED

Daniel Dunglas Home, the most acclaimed physical medium of the nineteenth century, bitterly denounced psychics who sat in curtained cabinets in unlighted rooms: "When the last of the dark-séance mediums has abandoned his or her vocation in order to set up as a third-rate conjurer, and the last puppet-box, alias cabinet, is demolished . . . the golden day of our cause's triumph may be accounted at hand."

That time has not yet arrived. Tom O'Neill, the late publisher of the *Psychic Observer*, filmed two séances at Camp Chesterfield in Chesterfield, Indiana, in May 1960. Edith Stillwell's full-form materializations were the most amazing he had ever seen; he hoped to record them for future study. Infrared film was used with the permission of the medium. As the camera whirred in the dark, specters appeared and disappeared near the psychic's cabinet. To the naked eye there was no clue to the mystery, but when the ultrasensitive film was processed O'Neill and his friend Dr. Andrija Puharich saw clearly that the ghosts were living people masquerading in luminous cloth. Some O'Neill had seen earlier on the campgrounds. They came, the film disclosed, through doors, not from thin air.

O'Neill published the unlooked-for exposure in his July 10,

1960, issue and wrote: "The motion picture results of those proceedings will go down in history as the greatest recordings of fraud
ever in the movement of Spiritualism . . . . The whole sordid mess
is one of the bitterest pills I ever had to swallow."

Strange rapping sounds in the night had heralded the birth of
modern spiritualism March 31, 1848, in a frame farmhouse in
Hydesville, New York. Questions put to an unseen force in the
room where two children, Maggie and Katie Fox, slept were answered by knocks. Later Leah, their older sister who lived in
Rochester, discovered that she too was a receiver on the first spiritual telegraph. Soon there were few towns in New England where
similar signals, seemingly from the dead, were not being heard.

Six years later 15,000 spiritualists signed a petition which
James Shields of Illinois and Charles Sumner of Massachusetts presented to the United States Senate in Washington, D.C., April 17,
1854. A government investigation should be made, the believers
said, as the dead were so eager to communicate with the living.
Shields presented their case dramatically. An "occult force" seemed
to be "sliding, raising, arresting, holding, suspending, and otherwise disturbing ponderable bodies . . . . lights of various forms and
colors, and of different degrees of intensity, appear in dark rooms
. . . . Harmonious sounds as of human voices, and other sounds re-
sembling those of the fife, drum, trumpet, have been produced
without any visible agency."

The senators were in a jovial mood that day. When it was
asked to which committee the petition should be referred one
suggested the Committee on Foreign Relations: "We may have occasion to enter into diplomatic relations with the spirits." The laugh-
ter had scarcely subsided when another senator offered his opinion
that the Committee on Military Affairs might be more appropriate.
The petition was tabled.

If Congress was not willing to investigate, clergymen, skeptics,
and newspaper reporters were. In the next quarter of a century
hundreds of frauds were unmasked.

In the fall of 1876 a Mrs. Bennett, who was known in Boston

as the "West End medium," challenged the *Herald* which had printed stories of her deceits to prove their charges. A reporter was present as she produced the voice of "Sunflower" while seated in her cabinet, then materialized the body of her Indian guide. The reporter searched for concealed trapdoors and ripped up several planks in the floor. Hidden in a recess was the medium's thirty-year-old accomplice.

That same year the Rochester *Democrat and Chronicle* printed the confessions of a man named Jennings, the city's best-known materializer. Sometimes he worked alone, sometimes he used a confederate. "My accomplice used false hair, wigs, beards, etc., and put flour on his hands to give a ghostly appearance. For baby faces he had a piece of black velveteen, with a small round hole cut out. This, placed over the face, gave the appearance of the tiny features of a babe." One night Jennings used a painted mask which was rolled up and attached to one end of a wire. He "poked it through the screen, and then unrolled it by turning the wire. I also had a piece of thick, dark worsted cloth which I used as a beard for myself . . . . two faces appeared at once and almost threw the meeting into ecstasies."

In New York Henry Gordon was such an adroit performer that he convinced his clients that faces painted on cardboard, draped with luminous cloth, were spirits. He was not detected until overwrought sitters rushed the cabinet to clasp their departed loved ones and found Gordon and his devices in their arms.

W. F. Jamieson and his partner, a man named M'Queen, were suddenly in the spotlight in Kalamazoo, Michigan. A doctor in the audience struck a match after one of the psychics said he had levitated himself and was floating around the room playing a guitar. The illumination disclosed that the medium, whose voice came from near the ceiling, was standing on his chair whirling the musical instrument around his head.

D. D. Home was sorely distressed by the crude tricks of his contemporaries. He had never used a cabinet though he had performed some of his most fantastic marvels in the dark.

An extensive account of his most striking feat of levitation appears in the 1921 edition of *D. D. Home, His Life and Mission,* a book written by his second wife and edited by Sir Arthur Conan Doyle. It took place "in the presence of three unimpeachable witnesses, Lord Lindsay, Lord Adare, and Captain Charles Wynne." In December 1868 they were seated in the dark in an apartment on an upper floor of Ashley House in London.

"We heard the window in the next room lifted up, and almost immediately afterward we saw Home floating in the air outside our window. The moon was shining full into the room. My back was to the light; and I saw the shadow on the wall of the window-sill, and Home's feet about six inches above it. He remained in this position for a few seconds, then raised the window and glided into the room feet foremost, and sat down," was the way Lord Lindsay described it.

"We heard Home go into the next room, heard the window thrown up, and presently Home appeared standing upright outside our window. He opened the window and walked in quite coolly," Lord Adare wrote. Wynne, in a letter to Home dated February 2, 1877, added: "The fact of your having gone out of the window and in at the other I can swear to."

Other reputable observers attested they had seen the Scottish-born mystic produce spirit hands, elongate his body to an extent that was not humanly possible, and demonstrate that he was both fireproof and incombustible.

Tsar Alexander II, Emperor Napoleon III, and Queen Sophia of Holland welcomed Home to their courts. Lords and their ladies, counts and countesses, dukes and captains of industry, entertained him and were in turn astonished by his phenomena.

Daniel Dunglas Home, whose father was the illegitimate son of Alexander, the tenth earl of Home, was born in Currie, a town near Edinburgh, March 20, 1833.

His mother's sister and her husband brought him to Greenville (now Norwich), Connecticut, when he was nine. Daniel Home later wrote that he had seen visions before the Fox sisters attracted widespread interest in 1848 and that raps came in his presence too. His aunt was not sympathetic when a barrage of knocks shook the family breakfast table. She threw a chair at him. When other furniture moved mysteriously, her rage increased. Dan took refuge with friends who were more understanding.

His séances in nearby Willimantic and Lebanon in the early 1850's brought him invitations to stay with well-to-do families. The slender, gray-eyed youth with flowing auburn locks and a pale complexion began a way of life that was not to vary with the years.

It has been said that Home never accepted a fee for his services; rather, he became a perpetual guest whose expenses were paid and whose needs were met by his sponsors. He was never reticent in accepting expensive gifts, though he made it clear he could exhibit only when the spirits moved him.

In trances he prescribed herb remedies that effected quick cures for other sufferers. His own tubercular condition seemed beyond spirit aid. "I was often warned by my spirit friends against coming in contact with sick persons," he said. He took their advice. It was easy for young Home to find hosts who were healthy as well as wealthy, for he was a house guest of rare appeal. His conversation was amusing; he could play the piano and quote from popular authors. Older women, especially those with an interest in the spiritual side of life, were so charmed by the young man's attentions that they talked of adopting him. Doctors, clergymen, and professors who attended his séances were just as eager to have him to their homes not just for dinner but for as long as he wished to stay.

Three times in a single evening Home was levitated from the floor of a darkened room in the home of Ward Cheney, an affluent citizen of South Manchester, Connecticut. This was in August 1852, when Daniel was nineteen. Eventually he soared so high that his head and one arm touched the ceiling. Frank L. Burr, editor of the Hartford *Times*, had been holding the medium's other hand. Burr said that Dan's feet were twelve inches off the floor. As neither

Burr nor anyone else could see what was happening in the dark, he asked for an explanation.

Home, who had been gasping and trembling as he rose, replied when he recovered his breath: "*Somebody* put a girdle around me . . . and drew me up." It was clear the *somebody* Home referred to was a spirit.

Pale spirit hands also appeared during Home's séances and tugged on ladies' skirts, rang bells placed beneath a table, and played musical instruments.

By the time Home sailed for England in March 1855 (the spirits told him the climate there would be better for his health), his manifestations were the envy of every medium who knew about them in America. The Jarves family, with whom he stayed in Boston, paid for his passage.

Unlike Mrs. W. H. Hayden, who three years earlier had been the first American medium to introduce the new spirit phenomena to the British Isles, Home had more than rapping noises and cavorting tables at his command. It has been written that he was never publicly exposed. This is true—he never gave public séances. When he appeared privately, he was a guest, and as a guest could specify the conditions under which he worked. He gave firm instructions about how many people were to be in the room, where they were to be seated, and the degree to which they should participate in the séance. Nine or fewer was the number he preferred, though on occasion more were permitted.

Robert and Elizabeth Barrett Browning met Home during one of his stays with John S. Rymer, a wealthy solicitor, at Ealing. Dan was pleased to meet the celebrated pair. He admired their poetry; he was a versifier of sorts himself. During the séance that evening a spirit hand lifted a floral wreath from a table and placed it like a crown on Elizabeth's head. The hand was, Elizabeth wrote, "of the largest human size, as white as snow and very beautiful." She peered through her "glass" to get a better look at it.

Robert Browning was not as impressed, and his wife later

agreed with him that the hand had come from under the table. Perhaps he was provoked because the garland had not been fitted to his own brow; more likely the sheer audacity of the man he was to call a scoundrel and a trickster outraged him. Later he gave vent to his feelings in "Mr. Sludge 'the Medium'." The invective leaves no doubt as to how he felt about séances in general and one medium in particular.

Home was twenty-five when he met Alexandrina de Kroll, the seventeen-year-old daughter of General Count de Kroll, at a party in Rome. They were introduced shortly after midnight. She sat by his side as a late supper was served. "Mr. Home," she said, "you will be married before the year is ended." She explained there was a Russian superstition that this would happen if a man was seated, as Daniel was, between two sisters.

Sacha, as her friends called her, was right. In twelve days she was engaged to the medium, needing only the consent of her mother to make it official. She went on to Russia to prepare for the wedding. Home arrived in St. Petersburg later with Alexandre Dumas, the celebrated novelist, as his best man. Tsar Alexander II gave the bride his blessing and a diamond ring. When a son was born twelve months later, the Russian ruler sent another gift, an emerald pin rimmed with diamonds.

Count Alexis Tolstoy attended a séance at the Milner Gibsons' Hyde Park mansion in London. Home was in top form. The raps came; the table lifted. After the gaslights were lowered, one table placed itself atop another; a handbell rang in the air around the room; a sofa slid across the floor. Even more marvelous manifestations followed. Music came from the piano; Mrs. Gibson's bracelet "unclasped itself" and dropped to the table; and Home floated up toward the ceiling as Tolstoy grasped his feet in the dark. It was not the levitation that the count recalled as the most mysterious phenomenon of the evening, but the weird spirit hands "which were placed in mine and melted when I tried to retain them."

Home noted in his autobiography that skeptics had many explanations for his marvels. Some said "that I carried in my pocket a tamed monkey trained to assist me . . . that my feet are like those of a baboon . . . that I take with me wax hands and arms . . . . Others have stated that when I am said to rise in the air, it is only a balloon filled with gas in the shape of a man."

As to the rapping, he said some of the theories offered were "the snapping of toe-joints, others getting up to the ankle, while others maintain it to be in the knees, or thigh bones . . . . It has even been attributed to a strong beating of my pulse. Some say I rub my boots together, others my thumb nails, and that springs are concealed in the table and about the room."

The first rapping method Home mentioned is far from theoretical. In their later years the two Fox sisters, whose rapping noises gave birth to the phenomena, publicly revealed the source of the sounds. Sunday evening, October 21, 1888, at the New York Academy of Music, two thousand people saw and heard Margaret as she demonstrated the method and her sister Katherine looked on. To quote the next day's *Sun*: "Doctors from the audience went upon the stage and felt the woman's foot as she made the motions by which she used to do the rapping. Then she stood in her stocking feet on a little pine platform six inches from the floor, and without the slightest perceptible movement of the person, made raps audible all over the theater.

"She went into the audience, and there, resting her feet on another person's, showed how by the motion of the great toe the sound was produced."

The *Evening Post* summed up the situation. Margaret located "the origin of Modern Spiritualism in her great toe."

Thomas Henry Huxley, the noted British biologist, admitted in the *Pall Mall Gazette*, January 1, 1899, that for thirty-five years he had been able to produce what other people called spirit raps with the second toe of either foot. "I have merely to bend the toe and then suddenly straighten it."

Was Home an accomplished sleight-of-foot artist? Were his spirit hands actually human feet—his own? A letter written by a gentleman who attended a Home séance in August 1855 was printed in the *Journal* of the Society for Psychical Research in May 1903. I quote, in part:

> The medium sat as low as possible in his low seat. His hands and arms were under the table. He talked freely, encouraging conversation, and seeming uneasy when it flagged. After a few preliminary raps somebody exclaimed that the "spirit hand" had appeared, and the next moment an object, resembling a child's hand with a long, wide sleeve attached to it, appeared before the light. This occurred several times. The object appeared mainly at one or the other of two separate distances from the medium. One of these distances was just that of his foot, the other that of his outstretched hand; and when the object receded or approached, I noticed that the medium's body or shoulder sank or rose in his chair accordingly. This was pretty conclusive to myself and the friend who accompanied me; but afterwards, upon the invitation of one of the dupes present, the "spirit hand" rose so high that we saw the whole connection between the medium's shoulder and arm . . . ."

Dr. E. Barthez, a physician at the court of Napoleon III in France, almost attended one of Home's séances there in 1857. He was in the room when it began, but the entranced medium said there were too many people present and he was asked to leave. He wrote his wife that the medium's method had been discovered by Morio de l'Ile, who saw the procedure: "At the proper moment he [Home] throws off a slipper, and with his naked toes tugs at a dress here and there, rings a handbell, gives a rap on this side or that, and then slips his foot back into his slipper again."

Viscount Beaumont-Vassy spoke in his memoirs, which were published in 1874, of the impudent medium at the Tuileries who pulled his foot from his patent-leather boot and presented it under the table to Napoleon as the spirit hand of Queen Hortense.

Houdini in the 1920's delighted theatergoers by duplicating Home's marvels while sitting at a draped table on a stage. Although members of the audience held his hands and controlled his feet by pressing the toes of their shoes on his, a tambourine jangled under the table and words were written upon a slate. Then, as a handbell rang, one of his assistants pulled aside the cloth to reveal that it was Houdini's foot, not the spirits, at play. The end of his stocking had been cut off, and his bare toes were holding the handle of the bell and ringing it. I too have shown audiences how a foot may be slipped from a shoe, used to play instruments, then returned without the spectator who sits across the table realizing what has happened.

No one would have been so rude as to seize one of Home's "spirit hands" without his permission and hold it until it could be determined whether or not it was attached to the medium's leg or arm. Home was an honored guest, not a professional who exhibited before the public.

Until I began experimenting, the reports that Home's "spirit hands" dissolved when people pressed them puzzled me. I discovered almost by accident how this illusion could be produced. A slow pull of the bare toes acting as spirit fingers was obvious to the spectator, but a quick straight jerk gave him the tactile sensation that the "hand" had evaporated.

Home's ability to grow taller, then shrink at will has often been cited as one of his outstanding psychic accomplishments. It is scarcely necessary to invoke a supernormal explanation for this feat which has been done repeatedly by an honest showman who frankly explained the method. Sixty years ago Clarence E. Willard, a vaudeville headliner, achieved fame as "The Man Who Grows." For more than twenty years he appeared in variety halls in England and on the Continent as well as the United States, where he was born. Surrounded by a committee from the audience, the five-foot-nine-and-a-half-inch marvel would zoom up inch by inch until he towered high above the men who stood near him. In his prime Willard could add eight inches to his height, though newspaper critics who wrote about his act said he grew a foot or more. Keeping his feet firmly planted on the stage, Willard stretched up until his vest was high above his trouser top and his chin was over the head of the tallest spectator who came up to observe. Willard also stretched his arm, pulling on his right wrist with his left hand until it appeared a dozen inches had been added.

Willard could and did repeat his specialty in hospitals under medical observation and before scientists. He never claimed to be superhuman. By diligent practice he had learned how to stretch. He told me he got his inspiration for the feat while watching tigers extend their reach in a circus. To get the maximum audience effect he took a relaxed stance when he began his elongation.

An optical illusion aided his arm stretching. His extended right arm was relaxed and the palm was close to his sleeve. As the left hand grasped his right wrist and pulled it bit by bit away from the body, the right hand was drawn further out of the sleeve. Before the feat was completed a good ten inches of wrist and arm were extended from the sleeve.

In April 1958 Willard, who long before had retired from the stage, explained his techniques at an Open House session of the Society of American Magicians in New York. Though he was approaching his eighty-fourth birthday, he could easily pass for a man of sixty. He said that the constant stretching had actually added two inches to his height. He hadn't performed professionally with his elongation act for years, but he became a good five inches taller as he talked.

The fire-resisting feats of Home which so startled his friends in British drawing rooms were performed before, during, and after his time by "fire kings" who entertained at fairs, side shows, and theaters. The same tricks that amazed the countryfolk became incredible marvels when the slender medium repeated them reverently without fanfare. A charred piece of white pine, introduced among the burning coals in a fireplace, may be handled with ease. If the performer suggests others will be burned and his suggestion is strong enough they will feel intense heat and blisters will sometimes appear on the fingers. A stock feat among the outdoor fire workers was to put their faces and locks of their hair in the flames of torches and braziers; when Home repeated this demonstration in a private home his supporters said he was supernormal.

The downfall of Mrs. Suydam, a spiritualist who performed her fire tests for a paying public, was reported in a dispatch from Rockford, Illinois, printed in the *Chicago Tribune,* January 30, 1877. She bathed her face in flames during her demonstration at Brown's Hall. Dr. J. Phillips, who was in the audience, volunteered to repeat the ritual without spirit protection. He succeeded, as did another spectator, James Chandler. A Rockford doctor offered the psychic a ten-dollar bill if she would hold her thumb for forty seconds over a flame without moving it. Twenty dollars more were offered by other skeptics. Those who supported her and those who said she was a fraud almost came to blows. Only the arrival of the police ended the fracas.

How could Home levitate himself in a room with the lights out? One method used then, and later, by mediums is most convincing. In the dark the psychic slips off his shoes as he tells the sitters his body is becoming weightless. The sitter to the medium's left grasps his left hand, the one to the right puts a hand on the mystic's shoes, near the toes. Holding his shoes together with his right hand pressing the inner sides, the medium slowly raises them in the air as he first squats then stands on his chair. The man holding his hand reports the medium is ascending; so does the sitter who touches the shoes. Until I tried this myself, it was hard to believe that spectators in a dark room could be convinced an ascension was being made.

How could Home write his name on ceilings under these conditions? One explanation is that he may have written it there hours or even days in advance when alone in the room. Who will notice a name written on the ceiling unless it is pointed out? Certainly none of those who participated in my tests did.

I had read that bold mediums in dark rooms slipped off their shoes, put their hands in them so the shoes were held toes up, then extended their arms and announced they were about to float across an area where a window shade was dimly illuminated from a street lamp. The shadow of the coat sleeves seems to be made by trouser legs. I tried this, first approaching the window from one side, then when the shadow was across the blind swinging my arms so the "body," which was never seen, turned in the air. Spectators are not very observant. Some told me later that I had floated *across* the lighted area.

This brings us to Home's most famous levitation. Lord Lindsay, who in after years became the Earl of Crawford, Viscount Adare, who became the Earl of Dunraven, and Captain Charles Bradstreet Wynne, Adare's cousin, were with Home that Sunday evening in 1868 in a room at Ashley House in London. No one *saw* him float across the outside of the building. They assumed, because they heard a window open in the next room and because he came in from the outside of the window of their room, that he had floated between the two rooms.

Study their statements which were quoted earlier in this chapter. The problem is not to explain how Home floated but rather how he crossed the space between the two windows. Houdini once suggested that Home could have arranged a wire so that it dangled down from above outside the window in the second room, that he could have grasped its end and swung from one ledge to another. Trevor Hall, in *New Light on Old Ghosts*, examines the testimony of the three "witnesses" and the location of the windows. He suggests that the windows were so close together that Home could have stepped from one to the other.

It is unlikely we will ever know precisely how the famous medium crossed the gap, but it is obvious the men who authenticated the floating feat never actually saw it. The marvelous outdoor levitation took place only in their minds.

In his autobiography, *Incidents in My Life*, published by Carleton in New York in 1858, Home said that the best description of his phenomena had been made by Dr. J. J. G. Wilkinson, and he quoted him at length. On page 112, Wilkinson asked the medium's spirits if "jugglers [magicians] did their tricks by means similar to the agencies there present?" A "no" answer was rapped. He rephrased the questions. Did Indian jugglers? The reply "in a pronounced manner" was "yes." Indian magicians use their feet as adroitly as their hands and their greatest marvel, the Indian rope trick, is a legend.

Wilkinson asked Home another important question: . . . "Why the effects generally took place *under* the table, and not upon it?". . . This time the medium replied himself. "He said that in habituated circles the results were easily obtained above board, visible to all, but that at a first sitting it was not so. That skepticism was almost universal in men's intellects, and marred the forces at work." If you are willing to suspend reasoning and blindly accept marvels without proof you can still "see" them today.

PALLADINO

Most mediums are wary of investigators who seek to test their powers under conditions more rigorous than those with which they usually work. Eusapia Palladino was the exception. Distinguished scientists in Europe were utterly confounded by her manifestations, which seemed to violate the known laws of physics, biology, and common sense. The most famous Italian psychic of her time levitated tables and produced ghostly hands, raps, and a strange breeze which apparently came from a scar on her forehead.

Cesare Lombroso, the eminent psychiatrist and professor of criminal anthropology; Marie Curie and her husband, Pierre, the discoverers of radium and polonium; and Charles Richet, the physiologist who was later to win a Nobel prize, found her marvels beyond their comprehension. She sat for them and other noted investigators whenever they wished—as long as they paid for the privilege of observing her.

She was not an easy person to study scientifically. The short, buxom brunette with large, black eyes, expansive mouth, and provocative manner performed with the intensity of a Sarah Bernhardt and the fire and drive of Otera, the Spanish dancer. Her expressive face contorted, her small hands twisted, and her feet were seldom still. She groaned, gasped, hiccuped, and shuddered. It was obvious she was under a tremendous emotional strain. When a sitting was over, she not infrequently collapsed, drained of energy, a limp mass of olive-hued flesh from which the mysterious motivating force had fled.

Palladino was born January 21, 1854, in the mountain town of Minerverno Murge in the province of Bari in southern Italy. Her mother, she said, died shortly after childbirth, and her father was murdered by outlaws when she was twelve. She came to Naples as a laundress and serving girl, and there in her early teens first became aware of her psychic gift. A table tilted as she touched it during an impromptu séance with friends; her development as a professional medium was rapid. Though she could scarcely write her own name, Eusapia was little handicapped by her lack of formal education. Her grammar may have been poor and her expressions crude, but the sheer brilliance of her phenomena towered over the puny efforts of her rivals, much as the nearby Vesuvius dwarfed its neighboring hills.

Her Neapolitan contemporaries held their séances in dark rooms; Eusapia exhibited some of her marvels with the lamps on and often unshaded. She was married twice—once to a man who worked in the theater whose hobby was conjuring, and later to Raphael Delgaiz, a younger man who had a comfortable income from a small shop. Age and pasta added pounds to Eusapia's shorter-than-medium-height frame, but even in womanhood she was as dexterous as she had been as a child.

She was thirty-six when the sixty-four-year-old Lombroso came to Naples to see her perform. She was a challenge of a sort the famous professor had never encountered—an intriguing mixture of charlatan and saint, a mature female with childlike emotions who was given to great rages and unusual tenderness. He learned in time that some of her manifestations were produced by trickery, but others seemed to him beyond the scope of human powers. "The Master of Turin," a skeptic until he met Palladino, had no answer to the psychic riddle. He was so overwhelmed that eventually he became a spiritualist.

There was almost a father-daughter relationship between the two. She saw in him a substitute for the parent she had mourned as a hill girl, a bearded patriarch of great learning who treated her kindly, who was pleased as well as puzzled by her strange accomplishments. Endorsed by Lombroso, she went on to Milan, Warsaw, St. Petersburg, and Paris to be studied by other men of repute. Dr. Julien Ochoworits, the Polish psychologist, offered a theory to explain what he saw: Eusapia had a second fluidic self which emerged from her body to carry out her demands. How else could the table soar, objects come from the cabinet behind her, and phantom hands appear over her head?

The British Society for Psychical Research was more interested in mental phenomena than physical manifestations and dubious of professional mediums. Still the reports from the Continent of Palladino's triumphs were well attested. She was brought to Cambridge in 1895 for a series of sittings. Richard Hodgson, secretary of the society's American branch, was positive she released her hands and feet, though they seemed to be held by the investigators. Similar charges had been made in Europe. The "control" was of her own devising. A sitter to her right grasped her right wrist while her left fingers touched the hand of the sitter on the left. This was in the dark, after preliminary table tilting. It was reported that she gradually moved her hands closer together and eventually lifted her left fingers and placed her right fingers in their place. This gave her free use of her left hand. In the same way she made one foot play the part of two, which permitted her to use the released leg whenever she wished. The leading British conjurer of the time, John Nevil Maskelyne, who participated in the investigation at Cambridge, shared Hodgson's views. He saw nothing that indicated Palladino had supernormal powers. Professor Henry Sidgwick, his wife, and Alice Johnson concurred. A complete account of the Cambridge séances was never published. It was said that when the mystic from Naples was in Cambridge she even cheated while playing croquet.

Eight years later, after further detailed European reports of Eusapia's marvels under scientific supervision had been received, the S.P.R. sent a three-man commission to Naples. The Honorable

Everard Feilding, second son of the Earl of Denbigh; Hereward Carrington, the British-born investigator who lived in the United States; and W. W. Baggally, who was skeptical of almost every phenomenon except telepathy, agreed unanimously that she had produced manifestations in their room at the Hotel Victoria which could be explained only in terms of a psychic force.

Earlier that year Carrington had written a book, *The Physical Phenomena of Spiritualism*, in which he had explained many methods of fraudulent mediums. Following the Naples tests he stated unequivocally that in the ten years he had tested psychics "all had been fraudulent, without a single exception." All, that is, except the medium in Naples.

On his return to the States Carrington wrote a 353-page volume extolling *Eusapia Palladino and Her Phenomena* and sought financial support to bring the fifty-four-year-old wonder to New York so that she could be studied by American scientists before she died.

It was Carrington's ambition to head a well-endowed laboratory for occult investigations. He believed that Palladino, under his management, would create such a sensation, such a national furor, that his dream would materialize.

By early November 1909 Eusapia was on the high seas bound for New York. It was almost inevitable that she was recognized aboard the Italian ship and persuaded to give a demonstration for the officers and a few of the most important passengers. They were more anxious to talk to the dead than see phenomena, but phenomena there were and in plenty. A lurid account of the sitting was printed after a ship's news reporter talked with some of those who had attended. A Dr. Oteri had asked to see his father.

"In answer to my call, we were all overcome by the filmy manifestation that rested on my right shoulder. It was the head of a man, but I did not recognize it as anyone I had ever known. I do not remember my father very well. The impression I got from the manifestation was that it was ghastly, horrible, unexplainable, mysterious."

Before Houdini performed his underwater survival test, a doctor gave him a thorough examination. Swimmers stood on the top of the submerged airtight box during the demonstration.

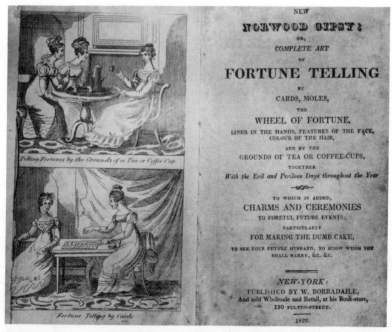

Frontispiece and title page of the *New Norwood Gipsy; or, Complete Art of Fortune Telling,* which was published by W. Borradaile in New York in 1823. Futures could be read, it said, in cards, tea, coffee grounds, and moles. Charms were explained which purported to reveal if the subject would marry or remain single.

Milbourne Christopher explains two methods of table levitation on the NBC-TV "Tonight Show." Here Johnny Carson and Ed McMahon use their thumbs to lift the top.

Christopher employs the Palladino hand-and-foot clamp method for this levitation. When he lifts his right foot and presses firmly with his right hand to keep the top level, the table soars up.

With his free hand Christopher pulls a "reaching rod," a collapsible metal pole, from his pocket, so he can have the "spirits" touch Kay Ballard's arm. This is done in the dark.

During Eusapia Palladino's visit to the United States in 1909, she became the target of newspaper cartoons. Here F. Opper shows how the "Kink of Denmark" reacts to the news that she has been exposed in New York.

When table turning became the rage in France in 1853, Honoré Daumier drew a series of satirical scenes showing how "Fluidomanie" affected Parisian life. Even the actors were tilting tables in the wings during theater performances.

Another Daumier lithograph depicts the guests at a party trying to make a giant key turn and endeavoring to move an uninterested cat.

The eclipse of the sun, September 5, 1793, intrigues the star gazer in the frontispiece of Volume 1 of *The Astrologer's Magazine*, published that year. It was the first periodical devoted to devotees of the horoscope.

POWELL, THE FIRE-EATER

Feats that mediums later claimed were evidences of their psychic power were performed in England by Robert Powell, the fire king, between 1718 and 1780. He ate red-hot coal "as natural as bread."

Signora Josephine Girardelli put her arms and hair in flames in 1814. She stood barefooted on red-hot metal and performed other seemingly impossible feats.

SIGNORA JOSEPHINE GIRALDELLI.
The Original 'Salamander'.
Published March 16, 1814, by R. S. Kirby, 11, Warwick-Lane.

On Monday Evening, Jan. 4, 1819,

And on Wednesday, Friday, and Saturday Evenings,

By Permission, and under the Patronage of the Nobility and Gentry,

At the KINGSTON ROOMS,

THE TWO WONDERFUL RUSSIAN

FIRE-PROOF

PHENOMENA,

Monsieur and Mademoiselle CHABERT,

(Brother and Sister,) who have had the Honour of exhibiting before the University and City of Oxford, with univerfal Approbation; of whom the London Papers have made fo much mention, and who lately caufed fo much Aftonifhment in London and Paris, alfo at Peterfburgh, by going into an OVEN, in Prefence of the Royal Faculty of Phyficians, with a LEG of MUTTON, and remaining with it until the Meat was well baked. This Experiment he will have the Honour of performing again, whenever a liberal Subfcription fhall be made for that Purpofe, as has been mentioned in the *Courier* of Saturday October 31ft, 1818.

Mons. and Mad^elle. CHABERT,

The only real Incombustible Phenomena,

Have the Honour refpectfully to announce, that their Public Exhibition will take place for one Week only, previoufly to their going to London to perform, by Subfcription, that extraordinary Spectacle of *their both going into an Oven with a* SHOULDER of MUTTON *raw*, and to come out, when they prefent it *cooked* to the Company.— The Subfcription is for *Five Hundred Pounds*, two Hundred of which has been already received at No. 29, Great Suffolk Street, London.——The Performances will confift of the following extraordinary Proofs of their fupernatural Power of refifting the moft INTENSE HEAT of every Kind; and Mr. CHABERT pledges himfelf that no SLEIGHT-OF-HAND (as is ufual in thefe Things) will be practifed.

1. Will bear a lighted Candle under his Feet for feveral minutes
2. Will Forge a plate of Red Hot Iron with their Feet
3. Will undergo the Torture by Fire as ufed in the Spanifh Inquifition
4. Will pofitively drink Boiling Oil
5. Will drop on his tongue a quantity of Sealing Wax, from which any of the Company may take the print of a Seal
6. Will eat Burning Charcoal
7. Will bathe his Feet in Boiling Lead
8. Will pour Aqua-Fortis on Steel-Filings and trample on it
9. Will rub a Red Hot Shovel on his Tongue, Arms, Legs, and on his Hair, until it is fo hot that a perfon cannot bear his hand on it
10. Will pour Vitriol, Oil, and Arfenic into the Fire, hold his Head in the Flames, and inhale the Vapours
11. Will pour Aqua-fortis on a piece of Copper in the hollow of his Hand
12. Will put Boiling Lead in his Mouth with his Hand
13. Will eat of a Torch as if it were a Salad.

Admission, 3s.—Children, Half-Price.——A Band will attend.

Mr. CHABERT refpectfully informs the Nobility and Gentry, that if the Amount of £10 is fubfcribed, a beautiful Difplay of FIRE-WORKS will play on him until his fhirt is burnt from his back.

The Nobility and Gentry are refpectfully informed, that every facility will be given in affording the means of examining as clofely as poffible into Mr. CHABERT's Performances. The Amateurs of Chemiftry are requefted to bring with them any Materials they may think proper, to put the Exhibitor's FIRE PROOF to the Teft.

Between the Hours of Performance, Mr. and Mifs CHABERT will be happy to attend any Ladies or Gentlemen at their own Houfes, if required, for any Performances.——Mr. CHABERT fpeaks French, Italian, German, Ruffian, Spanifh, and Polifh; Mifs CHABERT will converfe in the Ruffian and Englifh, being educated at an Englifh Boarding School.

In Cafes of fudden Fire, Mr. CHABERT will be happy to be called upon to help any Fellow-Creature in danger.

☞ Doors to be opened at SIX, and begin at SEVEN o'Clock.—Addrefs, Mr. CHABERT, 12, STALL-STREET.

Richard Cruttwell, Printer, Bath Chronicle Office, St. James's Street.

J. Xavier Chabert and his sister presented their "Fire-Proof Phenomena" in London in 1819. Their most impressive stunt was to enter an oven carrying a leg of mutton and stay inside until it was cooked.

C. A. George Newmann, a noted American thought reader, performed the blindfold carriage drive, which had been introduced by Washington Irving Bishop, to attract audiences to his theater shows.

An Oriental method of predicting the future involved shaking marked sticks in a cannister. Those that toppled out and fell to the ground indicated whether good or bad influences would control events.

Professor Manlio Smeragliolo wanted to reach his mother. Something made the sign of the cross: "I distinctly felt the touch on my forehead, then on my breast, and then on each shoulder. . . . After that I distinctly felt a kiss on my lips, and after that two kisses on my right cheek."

With the press hot on Palladino's trail, Carrington managed to spirit her away from the docks without a personal interview and take her to the 113 Street apartment where she was to stay with her husband's sister and the sister's husband. The demand for press coverage rose to immense proportions. Carrington announced that he would admit reporters free to the first New York séance "provided they left us alone thereafter." He knew that nothing so stimulates the press as a story that is difficult to cover; an uncooperative Garbo gets ten times as much space as a more willing star.

Carrington had said he was bringing Eusapia to America so scientists could test her unparalleled phenomena. There were no scientists present on the evening of November 14, 1909, nor had investigators from the American Society for Psychical Research been invited. The star sitters were William A. Brady and his wife Gladys George, the actress. Mr. Brady was a Broadway producer.

Carrington knew from experience that the Italian medium worked alone. Still he made a great show of sealing the windows of Room 328 in the Lincoln Square Arcade and pointing out that burglar alarms had been installed which would ring if anyone attempted to force open the windows. He also attached heavy bolts to the doors. Photographer Vander Weyde took publicity shots of the celebrities. Cecil B. DeMille couldn't have staged a première more effectively.

A light, oblong, four-legged pine table had been constructed to Palladino's specifications. It was, the reporters found, that and nothing more. There were no concealed springs in its legs, no loose planks or hidden mechanisms.

A few feet behind the table in an alcove of the room was a cabinet about three feet square and seven feet tall. Black drapes covered the front. There were also a number of objects in the cabi-

net which the medium had been known to use during her manifestations: a toy piano, a flageolet, a music box, a small stool, a man-
dolin, and an accordian.

Though Eusapia had not been searched in Naples until after
several séances had been completed, Carrington announced she
would disrobe behind the curtains of the cabinet and permit the reporters to examine her clothes.

The signora who supervised this operation in Naples recorded
a description of the medium's apparel for posterity:

> Madame Palladino first took off a black serge bodice and skirt
> of the same material and colour . . . a white knitted stay-cover . . .
> a white linen scarf a little over a foot in length and about four
> inches wide . . . a long dark blue petticoat with white embroidery
> round the bottom . . . a short white flannel one . . . a pair of pink
> and brown stays . . . a long shift of coarse white linen.

When this bulk had been removed the bulging mystic was still
well covered with:

> a pair of grey, wooly, divided combinations, that is to say,
> body and drawers . . . white stockings, black elastic garters under
> her knees and a pair of brownish coloured boots, with heels, which
> are only buttoned by the top button.

The *New York Times* reporter, Will Irwin, was more interested in Eusapia's phenomena than her plumage. He wrote: "Mrs.
Brady brought out her outer garments for the inspection of the
men. They seemed above reproach."

To fill the stage wait while his star dressed, Carrington lec-
tured on the lighting system. Suspended above the far end of the
pinewood table, opposite the chair where Palladino would sit, was
a five-globe fixture. In it were a white sixteen-candle-power bulb
and four four-candle-power bulbs, one bare, one covered with two
thicknesses of white tissue paper, another covered with two thicknesses of red tissue, and still another with four wrappings of the
red paper.

The sitting would start with the brightest light, then, whenever

Eusapia wished, this would be switched off and a dimmer one used. Each had a separate switch.

It should be noted that the fixture was not over the chair where the medium would work but some five feet away. The lights were *above*, thus insuring a shadowy area under the table.

The medium emerged from her improvised dressing room and protested, through her interpreter, that there were too many people seated around the table. Chairs were pulled away. She placed Brady, the theatrical impresario, to her right. Next to him on the long side sat the reporter from the *Sun*. At the far end of the table was the man from the *World*. On her left was J. W. Morrisey, one of Brady's representatives. Between Morrisey and the *World* reporter sat Brady's wife. The other observers were a short distance away.

Seated at the narrow end of the table with the cabinet behind her, Palladino, in her black dress, resembled the high priestess of an ancient cult, which in a way she was. Her hands and feet touched those of the men to her sides. She bent forward, her eyes almost closed.

At 9:43 a rap was heard. A minute later the table began moving, tilting first on two legs, then swinging on one. At thirty seconds past 9:53, under the faint red glow of the four-candle-power bulb wrapped with two sheets of colored tissue, all four legs were off the floor for three seconds. Later only the bulb with four thicknesses of red tissue was used. The curtain behind Palladino bulged forward as she groaned. A pale hand was seen extending from a drape, though the men affirmed they held both of the medium's hands. The stool came from behind her to land upside down on the tabletop. Brady was grabbed by something he couldn't see. Morrisey felt a cold wind on his head. More raps were heard, the white hand was seen again, and there were other phenomena. Even when the table legs closest to Eusapia were inserted in a special sheathing device, designed to prevent them from being manipulated by her feet, the table still tilted and rose.

It was the complete levitation of the table, the *Times* reported, "which sent the reporters away believing—if not in spirits, at least in a mysterious personal force which contradicts all known laws of matter."

Carrington played his part well. Rather than acclaim each manifestation, he sometimes suggested the effects could be accomplished by trickery. This provoked the sitters to declare that the medium was under perfect control.

Someone rapped on the table with a rhythm, and echoing sounds like the beat of a muffled drum duplicated the pattern. Carrington cautioned: "One method of producing raps is by sliding the hand along the tabletop. Watch her hands, and see that she does not move them along the surface." When, with everyone standing, the table soared up, he called out for the reporters to make sure that neither Palladino's feet nor knees touched it.

As the cabinet drape "blew" forward, Carrington said this sometimes happened when she released a hand without the holder's knowledge. There were instant denials that this had happened.

For two hours and thirteen minutes Eusapia gave a virtuoso performance. When it was over she was exhausted. She could scarcely lift a glass of water to her lips and had to be helped from her chair. Then she stretched out to recuperate on three other chairs which had been placed side by side. Eleven minutes past midnight she recovered enough to accept the congratulations of Carrington and his wife.

Two nights later, when the second séance was staged, the most prominent sitters were S. S. McClure, of *McClure's Magazine*, who it was rumored had provided most of the backing for the American appearances, and Dr. Saram R. Ellison, a founder of the Society of American Magicians, one of Carrington's old friends. Carrington, who kept no formal record of this séance, asked the doctor to write him his frank opinions on the phenomena. Ellison, who had one of the largest collections of conjuring books in America, was impressed with Eusapia's showmanship, but far from convinced that the phenomena were real: "By substitution of hands and feet she could have done any of the manifestations. I certainly lost control of her knees on many occasions and have doubts of her hands and feet." It was not through carelessness on his part, he explained; the medium moved constantly. When he tried to take a firm grip she complained about the pressure.

Two physics professors attended the third séance: Robert W. Wood of Johns Hopkins University and Augustus Trowbridge from Princeton. They were there, with other sitters who paid fifty dollars each for the privilege, not to conduct scientific tests but to observe. Hugo Münsterberg, professor of psychology at Harvard, attended two of the séances. Carrington was to regret he had been invited. The professor's article in the February 1910 issue of *Metropolitan Magazine* revealed that Palladino had been caught in a fraud. The red-tissue-wrapped bulb provided so little illumination that one of the sitters (Edgar Scott) had been able to leave his chair and sprawl on the floor, behind and to the left of the medium. When the stool moved noisily in the dark he reached out to grab whatever was motivating it. Eusapia's left foot was trapped in his hand. She screamed, he released the foot and returned to his seat. He didn't mention the incident until he had left the séance. Munsterberg thought her hand had touched his arm several times in the dark. When he heard Scott's story he decided the medium's foot was responsible.

After Carrington read the article, he replied that no mention of a sitter grasping the medium's foot had been made during the evening. The full report of *The American Séances with Eusapia Palladino* was not published until 1954. In the notes for the ninth sitting, it is recorded that at 11:44 she "screams sharply. Reason not known." Carrington adds that she told him she had shrieked because "a human hand had grasped her left ankle, pulled it sideways . . . . No one was near her at the time and we were unable to find any explanation for this incident."

If a sitter had caught her in the act, Carrington added, it would "merely prove that she had attempted fraud on this particular occasion." He went on to ridicule the suggestion that she "had slipped her foot out of her shoe . . . since she was wearing high boots at the time." With the floor-length dresses Palladino wore, it was impossible to tell how many of the buttons of the boot had been fastened at the start of the evening. In the dark it would have been easy for her to undo them. As to slipping feet in and out of boots, other mediums of the time had been detected in precisely the same action. European investigators had noted that though the toes of her shoes protruded from the edge of her skirt she could have used a free foot hidden by the folds of her dress to help lift a table.

In January 1910, two months and twenty-four séances after her arrival in New York, Palladino was engaged for a series of tests in a physics laboratory at Columbia University. Tests is scarcely the right word—no special scientific devices were employed; the professors chose to rely on their senses of sight, sound, and touch. At first Edmund B. Wilson, the biologist, thought her hands were under perfect control in the dark. He had a firm grasp on her wrist when he was seated to her right. Later when he took a place at her left he was not permitted to hold her left hand; instead she touched him with her fingers. He reasoned she was making one hand play the part of two—the ruse that had been detected frequently before.

In the light when she made the table tilt away from her, Wilson said she pushed it up with a palm of one hand, which rested on the edge of the top on her side. During this portion of her performance her hands were not controlled. He also noted that when a wire was passed between the tilted table and the medium's body in an effort to discover if a thread or rod kept the table balanced on its two far legs, she had both hands pushing on the top. She lifted first one, then the other but always had one on the table to maintain its position.

A report on the four séances at Columbia was printed in the May 20, 1910, issue of Science. The New York Times and other newspapers quoted it at length:

> So far as these sittings afford data for judgment, the conclusion of the undersigned is unfavorable to the view that any supernormal power in this case exists.

It has been said that Eusapia finds trickery more easy than the exercise of her supernatural power; that she consequently resorts to the former whenever the control by the sitters permits it, and that the only fair test is had when there is such control as makes trickery absolutely impossible. During a fourth sitting, at which the undersigned were present, something like this control was exercised, and while this was the case none of the so-called evidential phenomena took place.

The names of the investigators followed: Charles L. Dana, M.D., Professor of Nervous Diseases; William Hallock, Professor of Physics; Dickinson Miller, Professor of Philosophy; Frederick Peterson, M.D., Professor of Psychiatry; W. B. Pitkin, Lecturer on Philosophy; Edmund B. Wilson, Professor of Biology; and two professors from other universities who had aided in the tests: Augustus Trowbridge of Harvard and R. W. Wood from Johns Hopkins.

Professor Miller, who had arranged the sittings at Columbia, also booked the medium for two séances in April. If Palladino cheated, he wanted a precise description of her more baffling feats —the complete levitation of the table, for example. He met with Winfield S. Davis, who for many years had appeared professionally exposing spiritualistic marvels. Davis had given his friend Richard Hodgson the secrets of hand and foot releases before he went to England to test Palladino at Cambridge. Davis suggested that magicians who knew mediums' methods should control her. James A. Kellogg, John William Sargent, Joseph F. Rinn, and Davis met at the home of Professor Herbert G. Lord to discuss their strategy. Davis, Kellogg, and Rinn were also officers of the Metropolitan Psychical Society; Sargent was a past president of the Society of American Magicians.

Rinn was chosen as an undercover man, and Warner C. Pyne, the student who had taken shorthand notes during the sittings at Columbia, volunteered to be his assistant. The two séances with the magicians in charge must have been the strangest Palladino ever gave. For long periods there were no manifestations; then the phenomena were produced as strongly as ever; then they ceased again. She didn't know why until Professor Joseph Jastrow pub-

lished his article in the May 4, 1910, issue of *Collier's Weekly*.
The conspirators had arranged for Davis to cough as a signal
for them to tighten or relax their control. During the relaxed period raps were heard, and the table tilted and floated. A cough terminated the activity as the magicians took firm grips on both her
hands and feet. Not until another cough did they give her leeway
to go into action again.

Her greatest surprise must have been when she read that Rinn
and Pyne, clad in black from head to toe, had crawled into the
room when the lights were dimmed and hidden under chairs occupied by two ladies. With their heads close to her feet they had
seen her strike the table leg with her shoe to produce raps. They
also saw her put her left foot under the left table leg as the table
tilted to the right. When she lifted her foot, all four legs rose from
the floor. She had pressed down with her left hand on the tabletop
to clamp the table between hand and foot. With the table held by
this pressure, it would go up when she lifted her foot, down when
she lowered it.

I have demonstrated Palladino's technique not only during my
stage performances but also on Johnny Carson's NBC-TV "Tonight
Show" and in my television special "Houdini: The Impossible Possible."

The explanations of Palladino's tricks in widely circulated
newspapers and magazines shattered Carrington's hopes for a
richly endowed psychical research laboratory. She became the subject of numerous editorials and cartoons denouncing occult deceptions. Yet he refused to waver from his firm position that though
she occasionally cheated she also produced genuine manifestations.
To bolster his case he took Howard Thurston, then America's leading stage illusionist, to see the Italian mystic in her apartment on
113 Street. Thurston was amazed. He wrote: "I am convinced that
the table was levitated without fraudulent use of her hands, feet,
knees or any part of her body, or by any mechanical contrivance."
He offered a thousand dollars to anyone who could prove that she
cheated.

Thurston, who began his career as a card manipulator, could

produce fantastic spirit effects on the stage. In that area he was an expert; at psychical research he was a novice. His thousand-dollar offer was safe, for unless Palladino agreed to perform under test conditions no one could really prove that she had used the methods that had been revealed.

Joseph Rinn, who in his black coveralls had been beneath Palladino's table, made a counteroffer. He would give a certified check for a thousand dollars to her if she could produce genuine phenomena while laced up in a canvas bag. Eusapia replied that once she had been tied up in a sack in Vienna and had nearly suffocated; never again. Rinn made another offer. They were both to be tied in exactly the same way. If he couldn't duplicate any manifestation she produced in these circumstances, the money was hers.

The *New York Times* of May 18, 1910, reported that Eusapia had accepted Rinn's second challenge. She said she would permit a complete examination to be made of her body and the objects she planned to use and that she would allow a committee to bind her legs to a chair. The ends of the cord would be nailed to the floor. Her wrists were to be tied with a ten- or twelve-inch space between them. Other cords would run from her wrists and be tied to those of sitters on her right and left. She specified that her upper arms were not to be tied to her body.

She said she would submit to this test "in the name of science," as she had succeeded in the past when tied in this fashion. However, she could not promise what the outcome would be.

This was not the way Rinn wished her to be bound; there would be too much slack in the bonds on her hands and legs; when tied this way in Europe the restraints had not hampered her movements. He insisted that she be tied more securely. Carrington replied that Rinn was demanding unfair conditions. Eventually they agreed on terms. Professor Joseph Jastrow; the Reverend Henry Frank, pastor of the Berkeley Lyceum Church; and Thurston, the magician, were to make up the committee. Carrington was to be the master of ceremonies.

The date set for the test was Sunday evening, May 22; the

place, an office in the Times Tower on Broadway. The newspaper had a cabinet constructed to the medium's specifications. Carrington was to supply everything but the cord, which Rinn would bring. Kellogg and Davis were to tie Palladino under the supervision of Sargent and Rinn.

Everyone came that evening except the medium. Eusapia sent word she would not permit Jastrow to be on the committee. She also demanded twelve inches of slack between her tied hands and legs. With this much play Rinn knew she could produce raps and lift the table with her foot. She had said that even if she produced only a single manifestation this would entitle her to the award. Her last message that evening said she had decided to withdraw from the contest.

Rinn issued a new challenge. If she could cause an ordinary lead pencil to rise even a few inches above a table without touching it, he would give her *two* thousand dollars. Eusapia ignored him.

Palladino sailed for home June 18, 1910. When Everard Feilding read of her fiasco in New York, he recalled the startling phenomena he had seen in Naples scarcely more than a year and a half before. Was it possible that he could have been deceived by such ridiculously simple tricks? With his friend William Marriott, a magician who had exposed psychic fraud for *Pearson's Magazine,* he went to Italy again. This time her deceptions were obvious. When one knows how a feat can be done and what to look for, only the most skillful performer can maintain the illusion in the face of such informed scrutiny.

Eusapia Palladino died May 16, 1918, at the age of sixty-four. Her fame was perpetuated by Hereward Carrington in the many books he wrote after her death and by Sir Arthur Conan Doyle, Nandor Fodor, Harry Price, and others who, though they never saw her, believed at least some of her phenomena were genuine.

The magicians I have known who attended her séances in New York and who took part in the exposure said that she was an excellent showman, but they saw no evidence of psychic force. She frequently varied her methods. Raps can be produced by pressing firmly on a tabletop and sliding the fingers ever so slightly. In addition to actually striking a table leg with the edge of one's sole, raps can also be made more subtly. If the edge of the sole is pressed firmly against a table leg while the foot is on the floor, a minute forward movement will produce a scrape which sounds like a rap on the surface of the table.

How did she levitate the table when the legs nearest her were encased in square protective wooden sheaths? Joseph Rinn, who was a fellow member of the Society of American Magicians, assured me that she used her released left foot. In this instance it was not put under a table leg, but extended horizontally so that the center of the table was balanced on her toes. Her table was light, less than twelve pounds, and she had short, muscular legs.

Using the techniques described earlier to release either a hand or a foot, she could produce her impressive manifestations without the sitters' being aware of what she was doing. She could remove her foot from her shoe or boot and those who looked beneath the table would see the tips of both shoes protruding from her long skirt, never realizing that the foot was free. As a séance progressed she moved her chair bit by bit closer to her cabinet. With her free foot she could reach back and bring the stool or one of the musical instruments forward until it was by her side. Then, with her foot under it, an upward kick would send the object into the air, or she could lift it to the tabletop.

W. S. Davis explained how Eusapia levitated a table while she and the sitters were standing. First with hand pressure she rocked it back and forth, then tilted it away from her; when the left table leg was off the floor she pushed her free foot forward and caught the leg on her foot, the black skirt material hiding this action. A sharp kick upward caused the table to "float," then drop to the floor with a bang.

What Carrington described as the "blowing out" of the drapes behind the medium was brought about by her free hand, which reached back and swept the panel forward. This was done when a bulb wrapped with red tissue was the only illumination.

Palladino's years of practice, knowledge of how spectators could be diverted away from the point of trickery with a word, a nod, or a squirm, enabled her to baffle the distinguished men who were experts in their own fields but unfamiliar with mediumistic chicanery.

What about the cool breezes that sitters felt during the séances? Hold your hand, palm toward your mouth at a distance of twelve inches. With your lips almost, but not quite, closed blow forcibly toward your palm. You will feel the chill air. Most people believe human breath is warm and it is if you are very close, an inch or so away from the source. However, as it travels through the air it becomes cold.

On occasion Palladino used strong human hairs to move objects. Camille Flammarion, the French astronomer, detected her as she caused the balance of a scale to tip with a hair. Carrington also caught her in the act during the ninth American séance. He saw her pull a hair from her head, stretch it taut between her hands. When her hands, each several inches away from the tray of the scale, moved downward, the hair forced the tray down too.

Other mediums have lifted tables with small rubber suction cups attached to their hands, or with a slotted finger ring which engaged the head of a nail in the tabletop. Tables have been lifted by horsehair and by metal bars which were strapped under the medium's sleeves to their arms. Some of these devices are ingenious. The bars are in tubes and extend only when the operator drops her hands. When her palms are placed on the tabletop the bars extend under it. A lift of the hands and the table floats. A hook attached to a leather belt around the medium's waist has also been used to support a table while the performer walks about a room with only fingertips, seemingly, touching the top.

Mediums can make tables float without touching them, though they stand several feet away. Confederates carry out the necessary actions. I have seen observers whose eyes never left the medium's hands completely baffled by the simplest of deceits. Two confederates, one to the medium's right, the other to the left, had their fingers on the tabletop but their thumbs under it. When they raised their hands their thumbs lifted the table.

W. S. Davis used a simple device to cause a table to remain tilted though he did not touch it. This was a slender black rod about six inches long. This was positioned between his body and the side of the table closest to him. His hands and feet were under control and away from the top and legs. When he moved his stomach forward the rod pushed the table up until it was balanced on the two far legs. When he relaxed his forward thrust the black rod dropped unseen and unheard to the carpet and the table banged back in place. In a dimly lighted room the black rod could not be seen even while it held the table at an angle.

Palladino's great strength was that she required neither special equipment nor confederates to perform her most talked-about feats. She was a master of séance-room psychology. Even when intelligent men caught her cheating, she could usually convince them that the feats they had not detected were legitimate phenomena.

D'ANGELO'S INVISIBLE HAND

In a dark room it is a simple matter to produce mystifying phenomena. Believers never suspect that the shroudlike ghost is a piece of luminous cheesecloth or that it is the medium's hand, not a ghost's, that lifts a trumpet and brings it to her lips so that the "departed" may speak. They are not aware that the tiny blue lights that flicker over the medium's head are her beads coated with Strobelite, a phosphorescent paint that glows in the dark. The beads are exposed to light before the séance begins; then she covers them with a scarf around her shoulders. In the dark they are raised, shaken, and dropped back in place to be covered again with the scarf. At one séance I saw a mysterious green streak in the air and only when the lights were turned on did I realize it had been made by the luminous dial of a sitter's wristwatch as he reached up in the dark to brush his hair.

One doesn't expect psychic wonders in broad daylight or even in an office with sunlight streaming through the windows. Yet in the 1950's it was reported that a Neapolitan medium could generate a psychic force so powerful that it could punch as effectively as a fist; he could produce the force in a brilliantly lighted room.

It was said that he discovered this invisible extension of his personality when he was sixteen. A voluptuous young girl in a summer dress was walking down a street a dozen or so feet away. He found the desire to touch her overwhelming. He made a caressing gesture and was amazed when she swung around ready to slap the face of her molester. When she saw that no one was close enough to touch her, she fainted. He ran away. Finally, exhausted, he fell to the ground. He was in the graveyard of a church. Perhaps his surroundings influenced him, for he vowed he would never again use this strange new power so capriciously.

Achille D'Angelo became famous for his psychic cures. A few waves of his pudgy fingers, and pain would cease, the lame would walk, and those who could scarcely see regained their vision.

John Zischang, a United Press reporter, phoned me in 1952 with the news that the celebrated medium was in New York. The Neapolitan healer had planned to make the visit incognito; he hadn't seen his brother or sisters who lived here in thirty-five years. Long before his arrival, however, the Italian community knew he was coming. D'Angelo had been interviewed by the Paris representative of Manhattan's WOV radio station.

The tape, which had been sent by plane, was aired while D'Angelo's ship was still on the Atlantic. The broadcast in Italian, word-of-mouth accounts of his cures, and the many stories that had been written of his wonders in the Italian press created a near sensation among the Italo-American population. One of the most unusual welcoming crowds that ever assembled on a New York pier awaited the arrival of his ship. Old men with bandaged heads, women in wheel chairs, and children wearing braces as they leaned on crutches pressed against the barrier to the customs area hoping to glimpse the man who could cure their afflictions. Some had his likeness, torn from newspapers and magazines, to be sure they would recognize him.

The noted psychic was not a physician, and he was well aware that New York authorities were skeptical of those who healed with their hands. Moreover, he was here for a holiday, not to practice his art. He eluded the supplicants and reached the home of his brother in Mount Vernon, New York, without incident. A news reporter from WOV found him there. D'Angelo patiently explained that his visit was social, not spiritual. He would not give consultations; he wished to spend his time with his relatives and see the sights like any other tourist.

Their Italo-American listeners should know this, the reporter said, otherwise D'Angelo would be mobbed wherever he went. D'Angelo agreed to come to the station for an interview. The broadcast announcement that he would appear the next day produced telegrams, special delivery letters, and phone calls from three states. He had to fight his way through a crowd on the street to enter the studio. Hundreds were pleading for a personal session with the great healer.

John Zischang succeeded where the multitude failed. He was interested in the medium's phenomena, not his cures. Rino Negri, an executive with a Manhattan advertising agency, brought D'Angelo to the offices of the United Press. There the reporter, in the presence of Gay Pauley, another member of the staff, had an experience from which he had not fully recovered when he called me.

He had felt the full force of D'Angelo's invisible hand. Though Zischang's eyes were closed, Miss Pauley verified that the medium had not touched him. D'Angelo had agreed to give another demonstration. Would I be interested in seeing it?

The reporter had assembled specialists in several fields for D'Angelo's second séance: Mrs. Laura Dale, from the American Society for Psychical Research; Dr. John Greig, associate professor of physics at New York University; Paul Morris, then chairman of the board of the Parent Assembly of the Society of American Magicians; and Robert Hewitt, another United Press reporter.

The suite in which we met consisted of a waiting room and an office, longer than it was wide. From the windows of the office one could see the street far below and feel the heat of the afternoon sun.

D'Angelo was neatly attired in a dark blue suit, white shirt, and pale blue silk tie. His black shoes were polished to a gleam and he had an illustrated Italian book under his arm which detailed the highlights of his career. He was shorter and plumper than I had expected. His white wavy hair and dark eyes were his most distinguishing features. I would imagine he was in his early fifties.

He specified in English that no more than four people could enter the office to see him perform, then added he would repeat the demonstration for those who waited.

Mrs. Dale, Greig, Morris and Hewitt followed him as he went through the doorway, and shortly the door was closed. As we sat in the waiting room I asked Zischang if he had any idea how the psychic thrusts were made. He replied he hadn't, that was why he had invited us to observe.

The door to the inner office opened. Four puzzled people filed out. I took Paul Morris aside and asked him what he had seen. "Nothing," he replied, "I volunteered to act as the subject." He had been seated in a chair and told to close his eyes. After a short wait he felt a blast of icy air on his neck, then two sharp jabs as though a finger had poked him. Those who looked on said D'Angelo had not been responsible—at least not physically—for the jabs. Were the observers on all sides? No, Paul answered, his chair had been at one end of the room, they were seated at the other. We agreed that if Paul could see the repeat performance he would be on one side of D'Angelo and I on the other so that we could keep him as much in view as possible.

By then, D'Angelo announced he was ready. It was warm in the office, and the medium had removed his jacket. His shirt sleeves were summer length, just above his elbows.

Dr. Greig, who had seen the previous demonstration, volunteered to act as the medium's subject. He sat in a chair at the far end of the room near the windows and to the left. Paul and I walked forward to stand several feet away on either side of the chair. D'Angelo waved us back and indicated where we should sit.

Greig closed his eyes. D'Angelo rubbed his hands together briskly, then making hypnotic gestures began to circle his subject's chair. As he walked slowly around Greig, constantly waving his hands, he tripped on the cord from a telephone which was resting on a nearby desk. He toppled against Greig's shoulder, smiled, shrugged, then continued his orbit. When he had completed the circle, he asked his subject to open his eyes again.

Greig was bombarded with questions. What had he felt? Would he describe his sensations? The physicist thought a moment and said he had felt a push, rather firm, on his left shoulder. This, we said, must have been the medium falling against him. Then he was aware of a steady stream of cold air on the nape of his neck. He indicated the spot. No, there were no jabs, such as Paul Morris had experienced.

Paul and I thought there was a good reason why no jabs had been forthcoming. When we had been moved back by D'Angelo we sat as far apart as we could and we had the medium almost constantly in view. Any false move would have been immediately apparent.

Houdini used to make an offer to mediums. He would give them a thousand dollars or more if, after seeing one of their feats three times, he couldn't duplicate it. The first view was to get the normal audience reaction, the second was to check out telltale moves, the third was to verify the previous observations.

I asked D'Angelo if he would use me as a subject. He smiled and shrugged; he was exhausted, he said, and his psychic power was depleted.

We thanked him for his demonstration, and before he left, by way of slight reciprocation, I produced a flash of fire in the air and caused a small ball to vanish from my hand and join the one D'Angelo held tightly in his fist. Until then he hadn't known I was a magician. I wondered what his reaction to the conjuring would be. He winked and said, "That should make you popular with the girls."

Mrs. Dale said later that while she did not know how the jabs and cold air had been produced, she would have to see further demonstrations before she was convinced D'Angelo had used psychic force.

Dr. Greig agreed. Both the wind and the punches could be

simulated, he said, by a variety of devices. For instance, a compressed air container or a tube and a bellows for the cold breeze, a sort of peashooter concealed in the mouth which could eject balls of some transparent substance for the jabs. He admitted, however, that he had seen no evidence such contraptions were used.

Paul Morris maintained that it would be impossible for investigators to observe fully what happened until D'Angelo performed completely surrounded. What we had seen were demonstrations under the medium's conditions.

I questioned John Zischang about the earlier séance when he had been the subject. He mentioned a detail I had not known before. After D'Angelo had made several gestures, Gay Pauley told him, the medium had crossed the room, jabbed her lightly in the neck, and indicated that this was what Zischang was feeling at that precise moment. Then the medium returned to complete his circling of the chair. Zischang had felt cold wind, a light tap on the forehead, another on his shoulder, and, after a brief interval, the jab in the neck.

The solution to D'Angelo's phenomena seemed to me so obvious that I hesitated to mention it until I tried out my theory and tested its effect. Psychic power was not needed.

I invited several friends to my apartment. One sat with eyes closed in a chair. I made mysterious gestures toward him as the others looked on. At one point I came over to a watcher, jabbed him twice in the neck, and whispered that this was what the person in the chair felt at that precise moment. Then I circled the chair again.

When my subject opened his eyes and was asked to describe his sensations, he told of feeling a chill wind and two strange thumps in the neck. "Did you see him touch me?" he asked my other guests. All agreed I hadn't.

Did D'Angelo use psychic power for his demonstrations? I didn't. I produced the chill wind by using the trick of an earlier Neapolitan medium, Eusapia Palladino. With my lips slightly open I blew a blast of air through them as I walked around the chair.

When I was behind my subject's head and momentarily one hand was out of view of the onlookers I jabbed my index finger twice in his neck. Then I had approached one of the watchers, jabbed him, and explained that my subject would feel these jabs. Back near the chair I made a few more passes with my hands, then asked him to open his eyes.

It sounds so simple when one reads a description of this technique, it is hard to believe that anyone could be fooled by such trickery, let alone attribute the cause to psychic force. I can assure you that many of the most baffling mediumistic feats are equally uncomplicated. The public expects trickery from a magician, miracles from a medium.

Years later John Kobler, who had been in Europe gathering material for an article on ESP, called me to tell of a weird experience he had had in Italy: cold winds and ghostly touches. "Think of the medium's name," I said, then pretending to read Kobler's mind, I spelled out Achille D'Angelo.

When Kobler told me how baffled he had been by the Italian mystic, I described my experiments and mentioned there were many other ways to produce chill winds and ghostly touches. The movement of the hands making the passes can generate enough air current to simulate a fair breeze. The use of a long hair clipped between the fingers of one hand can cause the skin of the subject with closed eyes to tingle. As the hair is invisible at a distance of a few feet, witnesses will swear that the hands did not come close enough to touch the subject. Gusts of wind also can be produced through a thin rubber tube, running down one sleeve, under a coat. One end is fastened to a finger ring or held between the fingers, while the rubber bulb on the other end is concealed under the armpit and pressed by the arm.

When a subject's eyes are closed, deception is easier. Try this. Extend the forefingers of both hands. Hold the tips of the fingers three inches in front of a friend's eyes. Tell him to shut his eyes so that you can put a finger on each lid. When his eyes are shut, immediately extend the second finger of your right hand, put the forefinger on his right eyelid, the second finger on his left eyelid. Say that you will cause a spirit force to tap him on the back of his head. Use your free left hand to reach across and thump. Quickly bring this hand with the forefinger extended back to its original position. As you lift the two right fingers from his eyelids, bend the second right finger back as it was at the start and move both hands away as though the index fingers of both hands had been on the eyelids. The subject opens his eyes when the finger pressure is removed. He sees the index fingers and cannot understand how the mysterious tap was produced with these on his eyelids.

I have seen a professed psychic demonstrate the force which she said emanated from her index finger by pointing it toward a cigarette on a table. As her finger approached the cigarette, it rolled away. Previously she had rubbed the finger briskly on her silk dress, implying that static electricity had something to do with the uncanny action of the cigarette.

You could rub your finger on silk for years and still never duplicate her marvel. However, if at the moment you extend your finger toward the cigarette you also send a stream of air from between your almost closed lips in its direction, as she did, you would have seen the cigarette suddenly take on life and move.

On the subject of objects moving though untouched by human hands, three members of my World War II platoon saw something in the bar of a small inn near Morlaix which made them doubt their sanity. A Norman farmer put the drawer from a match box upside down on a table, made several gestures over it, then walked to the other side of the room. He wiggled his fingers. The object moved slightly. Now he opened and closed his fingers extending them toward the table. Slowly the match box drawer slid three inches across the surface. They looked under the table, felt for strings or hairs. There seemed no possible explanation. The Frenchman laughed and lifted the drawer. The howl which came from the soldiers could be heard, I am told, above the dull thuds of artillery shells which were traveling toward Brest. Under the drawer was a big black bug struggling to escape.

ASTRAL PROJECTION

The first person I met who claimed he could leave his body was Harold Sherman, the president and executive director of ESP Research Associates Foundation, which has its headquarters in Little Rock, Arkansas. I was introduced to the stocky man with white hair before we were interviewed at the WINS radio studio in New York in 1965. I had read in his book *How to Make ESP Work for You* that once, while on a table in his doctor's office, he had emerged from his physical self and gazed down as the doctor lanced a water blister on the toe of the now spiritless body. Another time, when he was relaxing on his studio couch, he had projected himself astrally. I had never seen anyone perform this remarkable feat, and I hoped Sherman would demonstrate his unusual talent in the studio. I watched him closely for thirty minutes, but not once did he say that his inner self had left his skin.

Both saints and sinners in the past reportedly sent their psychic doubles through space. On Holy Thursday in 1226, Saint Anthony of Padua allegedly appeared at the same time in two places. Religious officials at a monastery in Limoges said he was there participating in their ritual while he was seen on his knees, head covered with his cowl, during his service across town in the St. Pierre du Queyroix church.

In 1774 Alphonse de Liguori fasted during his imprisonment at Arezzo, then slept, it is said, for five days. When he awoke he claimed he had been in Rome by the side of Clement XIV. Those who attended the pope during his last hours verified that de Liguori had been present.

Count Alexis Tolstoy asserted he had seen the psychic double of Daniel Dunglas Home, the nineteenth-century medium, at a railway depot three hours before his train pulled in and Home arrived in the flesh. Ophelia Corrales, a Costa Rican singer, could apparently project her voice if not her spirit. When she sang, her voice is reported to have been heard miles away from her physical body, although she herself was unaware of the sonic projection.

The Reverend Arthur Ford, America's best-known trance medium, told me as we talked of his career in 1968 that he, too, once had an out-of-the-body experience. As he was being operated upon, he left his body and watched the surgeons work. It was not something, he admitted, that he could do at will.

The Reverend Dr. Gilbert N. Holloway, however, is perfectly willing to travel spiritually to any place in the world at the behest of those who attend his inspirational meetings. I saw him on the "Alan Burke Show" on New York's Channel 5 in 1968, and six of the seven members of the studio audience who asked him to project astrally said he accurately described the places to which they had directed him.

As I listened another night to Barry Farber's WOR radio show, it was obvious when Holloway described my friend Felix Greenfield's apartment that his ethereal spirit had gone to the wrong address.

Gilbert Holloway was born in Minneapolis in 1915. According to the jacket of his book *Beyond ESP*, he was "a brilliant student," made Phi Beta Kappa at the age of nineteen, earned his B.A. at Stanford University, studied at Union Theological Seminary, and received a master's in education and history at Columbia. He started his present career "as one of America's outstanding spiritual teachers" at the age of twenty-one.

Holloway does not fit the usual notion of a psychic in appearance. He is an affable, exuberant man with an oval face, receding gray hair, and a gift of gab. If you ran across him in a hotel lobby, the chances are that you would think he was a Rotarian or an automobile salesman on his way to close a deal.

His conversation gives a clue to his calling. His talk is sprinkled with such phrases as "advanced thinkers," "the vestibules of truth," "the powers of the spirit," and "thirsting souls."

The press release announcing Holloway's book in November 1969 said that he had predicted Richard Nixon would win the election. Let's see what he said in New York before voters went to the polls: "And about a year ago in Texas, in the central part of America, long before the heating up of the present election, I saw that the real dark horse of the 1968 campaign would be the candidacy of George C. Wallace . . . tonight just ten days before the election, I have seen this go into a tremendous momentum, as I predicted, and there is still the strong possibility, as I mentioned months ago, of Mr. Wallace not only getting an extraordinary vote, and he will as I believe in prophecy, but he very well may be elected President of the United States."

That was Holloway's public statement less than thirty minutes before I gave him a name and address for his astral spirit to visit. I attended six of Holloway's lecture-demonstrations in New York in 1968 and had transcripts made of his statements so that I could fully assess what he said.

As he "attuned to the person," Holloway explained, "I immediately receive a stream of impressions, they run through my consciousness and I speak of these, give these forth quickly and they usually pertain quite accurately to that person. If I were perfectly attuned to the spirit, I'd never make a mistake, I'd be a hundred percent all the time, but this is very difficult. My batting average will run around eighty-five or ninety percent usually."

Standing on a platform in a hotel assembly room with several baskets of flowers behind him as a background, he shut his eyes and asked me to repeat the name and address. I did. Here are his statements and my assessment of their accuracy. This reading is given in complete detail so the reader may see the generalities which, with even a little luck, will apply to many people.

"As I touch this person and this place this lady is very attractive [yes] and has unusual eyes [no]. She doesn't use a great deal of eye makeup, just a bit to highlight this feature. [No.] I hear music around her. Even right now, if you were to call her I think there's music playing in this apartment [I made a phone call immediately afterward. Neither radio nor television set had been on. There was no music] and this lady is a gifted person. She is sensitive along this line—in fact she is so gifted that if you were to check right now she would be aware that some kind of spiritual or psychic contact was being established with her. [She has no gift or even interest in psychic affairs and did not know that Holloway's spirit was visiting.] She might even see me in the spirit standing in the room. It's possible that she would be aware of something of this nature. [Not so, as mentioned earlier.]

"This lady has had an illness [no] and I see her overcoming this as she has largely done so, but I can see her feeling weak [yes, she was recovering from an operation done four months earlier] and very dejected and very, very sad for a time [she insists that she was neither dejected nor sad] and she's come back from this and seems to be back more in her full powers at present. [Note he said she was ill, not that she had had an operation.] I see the symbol of Mercury here and it's full of lights, a very lively person. [Her astrological sign is Libra, but she is a lively person.]

"I see lively colors in this apartment as I—as I go here—and also some very clever ideas in decor. [Yes, but I was hoping he would tell me what they were.] I see green here, I see there's some red or some very dark orange red, a very unusual shading on a piece of furniture here or even partly on one wall. [This is difficult to evaluate, these colors and many others are in one way or another in the apartment. There is no "unusual shading on a piece of furniture or partly on one wall."]

"And I get a fiery effect here, something to do with fire, I don't know whether it's a representation of fire or something else, but there's a strange effect here. [There is a painting in the bedroom of a fire walk.]

"This lady is interested in the ethereal conditions [not even slightly], and she has created the decor here in overall almost like an ethereal effect. [She didn't create the decor; it is not ethereal.]

"She also meditates and prays in some unusual way [no], is aware of some other kind of Eastern religion [no], and I get a spiritual vibration in this place as I go here. [I can't imagine why.]

"There's an unusual rug here too, which is of a golden color like a throw rug in part of one of the inner rooms of the apartment as I touch this. [No.]

"I see books here. [Yes.] This lady writes a great deal, she has an extensive correspondence. [She is a writer, but carries on a limited correspondence.]

"One of her eyes bothers her. [No.] And I see her sometimes rubbing her eyes this way. [Yes, everybody does in the way he demonstrated.] And also, too, I feel a very careful diet. [No.] I see a juicer here. [Possibly; there is an unused one in the storeroom.]

"She has studied diets. [No.] She reminds me of Gloria Swanson a little in this regard [few things would appeal to her less than Miss Swanson's organic food diets] and is careful in what she eats [no], because if she were to eat carelessly or just eat most anything as a lot of people do she would have a severe stomach ache or gastric difficulties and she seems to guard against this. [All wrong.]

"There's a male person, a male presence here of whom this lady is very proud. [She was alone.] Whether this person is there all the time I don't know, it could be a son [she has no son], or a protégé [she has no protégé], but it seems he is not here part of the time as he may be out on business or even out of the city but is much loved.

"This lady is telepathically inclined [far from it] and often feels herself to be in rapport with loved ones at a distance. [No.]

"And someone, I don't think it is she, it may be someone else in the apartment, has what is called necrophobia, or the fear of death. [No, the other occupant of the apartment who was not there at the time has no such phobia.]

"And this lady, they do not permit any morbid things here, no death's head jokes [a family joke is a puppet skeleton which hangs in a closet], because there is a tendency, this is a curious thing to say, but I see it and I mention it, some tendency of necrophobia here and an effort is made to keep things light, happy and the spirit is redirected shall I say, very much to the accent on the living and on the positive and beautiful side of life. [Again no to the necrophobia idea.]

"You know this lady is very sensitive to noise [no], and there's a fire station not far from here [no], and I can hear the fire trucks outside the window [no] and she puts her window right up right away [no], maybe because the scream of a police siren or a fire truck bothers her and upsets her. [She has never been known to complain about sirens or open a window to see a fire or police vehicle.]

"And the last thing I'm trying to say before I withdraw from this address and this person is that she's very tenderhearted [she says she isn't] and she can feel through empathy the sufferings of other persons even at a distance and I see her at times praying to have released from her the feelings of a suffering in a distant person. [No.]

"And, oh, I must add this too, this lady has visions and unusual psychic experiences at times. [No.] Some are similar to what I do and what I'm doing. [Definitely not.] That's why I thought perhaps she might even be in rapport with me in some degree even as I am in touch with her. [She didn't know he was there.]

"And her mouth bothers her here at times [Holloway touched his jaw. She never had a pain in that area] and there's some dental work that needs to be done here, but she doesn't like the dentist much, she's avoiding this [she had been to the dentist the week before and received a clean bill of health, not even a cavity this visit], but I do feel a need to have something done here in the lower jaw. [There was nothing wrong in that area at that time or since.]

"This is Dr. Holloway reaching out in the projection of spiritual consciousness to this lady, now withdrawing and here I'm back with you."

He opened his eyes, smiled, and asked me: "All right? Was I there?"

I told him that to be fair I would have to evaluate what he had said, which I have done above. The lady, of course, was my wife. Our apartment is practically a museum of magic. It is filled with books on the subject in many languages. The walls are covered with paintings, engravings, and old prints of conjurers. There are statuettes of magicians, automaton cup-and-ball players, and even a bust of Houdini. I was surprised he had not noticed this very special motif.

Once when I attended a Holloway meeting, a man I knew gave him a fictitious name and an address which, had it existed, would have been under the waters of the Chesapeake Bay. Holloway apparently thought a house was there for he described the colors in several rooms, saw some books, a throw rug, and a family pet.

When I asked Holloway to travel astrally the second time, I gave him the address of one of my friend P. C. Sorcar's three houses in Calcutta, India. He did not seem to be fazed. He asked, however, if Sorcar was a man or woman. Sometimes when he neglects to do this he describes a female as a male. He shut his eyes and stated he was in Calcutta. He said Sorcar had an unusual face, "almost like a chisel . . . a triangular face." P. C. has a round, cherubic face. He said, "I see bird symbols around him." I didn't when I visited Sorcar.

Holloway thought "he may have been a protégé of Nehru." He wasn't. He scored, however, when he said the man "traveled a great deal" and that I had "a rapport with this man . . . there's a certain understanding here, a certain tacit understanding." He didn't mention Sorcar's business; Sorcar is the best-known Indian stage magician. Twice I have arranged for him to come to the United States to appear in my network television specials. There's an understanding between us, but it has never been tacit.

When I attended Holloway's meetings, I struck up conversations with other people for whom he had given readings. There were few skeptics: no one bothered to write down his statements and almost everyone could say afterwards that many of the things he had stated were true. Some even went a little out of their way to confirm his pronouncements.

He told one woman during a personal reading: "You have a strong mystical, spiritual, idealistic flavor in your personality." She was delighted. He went on to say her life had not been an easy one. "You have reached out for things and not been able to grasp them all. . . . You have a goal, you have a sort of vision in your life and I see you following through to this, even though at times you have been very discouraged." There is, he continued, "a person very close to you who helps to sustain you in this goal, that is so dear to you." When Holloway was finished she said he was 99 percent right, but one thing puzzled her. Who was the dear person who was so close to her? Perhaps, she suggested helpfully, Mr. Holloway meant her cat.

BURIED ALIVE

Psychical researchers have been baffled when fakirs were buried in air-tight boxes for periods which medical men claimed were beyond human endurance. I learned when I was in India that so many holy men had been found in a condition that necessitated prompt and permanent reinterment when their temporary coffins were opened that the government had banned the dangerous demonstrations in 1955.

As a boy in Baltimore I had seen Rahman Bey, "The Egyptian Miracle Man," buried in a coffin under a mound of sand on the stage of the Garden Theater. I looked on many times as Chundra Bey, a Hindu, was enclosed in a glass coffin, then submerged in a tank of water that had transparent sides, during the performances of Howard Thurston, the great magician, at Ford's Theater. I also sat in the bleachers at the Oriole ball park, September 29, 1927, when Chundra Bey was buried alive beneath the playing field.

Since then I have witnessed other living burials, though none ever approached the extended time attributed to the most noted survivalists of the past.

"It has been related that two hundred and fifty years ago, in the time of the Guru Arjun Singh," wrote John Martin Honigberger in his *Thirty-five Years in the East*, published in London in 1852, "a *Jogi Fakir* was found in his tomb in a sitting posture, at Amritsar, and was restored to life. This *fakir* is reported to have been below the ground for one hundred years; and when he revived he related many circumstances connected with the times in which he had lived. Whether this tradition be true or false, it is impossible to say; but I am of the opinion, that he who can pass four months below the ground without becoming prey to corruption, may also remain there for one year."

Honigberger had been in India when Haridas, the best-known nineteenth-century practitioner of this mysterious art, was performing. Though he wasn't an eyewitness, he talked with several people who were. Maharajah Ranjit Singh, skeptical of the stories he had heard about Haridas, summoned the survivalist to his palace in Lahore. Just how long could the mystic survive a living burial? Ranjit Singh asked. For as long as the potentate wished, Haridas answered. Forty days and forty nights was the final decision.

After a period of preparation during which a small quantity of milk was his only food, the fakir fasted for a day, bathed, purified his intestines, then removed any possible impurities from his stomach by swallowing a thin strip of cloth three fingers wide and thirty yards long. When he tugged out the swabbing material and tossed it aside, he was ready for the long ordeal.

Haridas preferred not to be buried in the earth. Should a swarm of hungry ants attack him while he was in a trance, he could not defend himself. He sat cross-legged on a large piece of linen which was wrapped around him after he completed his ritual to suspend his animation and was locked, while in a sitting position, in a box with one of the Maharajah's padlocks. This took place, reported a Dr. McGregor, who was serving in the Punjab with the British Horse Artillery, "in a small apartment below the middle of the ground." The door to the garden house above the chamber was locked, and the entrance to a tall wall which enclosed the garden house was sealed with bricks and mud. Guards were posted by the wall on a twenty-four hour alert and the long wait began.

On the fortieth day the Maharajah, his grandson, members of his court, a General Ventura, Captain Sir C. M. Wade, and Dr.

McGregor waited anxiously as the barricade in the wall was broached. The door to the garden house was unlocked, then the key was turned in the heavy lock on the box and the front panel was opened. Everything was as it had been so many days before. Inside was the motionless, linen-shrouded figure. The cloth was gently unfolded. Haridas, in a sitting position with his arms close to his body and his eyes closed, gave no evidence of life. The procedure he had outlined before the test for resuscitation began. Warm water was poured over his head; a heated block of *otta*, a perfumed substance, was balanced on his crown; and one of the wax plugs that had been inserted in his nostrils during the pre-burial rites was removed. A blast of air came from the nostril. The second plug was taken out and his mouth was opened. The fakir's tongue, which had been thrust back against the roof of his mouth during his trance, was pulled forward and *ghee*, buffalo butter, was applied to it and to his lips. The stiff legs and arms were now massaged and relaxed, and the closed eyelids were dabbed with *ghee* and lifted. The eyeballs, McGregor said, were dimmed with liquid "like those of a corpse." The body, which had been warmer than normal, now appeared more natural. The pulse of one wrist, which had not been perceptible before, began to throb. Haridas attempted to speak, but his voice was too feeble to be heard. Eventually he gained enough strength to talk with the Maharajah. Ranjit Singh put a gold chain around the mystic's neck, gave him "rings, baubles and shawls," the guards fired their guns, and there were shouts of joy from the natives as the man who had lived forty days without food came out into the Indian air.

Though the people of the Punjab seemed to accept the fakir's miracle without question, the Scottish physician was dubious. If the man had been where he could be observed rather than shut in an inaccessible place, McGregor might have shared their wonder. As it was, he believed the fakir had access to food and drink, though as to how this was managed he would not "hazard a guess." Haridas also hibernated in Jammu, Jesrota, and Amritsar.

Raja Dhyan Singh told Honigberger that Haridas was buried

at Mammu for four months. His beard was shaved before the test, and when he was exhumed his chin was still hairless—proof positive to Singh that the body had not functioned normally.

Haridas' life above ground was not one of holy self-denial. So many complaints about his roisterous behavior reached Ranjit Singh that the Maharajah planned to issue orders that the fakir leave Lahore and never return. Haridas beat him to the punch. He took off to the mountains with an attractive woman and lived in the Himalayas until he died and his body was burned. He did not, as some of his followers may have hoped, emerge Phoenixlike from the flames.

Ancient chroniclers tell tales even more fabulous than those from India. "Epimenides of Creta" was said to have slumbered forty years in a grotto before awakening, and seven refugees from religious persecution, at the time of Emperor Decius, dozed for 155 years in a cave near Ephesus.

When Rahman Bey appeared at the Selwyn Theater in New York in May 1926, his "Miracles of Fakirism" and the attendant publicity stimulated American interest in the wonders of the East. Hereward Carrington, the prolific writer on occult subjects, introduced the slender, bearded mystic with a résumé of the stranger-than-science marvels of India and Egypt, and the promise that the Egyptian would amaze and astound the audience.

With the nape of his neck and the back of his feet resting on blades, Rahman Bey permitted rocks to be cracked by hammer blows on his unsupported stomach. He jabbed long needles through his flesh; apparently read minds; hypnotized a rabbit, a chicken, and a man; then, after a brief intermission, threw himself into a trance and was buried in a box on the stage under sand. The stage burial would last as long as the audience desired, it was announced. This was ten minutes on the opening night. Before the spectators left the theater they were given slips of paper on which were inscribed peculiar mystical symbols—talismans to bring them good luck.

Rahman could have used one of the talismans himself in July.

To publicize a forthcoming vaudeville tour across the country, he announced an underwater burial in the Hudson River. After the hoist lifted the bronze coffin in which he was sealed and was about to lower it under the water, an alarm bell rang. The coffin was returned to dry ground at the end of 79th Street, and workmen cut, tore, and ripped away the lid of the container. Rahman Bey's body was wet with perspiration. When revived from his trance, he denied having pressed the signal button. Perhaps, someone in the crowd suggested, his body had rolled on it as the coffin was being lowered.

Thirteen days later Rahman Bey entered another trance. This time he was sealed in a metal box and he stayed under the surface of the Dalton swimming pool on 59th Street for a full hour.

Houdini, the relentless crusader against fraud, was challenged by the fakir's manager to duplicate this underwater endurance test. If it's a trick, the manager taunted, show it up.

Though he was fifty-two, twice the age of Rahman Bey, Houdini could not resist the dare. He went to the Boyertown Casket Company, the firm which had supplied the bronze casket for Rahman Bey's Hudson River try. He was told by the director, a man named Spatz, that the casket held 26,428 cubic inches of air. Houdini ordered a duplicate of the galvanized iron box that Rahman Bey had used at the Dalton pool. It was made by the same man who had constructed the one for the fakir—Harold Williams of the Du Wico Electric Company on West 41st Street. Bey had used a single air cap on the lid; Houdini ordered two—five-inch bronze marine plates—reasoning that air would circulate more freely before two plates were fastened tight. He also had a telephone and batteries installed, which displaced an additional 100 cubic inches. This container, like Bey's, held 34,398 cubic inches of air—less the space occupied by the telephone gear.

There was only one way to find out how long he could survive in the box and that was to experiment. Houdini used a glass top rather than the metal one for his tests so that he could be observed by his doctor. The first secret try was made July 31 with Dr. Wil-

liam Stone, who lived at 48 West 88th Street, and his stage assistants looking on.

Houdini remained almost motionless. After a quarter of an hour
he began to perspire. He heard Stone say as he looked down
through the glass top: "I would not do that for $500." Later the
doctor said: "Oh, I guess he can do it for an hour." In the final
minutes of the test Houdini had been so conscious of the sweat
pouring from his body that he had tried to shout through the glass
several times: "Get me a towel." Each time he had to gasp for
breath he became so exhausted that he had to "pump with all my
might for air." This convinced him that panic shortened the lives of
those who were trapped for long periods in mine shafts or vaults.

An hour and ten minutes passed before the magician signaled
for the lid to be opened. He was dripping wet from head to toe,
but he had felt no pain. He was so comfortable most of the time
that he thought a bit of extra air must have seeped in.

The second secret test was made August 4. The inside of the
box had an extra lining of galvanized iron added to strengthen it
and make it completely airproof. A larger container was filled with
water and into this Houdini, in the glass-topped box, was lowered
about noon. Through the inch-and-a-half of water over the glass
top he was again observed. He was even more comfortable than he
had been during the first test; he knew now that he could beat the
fakir at his own trick. He was also colder; the water seemed to
chill the box. After fifty minutes he began taking longer breaths.
He was annoyed by the movements of people he saw through the
glass lid and the water; one of his assistants seemed to be swaying.
Despite his acute irritability he stayed sealed up for seventy minutes.

His public demonstration was to be staged the next day, August 5, in the swimming pool of the Shelton Hotel. For three weeks
the magician had been in training at home and in the back room
of the Boyertown Casket Company. His lungs, he thought, were in
remarkable condition for a man his age. He could stay under the
water of the bathroom tub in his house on West 113th Street for a

full two minutes. At sixteen he could hold his breath beneath the surface twice that time. He had no doubt he would succeed at the Shelton pool.

The night before Houdini had taken a purgative. The morning of the test he ate lightly, a fruit salad and half a cup of coffee. He was somewhat more nervous than usual, but he was sure that was because of the excitement, not fear. The twenty-inch-gauge galvanized iron box was thoroughly examined by newsmen at the pool. The exact inside measurements, from Houdini's records, were six feet, six inches long, and twenty-two by twenty-two inches square. Lengths of angle iron one-and-a-quarter inches wide and from three to four feet long were used inside, and two-inch angle-iron strips were fastened outside.

He prefaced his demonstration with a brief statement. He was about to prove that people were mistaken when they believed a man could not survive more than three minutes in an airtight enclosure. He would demonstrate that a trance, such as Rahman Bey claimed to use, was not necessary for survival. "If I die, it will be the will of God and my own foolishness."

Wearing black swimming trunks, Houdini stepped into the box and stretched out flat on his back. In less than eight minutes the metal lid was soldered in place. The two brass caps were tightened to cut off the last bit of air and the container was lowered under the surface of the pool. It was weighted with approximately 800 pounds of iron and eight swimmers stood on the top to keep it beneath the water line and level. Inside the submerged coffin Houdini was not as relaxed as he had been during the secret tests. The warm damp air in the swimming pool disturbed him. He felt the heat in the box long before the metal safety caps were fastened. He was more irritable than he had been during the tests. The men standing on the coffin seemed to be shaking it. After thirty minutes one of the swimmers misjudged his balance and fell, the others were jarred from their positions, and the box shot up above the surface. They quickly pushed it down and mounted it again. Houdini visualized the box splitting open and the water rushing in and drowning him; he forced the thought from his mind. Jim Collins, his chief assistant, used the telephone to explain the mishap and keep him posted on the passage of time. Collins' voice was jubilant when he announced Rahman Bey's one-hour record had been shattered. Fifteen minutes later Houdini told him that water was entering the box, but only in a trickle. At the ninety-minute mark, on Houdini's instructions, Collins helped lift the box from the pool. When the casket came above the surface line, Houdini had a sudden marvelous feeling of relief. It was as if the sides of the box, pressed in by the water, had snapped back to their regular condition.

One of the brass marine plates was unfastened. A happy Houdini pushed his arm through the opening as tinsmiths worked rapidly to unseal the lid. His pulse, Dr. W. J. McConnell reported, was 142; it had been 84 before the test. When the magician emerged from the box McConnell made further observations. Blood pressure, which was 84 when the lid was sealed, had dropped to 42. The heat of the interior of the casket had reached 99.2 degrees. Houdini was soaked in perspiration when he stepped out and felt a slight dizziness; otherwise he thought he was in good shape.

Later, at home, he added: "I counted my respirations, and averaged seventeen. When I was dictating this, I still had that metallic taste in my stomach and mouth; felt rather weak in the knees; had no headache, but just seemed listless.

"When Collins, my assistant, phoned me that I had been in the coffin for one hour and twelve minutes, I was going to stay three more minutes, but watching my lungs rise and fall, thought I could stand the strain for another fifteen minutes."

When the men fell and the coffin zoomed up he had felt water under his shoulders and when he reached for his handkerchief it was wet. He pressed it to his lips to test if the damp cloth would lessen his strain. It felt good against his lips and tongue so he kept it there.

"After one hour and twenty-eight minutes I commenced to see

yellow lights and carefully watched myself not to go to sleep. I kept my eyes wide open; moved on the broad of my back, so as to take all the weight off my lungs, my left arm being across my chest. I lay on my right side, my left buttock against the coffin, so that I could keep the telephone receiver to my ear without holding it, and told Collins to get me up at an hour and a half, thinking if I did go to sleep, he would get me up within that time."

Houdini was sure that if the air in the swimming pool had been fresh rather than heated he could have stayed under fifteen or thirty minutes more.

When he started his training for the endurance test he had weighed 168; the afternoon it was completed he balanced the scales at 157 1/2 pounds. Almost eleven pounds had been expended during the twenty-one days of rigorous training.

Houdini died in October 1926—not because of the aftereffects of the underwater survival, but because he had permitted a student in Montreal to take several hard punches at his midsection. The young man, while visiting his dressing room, had asked if it was true that Houdini could brace himself to withstand such blows. Houdini hadn't had time to flex his muscles before the first blow was struck. His appendix was ruptured, but he wouldn't admit it. He finished his week in Canada and went on to Detroit, where in great pain he completed his opening night performance; in the early morning he was taken to Grace Hospital. After two operations he succumbed on Halloween day.

Hamid Bey, a twenty-four-year-old fakir who said he came from Egypt to convince Houdini that living burials were superhuman feats, arrived in the United States three weeks after the master magician's death. By late January 1927, Hamid had convinced the bookers of the Loew circuit that he would be a strong theater attraction. Terry Turner, the press agent who had publicized Rahman Bey, was assigned the task of stirring up public interest in the new arrival. He announced that the handsome young mystic would attempt to break Houdini's record with a three-hour stay, not under water but under ground.

The site chosen for the exploit was the lawn of Walter A. Shannon, a theater manager, on Liberty Road in Englewood, New Jersey. Shannon had a special interest in the project—his wife was the former vaudeville mind reader Leona La Marr, "The Girl with the Thousand Eyes."

The New York *Evening Graphic*, with typical tabloid flamboyance, headed its story " 'I Shall Rise Again!' Declares Fakir, Buried Alive Today in Jersey." Thursday, January 20, was a cold, wet day. Before noon newspapermen chose a spot on the Shannon property by lot and gravediggers set to work to open a pit with an outer dimension of six-by-six feet. Even with picks and shovels it was hard work breaking through the frozen surface, but the ground beneath was softer and easier to manage. At a depth of four feet a narrower hole was dug. This was two feet wide, five-and-a-half feet long, and two feet deep.

Shortly after one P.M. the bearded Hamid Bey, wearing a white headdress, a long, thin, white robe which extended from his neck to his toes, and sandals, walked to the edge of the pit, followed by his attendants. Victor Bartelloni, also in sheikh headpiece and robe, said that as well as being Hamid's personal manager, he was a missionary in the Egyptian Copt cult that practiced catalepsy as a part of their creed. Zulicfer Effendi identified himself as a Turkish medium. Effendi wore a similar white robe and a red *gandourah*—headdress—which, like Hamid's, had flowing cloth past his shoulders. He carried a purple umbrella to protect the fakir from the drizzle.

At least a hundred people braved the light rain to see the spectacle. Most were reporters and photographers, but the crowd also included several children and a few barking dogs. When the photographers had their cameras ready, Bartelloni kissed Hamid on both cheeks for good luck. The fakir turned his face toward the overcast sky, pressed firmly with both hands on his neck and jaws, gasped, then fell back in a trance. Two doctors stuffed his ears, mouth, and nostrils with cotton. His rigid body was lowered into the coffinlike inner hole and his attendants threw a few handfuls of sand over his face and body. Any more than this, Bartelloni had explained, might disturb the trance as the sand was damp. The push button for an electric bell was placed by the side of the fakir's head, and its wire attached to a bell near the side of the larger hole on the ground. How he could sound the alarm while entranced was not explained. Boards were laid on the top of the small, casket-size pit, and the six gravediggers filled the larger hole with earth. Above the surface of this they extended more boards to form a platform.

The Shannons invited the reporters to their house for lunch and hot coffee. Hamid's two attendants took turns sitting in an old chair by the side of the grave, holding an umbrella over themselves and the signal bell.

An hour passed—Rahman Bey's limit, and just half an hour short of Houdini's mark. Perhaps to celebrate the fakir's progress but more likely in the hope of getting her picture in the newspapers, Senorita Heriberta Martinez, a brown-eyed Spanish dancer in full regalia, performed a spirited fandango on the platform above Hamid Bey's grave.

The *New York Times* report ignored the senorita but noted that the Turkish medium who sat by the grave claimed he was in contact mentally with his friend below the ground. From time to time he would report: "*Il est bien.*"

The ever-darkening sky was threatening both to the photographers and to publicist Turner. Some of the men had no flash equipment and without proper light they would have no pictures of the finale for their papers. The six gravediggers were instructed to start shoveling the earth from the pit. When the boards were removed from the inner compartment, Hamid Bey, still rigid as a log, was lifted out and brought to the surface. Bartelloni massaged and pounded Hamid's wrists, pulled the cotton from his nostrils, ears, and mouth, and reached in to bring his tongue, which Hamid had folded back to close his throat before the interment, forward. Soon the fakir was fully awake, shivering in the cold air, and trying to smile as he faced the cameras. He said "Houdini!" triumphantly. He had been buried for almost three hours.

Doctors Francis P. Weston and William Silverstein took Hamid's pulse and measured his respiration. Both were exactly the same as at the time of burial—72 and 18. The physicians were in disagreement on one point. Weston stated that Hamid had not breathed under ground, Silverstein just as emphatically said that he had.

The *Evening Graphic* had an angle on the burial not reported elsewhere. Their story said that somehow the clapper of the warning bell had been bent. Even if Hamid had pressed the emergency button his attendants on the ground above would not have known it. With the bent clapper the bell would not ring.

Hamid Bey's publicity led to a vaudeville tour. For a time Hereward Carrington, the well-known investigator and promoter of psychics who had been with Rahman Bey, was his lecturer.

Living burial in the ground using the Hamid Bey system of an inner grave protected by boards covered with loose earth is not difficult. Many magicians, who do not claim supernormal power or use trances, have duplicated it. There is sufficient air available for a three-hour stay. Hamid also claimed he could be buried three days and still survive. Is this possible? Yes—but not by using catalepsy. In the past, performers in India and elsewhere survived long burials by having their assistants secretly tunnel under the ground to the burial spot. In some cases the tunnels were made days beforehand. The box was lowered in a pit which had only a thin earthen wall between the lower end of the passageway and the end of the box. A panel that swung inward permitted the fakir to get out, dig through the barrier and crawl up to the ground. The far end of the tunnel was some distance from the burial pit, masked by a clump of vegetation or a nearby house. The mystic could live in comparative comfort, amply supplied with food and drink until the time came for him to burrow back and assume the trance position before the box was hauled up to the surface.

Among Hamid Bey's other claims were the ability to project his astral body wherever he wished when he was in trance, the power to send telepathic messages immediately to any member of his cult anywhere in the world, and the knack of picking up by thought waves the presence of crocodiles in a river. With these marvelous talents I wondered, along with the other magicians who saw him perform, why he was using tricks we all could do to perform his "telepathic" tests on the stage.

I knew him to display a sense of humor only once. That was when he told the story of his first public burial in Italy. He arrived in Brindisi with his brother as his press agent. The brother advertised that the "miracle man" could stay beneath the sod three days, then be in perfect health when he was revived.

The mayor of the city, Hamid said, honored him with a banquet the evening before the test. There he broke his fast, eating spaghetti to please the local dignitaries. Time and again they filled his empty plate.

Hamid entered his trance the day of the burial and was interred with a string which ran up to the ground and was tied to an old-fashioned bell. The unfamiliar pasta began to rumble in his stomach. His trance was broken; he pulled furiously on the string. Suddenly he saw a brilliant red flash, then passed out.

He was brought to the surface unconscious. The reporters thought he was dead and rushed away to write sensational stories. When he recovered, more sensational stories followed. When he was asked why he had not lived up to his promise to stay buried for three days, Hamid Bey turned his sad dark eyes on the questioners and explained truthfully that the spaghetti had defeated him. Though the burial was an artistic fiasco, it was a publicity success. The next day his statement was on the front pages under the headline: "SPAGHETTI IS STRONGER THAN THE MASTER. EAT MORE SPAGHETTI."

While both Rahman Bey and Hamid Bey enjoyed a considerable vogue in the United States, Tara Bey performed only a single night at Carnegie Hall in New York in May 1930. He had been a sensation in Paris five years before with feats of fakirism that earlier had astounded Mussolini, King Victor Emmanuel, and distinguished Italian medical men.

Tara's claim that a trance was vital for living burial was vigorously contested by Paul Heuzé, a writer, who proved his point by emerging unharmed after spending an hour under the earth himself. In December 1928 the two met face-to-face before a sold-out house in the Cirque de Paris—a special benefit show for charity. The bearded Egyptian pushed long needles through various parts of his body as the audience gasped. He pierced his neck with a thin sword, pulled it out without so much as a frown. He reclined with his bare back on a bed of sharp nails. He supported his body in midair with his neck resting on one metal blade and his ankles on another while a rock was cracked on his chest. There was wild applause.

Now it was the journalist's turn. He explained that anyone could do these seemingly supernormal wonders with practice. Heuzé thrust a needle through his own cheek. The crowd cheered. Heuzé went on to say that the other feats could be done too had he had time to train for them; the crowd jeered. They wanted a demonstration, not a lecture. Had Karma, a magician from Bordeaux, not been present Tara Bey would have won the confrontation. Karma came forward and duplicated the Egyptian's more spectacular feats with ease. Karma assured the audience that he was an entertainer, that he did not go into a trance or use occult powers.

The verdict of the investigating committee was predictable. Though Tara Bey had given an impressive exhibition, it was clear that powers beyond normal human skill were not needed for his feats.

The representatives of the Society of American Magicians who volunteered to serve on Tara Bey's committee from the audience at Carnegie Hall in New York shared this opinion. As to the fakir's burial on the stage, they thought this the least effective part of his repertoire.

Professor J. B. S. Haldane had discovered long before that there was sufficient oxygen in two and a half cubic feet of air to sustain a man for an hour if he remained motionless in an *airtight* chamber. Tara Bey, Rahman Bey, and Hamid Bey seldom were enclosed as long as twenty minutes in their stage coffins. Most audiences were satisfied with ten- or twelve-minute demonstrations.

The most astonishing aspect of living burial performances is the readiness of most spectators to believe that those who survive are superhuman.

No fakir of recent years has presented a more dramatic performance than Blacaman. Bearded, with a great mop of bushy, dark hair, he made an imposing appearance. Self-impalement and living burials played only a minor part in his exciting presentations. In April 1928, wearing only a loincloth, he entered a cage at the Circus Busch in Berlin and stared down the lions, which had been taunted by iron poles thrust through the bars. For Continental music halls he offered a full hour of "Indian Fakirism," assisted by fifteen attendants, fifty crocodiles, thirty lions, and fifty snakes.

An Associated Press dispatch from Moldes, Cordoba, Argentina, September 5, 1929, reported that Blacaman, the man "who has amazed thousands by his ability to emerge alive after being buried in a coffin," had been found dead the previous day "when the coffin was taken up after three hours in the ground. Examination showed that he had made strenuous efforts to release himself."

A photograph of the fakir standing with his arms folded in a coffin with a girl in a nurse's uniform at one side was printed in the December 1, 1929, *Baltimore American*. The story, which spelled his name Blakamann, said the mystic's final burial was on a theater stage in Argentina, the first night of an announced week's engagement, and that he was buried only fifteen minutes. When the coffin was opened, the fakir was lifted out and his assistants worked over his limp body, pumping his arms up and down and slapping his ashen face. "The audience," the account went on, "thought this was all a part of the performance until they realized the man was dead!"

The famous fakir did not die in 1929 in South America; the man who lost his life in Argentina must have been one of his many imitators. Blacaman was still performing with his crocodiles, pythons, and lions when I was in Europe seven years later.

FIRE WALKING

Fire is the most treacherous of elements. It provides heat and light, but it also causes death and destruction. Priest, witchdoctor, shaman, and psychic give graphic evidence of their seemingly superhuman powers when they demonstrate they are masters of its fury.

Westerners wince as they watch the Shinto priests of Japan walk barefooted across beds of cherry-red charcoal; tourists cringe as unshod fire defiers tread paths of burning embers or steaming stones in India, Tahiti, Trinidad, or Ceylon. Few exhibitions of supernormal talents are more exciting to the uninitiated.

The traditional Shinto rites begin when a section of the temple grounds is purified by prayer. Four tall bamboo poles with sharpened ends are embedded in the earth to mark its boundaries. Rope, with long, narrow paper pennants dangling from it, is strung from pole to pole. Bags of charcoal are emptied to form three mounds within the enclosure. The heaps are set afire and flames whip up as the burning coals are fanned. Soon the intense heat forces onlookers who gather by the barriers back to cooler ground. The glow from the red-hot lumps casts an eerie haze against the evening sky.

As the sky darkens the three fires are leveled into one with heavy iron rods. The fiery surface now extends over a plot approximately nine feet long and three feet wide. The sound of oriental music comes from the entrance of the temple. A procession, led by musicians playing hand-held instruments, walks with measured paces toward the steaming charcoal. The priests circle the fire, stopping at each bamboo pole to bow and chant. They command the evil spirits of the flames to flee and they purify the fire by tossing handfuls of salt from reed baskets on the charcoal.

Near one end of the fire the high priest removes his foot coverings. He steps with bare feet on a mound of salt, then takes the sacred *gobi*, a staff with a zigzag strip of white paper fastened to its top and, holding it aloft, steps calmly on the fire and walks confidently along the nine-foot path of burning coals. There are gasps from those who have never seen the ceremony before; these are all but drowned out by the music. He returns to the starting point by way of the adjacent unscorched ground and again shuffles his feet in the salt pile. His acolytes and the musicians have meanwhile removed their sandals. Now he leads the whole procession across the burning surface and the spectators are invited to participate. Men, women, and children take off their stockings and shoes; holding smaller *gobis* in their hands, they too walk on the sizzling coals without pain. Those who have faith and brave the ordeal are said to receive special protection from harm and suffering through the coming year.

This Shinto *Hi Watari* rite is also performed on burning wood, with the celebrants moving in single file across a narrower path of burning logs.

Fire walking has been practiced as a religious ceremony since ancient times. Strabo, the Greek historian and geographer who wrote before the birth of Christ, noted that the priestesses of Diana at the temple in Castabala, Cappadocia, were impervious to burning coals. The Hirpi in Etruria avoided service in the Roman legions by taking part in a similar annual rite at the temple of Apollo on Mount Soracte. Marcus Terentius Varro was not as amazed by this feat as the lawmakers. He surmised that a secret ointment that prevented blistering had been rubbed into the feet before the fire walk.

Shadrach, Meshach, and Abed-nego, the Bible says, survived

the fury of Nebuchadnezzar's furnace: "And the princes, governors, and captains, and the king's counselors, being gathered together, saw these men upon whose bodies the fire had no power, nor was a hair of their head singed, neither were their coats changed, nor the smell of fire passed on them."

Fire walking was also a part of religious festivals in India. When Indians migrated to the Pacific Islands, to Trinidad, South Africa, and other parts of the world, they continued to practice this ancient ritual. On the Maha Devi temple grounds in Suva, a coastal town of Viti Levu in the Fiji Islands, those who defy the flames spend ten days in study, meditation, and purification. They live apart from their fellows and abstain from drinking, smoking, and sexual relations. Early on the morning of the fire ceremony the participants immerse themselves in a stream to wash away the last traces of iniquity, then sit in a circle around their leader to pray and enter into the mental state which they believe is necessary to face the ordeal. The men thrust long thin skewers through their cheeks and impale wires through the flesh of their arms and bodies. The chief picks up his *khalasam,* an urn from which a stick with three points, representing the holy Hindu trinity, extends upward. Around it are leaves of mango and *heem* trees and flowers and fruit. Using both hands to keep the bowl in place on his head, he leads the initiates down the road to the temple. They shout, dance, twist, and turn to the beat of drums. It is a fantastic sight; dabs of red pigment on the top of the urn and the foreheads and bodies of the dancers might at first be mistaken for blood, but the skewers and wires produce no bleeding.

For more than a dozen hours the fire in the trench before the temple has been burning. After ashes are raked from the surface, the priest, still balancing the urn on his head, and wearing a long white cotton robe and garlands of flowers around his neck, stops briefly to pray before the pit, then strides across the hot ashes. He is followed by his coreligionists who are no more troubled by the heat than by the metal wires protruding through their skins.

Once, it is said, a woman fell as she crossed the fire, and her badly burned body was retrieved with one of the long-handled rakes. She confessed before she died that she had violated her oath of chastity during the purification period. Another story is told in Suva of a young Hindu who attempted to cross the fire without undergoing the ten days of preparation. He walked without prayer and without the sanction of the priest. He suffered no physical injury, but when the holy man predicted he would die in three months because the goddess was displeased, his nights became almost unendurable. He lived longer than the allotted time, but the natives say that the goddess eventually killed him.

British missionaries in South Africa had a peculiar problem. Conversion of the descendants of the Hindu immigrants in the province of Natal was almost impossible. Word pictures of the Christian hell where Satan tortured sinners didn't have the usual effect on Natal-born Indians. In 1928 when outsiders were first permitted to view the fire rituals at the Hindu temple in Durban, the missionaries understood why. The *Souris* ran sharp wires through their tongues and bodies without injury, and followed their leader in bare feet across a fiery pit without burns or blisters. Since they could endure such tortures in life, the threat of similar ordeals after death did not disturb them.

American Indian shamans of several tribes demonstrated their immunity to fire to early white settlers. As recently as 1921 a Cahuilla medicine man from Torres, near Palm Springs, performed this feat five times during the Morongo harvest moon festival at the Banning reservation in California. A fire was kindled of desert wood as the sixty-seven-year-old shaman stripped to his loincloth. With bare arms and in bare feet he danced around the flaming embers. Carrying a sheaf of feathers in his hands and wearing a strip of white cloth tied around his forehead, he called on the Great Spirit to remove the heat from the bonfire and to protect his "burning heart." As he chanted the prayer, the few older Indians who knew the words joined in. Waving the feathers in the air, he stepped on the glowing embers and scattered them with his feet. Tossing the feathers aside, he scooped up the burning coals with his bare hands and bending his head back, filled his mouth. Eyes closed, with his face toward the sky he held the smoking embers with his lips partially closed until the fire had been extinguished. Later a doctor from Banning examined the Indian's feet, hands, and mouth. He could offer no solution to the mystery.

In Raiatea, Tahiti, a fire is kindled in a pit three feet deep, twelve feet wide, and eighteen feet long. In the morning natives line the bottom of the outdoor oven with flat rocks, some as much as fourteen inches in diameter. Logs are placed over these and ignited. The flames from the burning wood produce a blaze six feet high. When only charred remnants of the logs remain, burning coals are heaped on the stones. Later in the afternoon the rocks are levered up and turned over with long poles so the stones rest on the surface of the red-hot fire.

The chief fire walker, who, like his followers, wears only a cloth which extends from his waist to his knees, carries a cluster of leaves in his right hand. He approaches the narrow end of the pit, implores the deity who controls the fire to grant him immunity, then bends to strike one of the steaming rocks three times with his sheaf. Standing erect, with leaves held high, he walks the length of the steaming stones. Nor is he the only human whose feet are impervious to injury; his attendants follow him one after the other across the smoking surface.

My friend Les Levante, the Australian illusionist, saw his first fire walk in the Philippine Islands. He traveled a day by boat, automobile, horseback, and foot to reach the remote village of Alfonso, Cavite. There at night, with only the light of the moon and the glow from a fire of flaming branches, he was a spectator to the tribal ceremony. The throb of drums, the clash of cymbals and gongs, and a waltz melody from a guitar added a theatrical flavor to the proceedings. Eleven men in bare feet walked effortlessly over the smoldering twigs. Levante had read that alum and other chemicals were used to protect the skin of fire defiers. "I examined their feet and looked for fakes of every kind, and found, like many more before me—nothing . . . they *did not* use any dope on their feet."

He arranged to take six Tagalog fire walkers to Australia, where they performed at the Sydney Exhibition as often as thirty times a day.

Is fire walking a demonstration of superhuman power or is it a trick? Ishii Black, an Englishman who lived many years in Japan and adopted the Japanese way of life, was of the opinion that when the burning charcoals were leveled the center section through which the Shintoists walked was thinner than the sides: "The heaped-up sides have the effect of burning up all the oxygen in the air, and so preventing the middle from getting enough to burn brightly; in fact, the center of the fire is nearly extinguished, though, on account of the glow from the sides, this is not noticed."

He believed the damp salt in which the priests rubbed their feet offered some protection, and that the handfuls of salt, which were thrown mostly on the center area, deadened the heat. He observed that the priests stepped firmly on the charcoals and that their weight "crushes out any fire under their feet before it has time to burn them."

When the spectators filed across the steaming bed, though the fire on the sides still flamed, the center path had been so trodden down that even those with tender feet could travel it without pain.

Samuel Pierpont Langley, secretary of the Smithsonian Institution and a professor of physics and astronomy, noted that the stones used in the ceremony he saw at Raiatea, Tahiti, in 1901 were of porous basalt and weighed between forty and eighty pounds. He took a hot stone immediately after the fire walker had trod upon it and immersed it in a bucket of water. The water boiled for twelve minutes, indicating that the basalt was a poor conductor of heat. Back in Washington Langley cooked the stone until it had the same appearance he remembered from the fire walk. Its temperature was approximately 1200 degrees Fahrenheit. He discovered that he could grasp one end of the stone without pain, though the far end, fired by a blowpipe, was red hot.

The Raiatea fire walk today is one of Tahiti's principal tourist attractions. Tanetoa, the priest who officiates, sometimes brings his heat resisters to Bora Bora to entertain visiting celebrities. G. M.

Feigen, a San Francisco surgeon, described the ceremony staged there for R. Buckminster Fuller, the noted American architect, in the July 12, 1969, *Saturday Review*. After the cinder bed had reached its maximum heat, the stones were pounded into place; their lower sections had a "ruddy blush." There was no doubt that the surface was hot. A leaf from a coconut tree thrown on it burst into fire and was reduced to ashes.

Before the ritual attendants brushed the tops of the stones with long pandanus leaves, clearing away stray cinders.

The priest, in white shorts and a white hat, carried a cane as well as the traditional ti sheaf. He offered a few words of Christian prayer before a call in his native language for protection from the flames. The fire walk has been modernized to appeal to the visitors from other lands. Six girls with grass skirts over their Tahitian *pareus* and as many men with grass skirts over their loincloths walked in pairs across the stones.

The visitors were invited to participate. Feigen was standing beside the priest in his bare feet almost before he knew it. Tanetoa said the proper protective words, then one of the men in grass skirts took the surgeon's hand and they were off across the hot stones. Feigen's feet and legs were cold rather than hot, though the rest of his body was conscious of heat. His soles tingled not as a reaction to the burning surface but because the tops of the stones were rough.

Part way across the pit one of his feet came down on a wood cinder but he continued on. Later he found he had been burned where the ember had touched his instep but it had been easy for him to walk across the fire.

In 1919 a British newspaper correspondent who lived in Papete, Tahiti, was too timid to remove his shoes when he took part in a fire walk. He reported that he felt no discomfort; neither the soles of his shoes nor the bottoms of his trouser legs were even slightly scorched.

Levante, the Australian magician who brought the Philippine fire walkers to Sydney, said that confidence and an even pace are the main requisites for a stroll through fire. He put this theory into practice and it worked. He observed the rituals in five countries. When wood fires were used they were made of short lengths of soft wood. The pieces were well charred before the walk was made. The walkers, according to Levante, never took more than six steps across the surface. The area adjacent to the fires was either grassy or of soft dirt. The grass or earth cools the feet afterward and extinguishes any chance ember that may have become lodged between the performer's toes.

In Rangoon in 1932 Levante noticed a heap of damp sand at each narrow side of the fire which Persian Mohammedans had built in an eighteen-foot-long trench. The ritualists spent hours chanting and beating themselves with lashes into a frenzy before they crossed the once fiery area. They continued running back and forth until the last glow was stamped out. One of Levante's assistants who had participated in the ceremony the year before told him: "The fire must be well burned, the ground surrounding it must be loose and cool," which tallied with his own findings.

My friend the late Harry Price, honorary secretary of the University of London Council for Psychical Investigation, arranged the first fire walks in England. Before then many adventurous men in various parts of the world had successfully duplicated the primitive rites without entering trances or using protective solutions on their feet, but Price was determined to find out why they could perform what seemed to be an utterly impossible feat.

His principal problem was to locate a fire walker. An advertisement in *The Times* produced correspondence from people who had seen the ritual abroad or were eager to be spectators, but no one volunteered to walk on fire. Price was about to give up when he heard from a young Kashmiri magician who introduced himself as Professor K. B. Duke. He said he had frequently walked across fiery pits during Mohammedan religious ceremonies in India. Clippings in his scrapbook verified his statement. The slender young conjurer agreed to submit to any scientific test Price or his committee could devise. As Kuda Bux, he became the star of the most publicized fire walks in history.

Price at fifty-four was the best-known psychical investigator in

England. A boyhood interest in conjuring led to a study of the occult. He assembled the most comprehensive collection of books and documents on the subject ever made. In his files were numerous accounts of fire walks in other countries, but he had never seen one himself. He arranged for Kuda Bux to appear at a dress rehearsal September 8, 1935, eight days before the formal test.

A pit twelve inches deep, twenty-five feet long, and three feet wide was dug on an estate in Carshalton, Surrey. Twenty-five copies of *The Times* were wadded up and tossed into the pit. Slats from old wooden boxes formed the next layer. Almost 300 eighteen-inch-long logs were spread on the slats to form the upper surface.

Price struck a match and tried to light the heap. It wouldn't burn. After ten gallons of paraffin were poured over the logs he tried again. In ten minutes the fire was blazing hot. More logs were heaped in place. In an hour the topmost logs were reddish embers, coated with white ash.

An hour and twenty-five minutes after the fire had been ignited, Kuda Bux approached the pit, removed a shoe and stocking, and touched the surface with his bare foot. He wasn't satisfied. He said there should be more fire and not as many unburned logs. Ten minutes later he touched the surface with his foot again. The fire, he announced, was ready for the final layer of forest-burnt oak charcoal. As this was spread the Kashmiri picked up a lump, bit into it, and crunched it between his teeth. He pronounced it perfect for the purpose.

There was a break for lunch, the twenty-nine-year-old fire walker from Akhnur followed his charcoal appetizer with a light repast. Fasting, obviously, was not necessary for his feat. When he looked at the fire again he was disturbed because the embers were not deep enough. In the past, he said, there had always been a nine-inch depth. Embers were raked from the far end of the pit to form a burning path twenty feet long.

Kuda Bux relaxed in a chair while Dr. William Collier, an Oxford physician, examined his feet. There was no evidence a pain-reducing solution had been applied. His right foot was washed as a precaution.

The 120-pound Kashmiri with black hair and a short moustache then stood erect on a wooden board at the end of the pit. He was dressed in a long black frock coat, dark trousers, a starched-collar white shirt, and a light tie. Had it not been for his bare feet one might have thought he was on his way to a diplomatic reception. He raised his left hand, intoned a short prayer, then turned his attention to the trench. Kuda Bux bent his knees, whisked away ashes from the embers within his reach, then straightened up and stepped on the surface. He took four long strides before he leapt away from the sizzling trench.

Three more times Kuda Bux walked briskly on the embers, but never more than four paces. He said the thin layer of embers was not conducive to a longer walk. His feet were examined again by Dr. Collier. They had not been burned, nor had the bottoms of his trouser legs been singed. Harry Price added a dramatic touch after Kuda's fourth walk. He tossed several sheets of paper on the embers; they burst into flames immediately.

One of the men who observed the tests was Digby Moynagh, editor of St. Bartholomew's Hospital Journal. An unconquerable desire to try the fire himself moved him to unlace his shoes and pull off his socks. Squatting near the trench, he gingerly touched the surface with a bare foot. He asked Price's permission to make an experimental walk. Delighted to have another human interest angle for the press, Price gave his consent.

Moynagh, in tweed slacks and a sweater, stood on the wooden platform in his bare feet like a hesitant diver on a springboard over a vat of boiling oil. He stepped off, touched his right foot to the surface, then his left, and as fast as he could he springjumped to one side of the pit. Yes, he admitted, the fire was hot and he had felt a tingling sensation. Half an hour later there were blisters on his feet. A nurse, who had been in attendance all day—just in case—applied picric acid and bandages.

For the formal demonstration September 17 the size of the pit, at Kuda Bux's suggestion, was changed. It was made shallower—nine inches deep; wider—increased from three to six feet; and a three-foot-long barrier of earth divided it into two eleven-foot sections.

The Kashmiri's feet were examined by Professor C. A. Pannett; the skin was soft and dry and there were no calluses. Both feet were washed and dried. A piece of zinc oxide plaster less than an inch square was fastened close to the arch of his right foot.

The surface temperature of the fire was 430 degrees Centigrade when Kuda Bux, in his frock coat, crossed the eleven feet to the dividing mound of earth with four long steps in exactly 4.5 seconds. He was not burned nor was the plaster on his instep scorched, though some loose strands at the edges were lightly browned. Three minutes later, with another four fast strides, Kuda Bux crossed the fire again.

Instruments were used to measure the temperature of the surface. Though the Kashmiri had not objected to this earlier, when he was poised on the wooden platform for his third walk he suddenly turned away. He told Price the instruments had desecrated the fire; if he tried again he was sure to be burned. Kuda Bux is a fine showman.

Digby Moynagh, who still had blisters on his feet from his attempt to walk across the pit at the rehearsal, was ready to try his luck again. Another two quick steps produced more blisters.

Another volunteer, a friend of Kuda Bux's, Maurice Cheepen, also found that two steps on the fiery surface were his limit: his feet were more severely burned than Moynagh's.

The worldwide press coverage of the British fire walks made Kuda Bux a celebrity. When I first met him a year later in England he was topping bills in provincial variety theaters with his eyeless-vision blindfold act; fire departments had vetoed the suggestion that fires be built on the stages so that he could repeat his famous feat indoors.

I was still in London when Harry Price announced a second series of fire walks. This time, Ahmed Hussain, an entertainer from

Cawnpore, India, was to brave the flames. Hussain, in colorful turban and festive Indian jacket and trousers, prayed and took three
long, quick steps without blisters. He claimed the power to transmit his immunity to others. Three Englishmen, John Craigie, N. W.
Marshall, and H. A. Bould, followed him across the pit. All except
Hussain were slightly burned. Two other volunteers walked alone.
Reginald Adcock crossed in three steps, A. I. Chesney in four. Both
received minimal burns.

When a B.B.C. radio commentator covered the April 9 tests,
the surface temperature of the fire was 750 degrees Centigrade—
320 degrees hotter than it had been for Kuda Bux. The length of
the walking area had been increased. Hussain took six rapid steps
in 2.3 seconds. This time the Moslem prayer did not protect him.
Six small blisters formed on his left sole and a tender pink area
was noted on his right arch.

Adcock took four paces and was again slightly burned, as he
had been two days earlier. A. J. Bould and D. C. Russell, two students from the University of London, also stepped on the steaming
surface; both were burned. Adcock participated in another experiment. He took seven steps across the fire wearing rope-soled shoes.
The bottoms were not scorched; only a few wispy strands of the
rope on the outer edges were browned.

So far the press, newsreels, and radio had covered the fire
walks. On April 20, 1937, a pit four feet wide, twelve feet long, and
nine inches deep was dug on the grounds of the Alexandria Palace
B.B.C. studios. Television cameras were focused on Hussain as he
took four steps across the hottest surface yet—800 degrees. Reginald
Adcock crossed the same area with three mighty strides. Neither
was blistered. This history-making open-air telecast was the first
remote B.B.C. pickup of a special event.

Price concluded that fire walking could be explained by "the
short contact-time of each foot . . . with a limit of immunity of two
steps per foot, the low thermal conductivity of burning or burnt
wood embers" and "confidence and steadiness in walking." He
found no validity either to the theory that sweat glands could be

controlled so that the feet were "abnormally dry" or to the "spheroidal state" theory.

Scientists who offered the latter explanation had suggested that perspiration on the feet of the fire walkers had protected them. Drops of water in a hot oven float on their own vapor. The globules do not boil, but quickly evaporate. This vapor cushion could act as a buffer between human skin and a fiery surface.

In the 1950's an inquisitive American scientist, Mayne Reid Coe, Jr., decided to test the "spheroidal state" theory at his home in Riviera Beach, Florida. If he could prove it worked, he could duplicate not only the fire walk but also the heat-resisting marvels of human salamanders. Legend says that salamanders, animals that are lizardlike in appearance, thrive on flames. The legend has long since been exploded, but the feats of Robert Powell, the British fire eater who performed in the eighteenth century, and Signora Josephine Girardelli, an Italian "Fire-Proof Lady" who appeared in England in 1814, were even more incredible. He ate "red-hot coals out of the fire as natural as bread," licked "a red-hot heater . . . with his naked tongue," and filled "his mouth with red-hot charcoal." She held "melted lead" in her mouth, stroked her hair, tongue, and arms with a red-hot iron, bathed her hands in boiling lead, and held her face, arms, and hands in open flames.

Coe's first experiments were with red-hot steel bars. He thought he wouldn't be burned if he touched the glowing end of one with a moistened finger, yet it took nerve to try. A quick tap produced no injury, only a slight tingling feeling of warmth. Soon he was stroking the bar with the tip of his tongue. He had used a rod three-sixteenths of an inch in diameter; now he tried a bar half an inch thick. There was less of a heat sensation than he had noticed with the smaller rod.

Completely confident now, he began dipping his fingers in molten lead. The climax of his research was a fire walk on Singer's Island, not far from his home. A pit was dug and lined with wood. When the embers were sizzling hot, he raked away the ashes, stood in bare feet at the narrow end of the pit, and, steeling himself, stepped forward with one foot, then the other. The heat was over-powering. He jumped clear of the fire. His left foot ached. He put it into a bucket of water. The sudden change of temperature felt good, soothing. Perhaps he hadn't been blistered as badly as he had imagined? He lifted his foot, looked at the sole. No blisters or burned areas were evident. Gradually the remaining pain faded.

Eventually he decided to try again. This time he would not sprint across as he had before, he would try to maintain a regular gait, slightly quicker than a walking pace. With four strides he crossed the fire. There was neither a burning sensation nor a vio-lent reaction to the intense heat that engulfed his body. Four more times he walked across the burning path without injury.

He and Harry Price had proved that there is nothing mystical about fire walking, that careful planning and confidence, not prayer, are the real secrets.

I met Kuda Bux again after he came to the United States to repeat his fire walk for a Robert L. Ripley "Believe It or Not" radio program in 1938. He is now a member of the Society of American Magicians, and four summers ago I had the pleasure of introducing him when he presented his eyeless-vision act during the society's annual "Night of Magic Under the Stars" in New York's Central Park. A dozen or so years ago he told me he was working on an even more astounding feat. He would try to walk on water; as yet he has not succeeded.

I was in India in 1966 when the newspapers announced that Lakshamanasandra Srikanta Rao, a hatha yogi who in the past had eaten nails, needles, razor blades, and glass, and who had walked on fire, would walk on water in Bombay. Some of the five thousand spectators paid as much as $70 for the choicest seats. An oblong concrete tank, twenty feet long and six feet wide, had been built for the occasion and filled with water. The white-bearded mystic ascended the steps to the edge of the basin. There he paused and prayed. With complete confidence he stepped on the surface of the water. As the huge audience gasped, Rao sank immediately to the bottom.

The quest for verifiable psychic phenomena, conclusive evidence for extrasensory perception, and authentic prophets continues. Exploded myths, revealed frauds, and shattered delusions do not deter those who are convinced that man has supernormal powers.

Let us hope that future investigators will be more cautious and better informed than those of the past, that they will not be misled by charlatans, unsound observations, or wishful thinking.

If any area of the occult is documented scientifically it will be a momentous occasion. Until then be wary of ESP, seers, and psychics.

BIBLIOGRAPHY

ABBOTT, DAVID P., *Behind the Scenes with the Medium,* Chicago, The Open Court Publishing Company, 1907.

ADAMS, EVANGELINE, *The Bowl of Heaven,* New York, Dodd, Mead & Company, 1926.

ANONYMOUS, *Table Turning and Table Talking,* London, Henry Vizetelly, 1853.

BRITTEN, EMMA HARDINGE, *Nineteenth Century Miracles,* Manchester, England, William Britten, 1883.

BROWN, G. BURNISTON, *A Report on Three Experimental Fire-Walks by Ahmed Hussain and Others,* London, Bulletin IV, University of London Council for Psychical Investigation, 1938.

BURTON, JEAN, *Heyday of a Wizard: Daniel Home the Medium,* with a foreword by Harry Price, London, Sydney, Toronto, Bombay, George G. Harrap & Co., Ltd., 1948.

CAPRON, ELIAS W., and HENRY D. BARRON, *Explanation and History of the Mysterious Communion with Spirits,* Auburn, New York, Capron and Barron, 1850.

CARPENTER, WILLIAM B., *Mesmerism, Spiritualism, &c.,* New York, D. Appleton and Company, 1877.

CARRINGTON, HEREWARD, *The Physical Phenomena of Spiritualism,* Boston, Small, Maynard & Co., 1908.

———, *Eusapia Palladino and Her Phenomena,* New York, B. W. Dodge & Company, 1909.

——, *Modern Psychical Phenomena*, New York, Dodd, Mead & Company, 1919.

——, *The Story of Psychic Science*, London, Rider & Co., 1930.

——, *The Psychic World*, New York, G. P. Putnam's Sons, 1937.

——, *The Invisible World*, New York, The Beechhurst Press, Bernard Ackerman, Inc., 1946.

——, *The American Séances with Eusapia Palladino*, New York, Garrett Publications, 1954.

——, and Nandor Fodor, *Haunted People*, New York, E. P. Dutton & Co., Inc., 1951.

CHRISTOPHER, MILBOURNE, *Panorama of Magic*, New York, Dover Publications, Inc., 1962.

——, *Houdini: The Untold Story*, New York, Thomas Y. Crowell Company, 1969; London, Cassell, 1969.

COHEN, DANIEL, *Myths of the Space Age*, New York, Dodd, Mead & Company, 1967.

CRAFT, AMOS N., *Epidemic Delusions . . . Especial Reference to Modern Spiritualism*, Cincinnati, Walden and Stowe, 1881.

DAVENPORT, REUBEN BRIGGS, *The Death-Blow to Spiritualism*, New York, G. W. Dillingham, 1888.

DE HEREDIA, C. M., *Spiritism and Common Sense*, New York, P. J. Kenedy & Sons, 1922.

DINGWELL, ERIC J., *Very Peculiar People*, London, Rider & Co., n.d.

——, and TREVOR H. HALL, *Four Modern Ghosts*, London, Gerald Duckworth & Co., Ltd., 1958.

——, *Some Human Oddities*, New Hyde Park, New York, University Books, 1962.

——, *The Critic's Dilemma*, Crowhurst, England, Author's Publication, 1966.

DIXON, JEANE, *My Life and Prophecies*, as told to Rene Noorbergen, New York, William Morrow and Company, Inc., 1969.

EBON, MARTIN, *Prophecy in Our Time*, New York, New American Library, 1968.

EVANS, HENRY RIDGELY, *Hours with the Ghosts*, Chicago, Laird & Lee, 1897.

FLOURNOY, THEODORE, *Spiritism and Psychology*, translated, abridged, and with an introduction by Hereward Carrington, New York and London, Harper & Brothers, 1911.

FORD, ARTHUR, in collaboration with MARGUERITTE HARMON BRO, *Nothing So Strange*, New York, Harper & Brothers, 1958.

——, *Unknown but Known*, New York, Harper and Row, 1968.

FORMAN, HENRY JAMES, *The Story of Prophecy*, New York, Toronto, Farrar & Rinehart, Inc., 1936.

GARDNER, MARTIN, *Fads and Fallacies in the Name of Science*, New York, Dover Publications, Inc., 1957.

GAULD, ALAN, *The Founders of Psychical Research*, New York, Schocken Books, 1968.

GAUQUELIN, MICHEL, *The Scientific Basis of Astrology*, translated from the French by James Hughes, New York, Stein and Day, 1969.

HALL, TREVOR H., *The Spiritualists*, New York, Helix Press, Garrett Publications, 1963.

——, *The Strange Case of Edmund Gurney*, London, Gerald Duckworth & Co., Ltd., 1964.

——, *New Light on Old Ghosts*, London, Gerald Duckworth & Co., Ltd., 1965.

HANSEL, C. E. M., *ESP: A Scientific Evaluation*, introduction by Edwin G. Boring, New York, Charles Scribner's Sons, 1966.

HARDINGE, EMMA, *Modern American Spiritualism*, New York, Author's Publication, 1870.

HEUZÉ, PAUL, *Les Morts Vivent-Ils?*, Paris, La Renaissance de Livre, 1921.

——, *Fakirs, Fumistes & Cie*, Paris, Les Éditions de France, 1926.

——, *La Plaisanterie des Animaux Calculateurs*, Paris, Les Éditions de France, 1928.

HOLLOWAY, GILBERT N., *Beyond ESP*, New York, Frederick Fell, Inc., 1969.

HOME, DANIEL DUNGLAS, *Incidents in My Life*, with an introduction by Judge Edmonds, New York, Carleton, 1858.

———, *Lights and Shadows of Spiritualism*, New York, G. W. Carleton & Co., 1877.

HOME, MME. DUNGLAS, *D. D. Home: His Life and Mission*, Edited with an introduction by Sir Arthur Conan Doyle, London, Kegan Paul, Trench, Trubner & Co., Ltd., 1921.

HOUDINI, HARRY, *The Unmasking of Robert-Houdin*, New York, The Publishers Printing Co., 1908.

———, *Miracle Mongers and Their Methods*, New York, E. P. Dutton & Co., 1920.

———, *A Magician among the Spirits*, New York, Harper & Brothers, 1924.

HOWE, ELLIC, *Astrology: A Recent History . . .* [British title: *Urania's Children*], New York, Walker and Company, 1968.

JASTROW, JOSEPH, *Fact and Fable in Psychology*, Boston and New York, Houghton Mifflin Company, 1900.

———, *Error and Eccentricity* [first published as *Wish and Wisdom*], New York, Dover Publications, Inc., 1962.

LEVINSOHN, RICHARD (Morus), *Prophets and Prediction*, translated from the German by Arnold J. Pomerans, London, Secker & Warburg, 1961.

LOMBROSO, CESARE, *After Death—What?*, translated from the Italian by William Sloane Kennedy, London, Leipzig, T. Fisher Unwin, 1909.

MACKAY, CHARLES, *Memoirs of Extraordinary Popular Delusions and the Madness of Crowds*, London, George Routledge & Sons, Ltd., 1892.

MACNEICE, LOUIS, *Astrology*, Garden City, New York, Doubleday & Company, Inc., 1964.

MASKELYNE, JOHN NEVIL, *Modern Spiritualism*, London, Frederick Warner & Co., 1876.

MONTGOMERY, RUTH, *A Gift of Prophecy*, New York, William Morrow & Company, 1965.

MULHOLLAND, JOHN, *Beware Familiar Spirits*, New York, Charles Scribner's Sons, 1938.

PIKE, JAMES A., with DIANE KENNEDY, *The Other Side*, Garden City, New York, Doubleday and Company, Inc., 1968.

PODMORE, FRANK, *Modern Spiritualism*, two volumes, London, Methuen & Co., 1902.

——, *The Naturalisation of the Supernormal*, New York and London, G. P. Putnam's Sons, 1908.

——, *The Newer Spiritualism*, London, Leipzig, T. Fisher Unwin, 1910.

POLGAR, FRANZ J., with KURT SINGER, *The Story of a Hypnotist*, New York, Hermitage House, Inc., 1951.

PRATT, JOSEPH GAITHER, *Parapsychology: An Insider's View of ESP*, New York, E. P. Dutton & Co., 1966.

PRICE, HARRY, *Leaves from a Psychist's Case-Book*, London, Putnam & Company, 1933.

——, *Confessions of a Ghost-Hunter*, London, Putnam & Company, 1936.

——, *A Report on Two Experimental Fire-Walks*, London, Bulletin II, University of London Council for Psychical Investigation, 1936.

——, *Fifty Years of Psychical Research*, London, Longmans, Green and Co., 1939.

——, *Poltergeist over England*, London, Country Life Ltd., 1945.

PROSKAUER, JULIEN J., *Spook Crooks!*, New York, Chicago, A. L. Burt Company, 1932.

——, *The Dead Do Not Talk*, New York and London, Harper & Brothers, 1946.

RAPHAEL, *A Manual of Astrology, or the Book of the Stars*, London, C. S. Arnold, 1828.

RAWCLIFFE, D. H., *Illusions and Delusions of the Supernatural and the Occult*, New York, Dover Publications, Inc., 1959.

RHINE, JOSEPH BANKS, *Extra-Sensory Perception*, London, Faber and Faber, Ltd., 1935.

——, *New Frontiers of the Mind*, New York, Toronto, Farrar & Rinehart, Inc., 1937.

——, *The Reach of the Mind*, New York, William Sloane Associates, Inc., 1947.

——, *New World of the Mind*, New York, William Sloane Associates, 1953.

RHINE, LOUISA E., *ESP in Life and Lab*, New York, The Macmillan Company; London, Collier Macmillan, Limited, 1967.

ROBERT-HOUDIN, JEAN EUGÈNE, *The Secrets of Stage Conjuring*, translated and edited with notes by Professor Hoffmann (Angelo Lewis), London, George Routledge & Sons, Ltd., 1888.

SHERMAN, HAROLD, *How to Make ESP Work for You*, Los Angeles, Devorss & Co., Inc., 1964.

SOAL, S. G., *Preliminary Studies of a Vaudeville Telepathist*, London, Bulletin III, University of London Council for Psychical Investigation, 1937.

——, *The Experimental Situation in Psychical Research*, London, The Society for Psychical Research, 1947.

——, and F. BATEMAN, *Modern Experiments in Telepathy*, London, Faber and Faber, Ltd., 1954.

——, and H. T. BOWDEN, *The Mind Readers*, Garden City, New York, Doubleday & Company, Inc., 1960.

SPRAGGETT, ALLEN, *The Unexplained*, foreword by Bishop James A. Pike, New York, The New American Library, 1967.

STEARN, JESS, *The Door to the Future*, Garden City, New York, Doubleday & Company, Inc. 1963.

TONDRIAU, JULIEN, *Du Yoga au Fakirisme*, Bruxelles, Presses Académiques Européennes, 1960.

VOGT, EVON Z., and RAY HYMAN, *Water Witching U.S.A.*, Chicago, The University of Chicago Press, 1959.

WOLSTENHOLME, G. E. W., and ELAINE C. P. MILLAR, editors, *Ciba Foundation Symposium on Extrasensory Perception*, Boston, Little, Brown & Company, 1956.

Previously unpublished notes and data gathered by Houdini; the personal scrapbook of Charles Howard Montague, the Boston editor who duplicated Washington Irving Bishop's feats, and other relative material in the author's collection have been used.

Special thanks are due A. H. Wesencraft, The Harry Price Collection, University of London; André Mayette in Paris; the late John Mulholland in New York; William W. Larsen, The Academy of Magical Arts and Sciences, Hollywood; Jean Monarque of Brussels; and the late dean of the Society of American Magicians, Jean Hugard.

INDEX